AN ONTOLOGY OF TRASH

SUNY series in Environmental Philosophy and Ethics
J. Baird Callicott and John van Buren, editors

AN ONTOLOGY
OF TRASH

*The Disposable and
Its Problematic Nature*

Greg Kennedy

STATE UNIVERSITY OF NEW YORK PRESS

Published by
State University of New York Press, Albany

© 2007 State University of New York

All rights reserved

Printed in the United States of America

For information, address State University of New York Press,
194 Washington Avenue, Suite 305, Albany, NY 12210-2384

Production by Kelli Williams
Marketing by Michael Campochiaro

Library of Congress Cataloging in Publication Data

An ontology of trash : the disposable and its problematic nature / Greg Kennedy
   p. cm. — (SUNY series in environmental philosophy and ethics)
   Includes bibliographical references and index.
   ISBN-13: 978-0-7914-6993-4 (hardcover : alk. paper) 1. Refuse and refuse
disposal—Moral and ethical aspects. 2. Refuse and refuse disposal—Philosophy.
3. Ontology. 4. Environmental responsibility. 5. Refuse and refuse disposal—
Psychological aspects. 6. Waste minimization. I. Kennedy, Greg, 1975– .
II. Series.

TD93.9.O56 2007
363.72'801—dc22

2006013724

10 9 8 7 6 5 4 3 2 1

To my parents, for their careful understanding

Contents

Preface

This book is something of an odd fish. Its title signals its oddity. "Ontology" literally means the study of being; it is a technical term designating a specific branch of philosophy that investigates why things simply are. "Trash" has no technical but many popular meanings. Contrary to "ontology" and the esoteric inquiry this word denominates, "trash" has at most a street-level significance, which rarely rises above the curb or, in worse cases, the gutter. By what right, then, do I couple the two here? Does their juxtaposition amount to little more than an author's wile to draw in the roving eye of the curious or blasé?

I can only hope that readers, whether slightly warmed by common curiosity or all aflame with academic zeal, will discover for themselves my innocence of guile. In neither title nor text have I undertaken to be clever. In fact, the entire present work evolved quite spontaneously out of an unconscious and even visceral discomfort I experienced in myself when dealing with the material culture of our society according to the norms of consumerism. To a great extent, the work simply embodies my need to scratch and thereby lessen this irritation. How did things become disposable? Why do we so readily and easily throw our goods away? What has happened, either in ourselves or in our material culture, that permits the former to trash such a huge quantity of the latter?

These questions immediately expose a problem behind our behavior as consumers. Despite its proximity and familiarity, we have no clear understanding of what trash truly is. In the face of landfill shortages and escalating disposal rates, some of us might ponder the best manner to handle the junk, but we neglect to meditate on the wider relation at work between our treatment of things and the status of their existence in the world we inhabit. Before we can throw an object out, we must conceive of it as disposable. Before we can arrive at this conception, we must first perceive the object in such a way that allows our minds to apply the definitive concept. It follows that something operating at the level of perception precedes all our habits of trashing. What is it about an object that makes us see it as disposable?

Perception so thoroughly informs our experience that we have great difficulty observing its operation. Fortunately, every perception has its content, which, if studied with an eye toward the very act of perceiving, will reveal patterns usually hidden within our perceptions. If we look at trash from the right angle, we start to see something more than a dirty collection of processed fibers, minerals, petroleum, and food scraps. Images of ourselves begin to emerge, uncanny images we could not otherwise behold except through this outside medium. By virtue of its sheer volume, trash now offers us the single greatest means for observing ourselves. An ontology of trash is ultimately self-exploration.

But even if this justifies a serious philosophical look at trash, why ontology? A study of trash cannot be anything but ontological because, with trash, *being* is most at issue. Trash is supposed to be nothing, a nonexistent; it is supposed to lack whatever legitimates the presence of an object in our world. In short, the disposable should not be. Yet obviously, and worrisomely, it is, and so remains, usually for a great many years. Ontologically, no other subject is quite so tantalizing as this very odd being that simultaneously resists and includes its nonbeing. Thus, the oddity of this work derives directly from 'the things themselves'. Its otherwise unhappy mixture of the academic and the pedestrian is prescribed by the subject matter itself. Hence, my honest desire to take trash up squarely has inevitably resulted in the queer incongruities of this book.

My thanks go to Ingrid Stefanovic and Claudio Cucciotti for encouraging me to release this odd fish into a larger pool, and to the State University of New York Press for supplying, as it were, the water. If the work has reached any level of maturity, this is due to the gentle guidance of Sonia Sikka, who led my often inchoate thoughts into a place of shelter, where they could grow and strengthen. My deepest thanks.

Introduction

Plastic bags, newspapers, pizza boxes, razors, coffee-filters, napkins, quartz watches, elastic bands, diapers, toothbrushes, j-cloths, mail-order catalogues, aluminum cans, ball-point pens, sticky-notes, hospital gowns, cosmetic compacts, cameras, holiday decorations, ink cartridges, running shoes, juice-boxes, boil-in-the-bag rice, lighters, rubber gloves, bottled water, missiles, glue-sticks, cutlery; two-year-old computers, cat litter, surgical instruments, drinking straws, plastic children's toys, cell phones, batteries, hairspray dispensers, Kleenex, lightbulbs . . . .

So many objects of our daily lives know but a fleeting presence. What does it mean that much, if not most, of our ordinary commerce with the world involves destruction? Does consuming disposable goods radically differ from using and maintaining durables? If so, then where does the difference lie—or is it buried irretrievably beneath the discards of a "throwaway society"? Does the evanescence of consumer commodities, from the paper plate to the fashions featured in last year's *Vogue*, reiterate the ceaseless flux of nature, or does it defy the ordered equilibrium to which nature, in the full revolution of its rhythmic cycle, intrinsically tends?

This study inquires into the meaning of disposable objects. It is an ontology because it seeks this meaning in the specific being of such objects. Beginning with the historical fact that things were not always as they are in the age of high technology, that "most Americans produced little trash before the twentieth century,"[1] the study asks how and why beings have become disposable.

Something far more urgent than mere historical curiosity motivates the inquiry. The historian has answers of her own to such questions as those posed earlier. "New materials," she explains, "especially plastics of all kinds, became the basis for a relationship to the material world that required consumers to buy things rather than make them and to throw things out rather than fix them."[2] Most of us now recognize that such a relationship, responsible for untold environmental degradation, threatens our existence. But how could our technological means to live endanger our existence? Ontology takes up the question of the meaning of trash because it perceives the dangerous paradox involved in the being of trash. It asks whether a discrepancy might divide our modern mode of being, the consumer lifestyle, from our true existence.

To bring up "true existence" is to invite further and thornier questions concerning human nature. Presumably, existing in a truly human manner would mean living in harmony with our nature or essence. But just what constitutes our essence? Indeed, do we not already begin to falsify our existence by searching for some immutable essence underlying it? If it is of the essence of a knife to cut, what analogous statement can be made of us? Is it essential to our being that we love, make mistakes, think, laugh, sicken, and die? A mere list of ordinary activities and attributes leaves our essence untouched. Empirical knowledge necessarily falls short here, owing to an intuition we all have felt that something of us remains outside any catalogue of what we do and how we appear. Sensory observation will never get at the object of this intuition. By their very nature, questions concerning human essence, even those that challenge the validity of all such questions, have a metaphysical direction.

To that extent, this study is also metaphysical. It attempts, through rational argument and evidence, to discover the unapparent truth of disposable items, human nature, and the relation between them. While, due to its material, the study cannot avoid metaphysics, it handles metaphysical speculation like a prudent apprentice would handle a potentially dangerous implement. "Metaphysics," according to Kant's classic definition, "is a completely isolated speculative science of reason, which soars far above the teachings of experience, and in which reason is indeed meant to be its own pupil."[3] It seeks answers beyond the immediate world of sense perception. A certain will belongs to such an endeavor, a will to ascertain, explain, and assert. These lofty goals at the same time render metaphysics incapable of practicing the humility of acceptance. The tendency of metaphysics to ascend to higher and higher altitudes of explanation betrays its intrinsic deficiency: it can neither accept nor fully appreciate the ground-level given as simply given. Metaphysics literally overlooks the sheer wonder of Being and consequently loses sight of it. If Socrates spoke truly, that philosophy begins with wonderment, then by questioning that experience, by striving to explain it and thereby in a way to possess it, metaphysics already initiates the end of philosophy.

Just as metaphysics responds at first to wonder and then subsequently loses it, so this study also sets off in response to metaphysics with hopes eventually to see beyond it. This is not to say that the study will gradually abandon argument and reason to end up mute and transfixed in the presence of the ineffable. Rather, remaining cognizant of the inherent tendencies and biases of explicative speculation, it will employ metaphysics with an eye to how the latter inevitably shapes the object of its inquiry.

For the study to make any sense at all of the historical phenomenon of disposable commodities, it must approach metaphysics not as a canon of concepts or a tradition of ideas, but much more a manner of being of those entities capable of ideation and thought. As reason's attempt to comprehend the cosmos, metaphysics is a certain human way of encountering the world. In seeking to grasp the world, metaphysics inevitably engages with and manipulates it. Peculiar to metaphysics, however, is the method of engagement, which disengages all human faculties and features except the rational intellect. This method is, in certain spheres, highly effective, and, if efficacy were the only outcome, our caution with respect to metaphysics would be unfounded. The problem, though, is that, when isolated, reason tends to become domineering and cruel. The innocuous will to explain can degenerate into a hostile will to dominate. Distinction and intellectual autonomy from the physical do not satisfy the metaphysical will, which, in Plato's words, "must escape the contamination of the body's folly." For, "as long as we have a body and our soul is fused with such an evil we shall never adequately attain what we desire, which we affirm to be truth."[4] From the moment when metaphysics supposes the physical as inimical to its projects, it starts to avenge itself on the physical. A paradox ensues. Shorn and scornful of body, emotion and whatever else ties a human being to its physicality, metaphysical reason attains unprecedented power over the material world. It gives birth, as will be seen, to science and technology, and thereby manages to subordinate the physical to its transcendent purposes. This study will get beyond the objectionable in metaphysics—its hostility—if it succeeds in reconciling thought to the humble physicality that our humanness, no matter how elevated its rational flights, cannot cast off.

"Physicality" is itself, of course, a philosophically burdened term originating from the metaphysical dualism established between reason and the body. To answer the tradition simply by valorizing a metaphysically conceived body over reason would remain squarely within that tradition. We know that facile reversals of metaphysical claims only reinforce rather than challenge their legitimacy. I hope that this study avoids recourse to such futile tactics. Nevertheless, the constraints of language, as well as the strategies of metaphysics throughout its history, urge me to cling to the term "physical" and its cognates. By approaching from a different angle its traditional connotations—such as limitation, finitude, imperfection, vulnerability, and so on—I will attempt to write about physicality in such a way that avoids the dogmatic dualism of mind and body and questions the metaphysical tendency to denigrate the latter pole.

Accordingly, I take pains throughout the study to maintain a conceptual difference between the metaphysical construal of the physical and a more holistic, less prejudicial interpretation. When speaking of matter as conceived within the tradition, I employ the term "substance," relying on the Cartesian echoes that this word creates. Descartes believed that the substance, and therefore the true essence of an object, consists of mathematical properties inaccessible to sensual perception and open to reason alone. Consequently, substance is matter completely divorced from our sensuality. In opposition to this, I wish to implant matter into our somatic sensitivity. For the purpose of this study, "physicality" implies the entire mystery of human embodiment, including the mysteries of death, finitude, sociability, the desire for transcendence, and so on. The physical always relates essentially to our embodied being-in-the-world. This by no means amounts to a repudiation of reason; rather it reflects, at least to my mind, the most honest and accurate appraisal of the homogenous complexity of reality. Everything we experience, know, or will we do so as embodied "worldlings." Thus "physicality" and the "human body" are here to be read as existential terms that encompass also mental phenomena. They are not to be confused with the reductive, segregating interpretations of metaphysics and empirical science. Again, I retain the otherwise problematic word "physical" in this manner in order to reveal the ultimate absurdity and impossibility of the metaphysical tradition's drive to exceed, if not exit it altogether.

Obviously, science and technology make disposables possible. The combined forces of mass production, cheap mechanized labor, globally interconnected transportation and communication systems, and intricate, nearly absolute mastery over raw resources give disposable commodities an economic advantage over and above sheer physical feasibility. Prior to the industrial revolution, labor was simply too dear, and materials too scarce; few people could afford to throw things away. Yet even among the well-heeled a different attitude toward things than ours held sway. Things were, as the cliche goes, built to last. Patina covered objects with special value. Ownership prized the historical continuity of use and possession that would mark, with increasing distinction, the aging of a good. Did this former reverence and attachment to things subside, thus clearing shelf space for science to market its innovations? Or did technology turn our collective head around, changing our gaze from past to future, amazing us with what we might buy and soon discard?

Most likely, attitude and invention changed together, dialectically. Today the dialectic has advanced to the point that disposable objects so predominate our daily lives that the distinction between disposable and durable has grown untenable. When, in 1923, General Motors introduced yearly model changes to its automobiles it, in effect, filed the phenomenon of durability and continuity in the archive of history. "For manufacturers of all kinds of products, the automobile was the ultimate test case for the principles of consumer marketing: if people could learn to discard cars that still worked, for reasons of style or new technologies, they could certainly come to think of anything else as disposable."[5] Some of us may continue to polish the patina of antiques and heirlooms, but even here the meaning of their longevity has changed. Now their meaning is determined by what market value they acquire in relation to the revolving door of constantly new and improved commodities.

Humanity has always had its garbage. Yet, in earlier times, things were usually worn out before they were thrown out. Most of the contents of modern garbage-cans, however, underwent little qualitative alteration prior to disposal. Apart, perhaps, from an imprint of lipstick on its rim, the polystyrene cup looks no different after the consumption of its coffee than before. Both its substance and its form are exactly the same, yet its being has fundamentally altered. Before consumption, the cup was a marketable and desirable commodity; after, it is only trash. What does the brief act of consumption involve that could cause such powerful ontological effects?

Recourse here to philosophy, let alone to ontology, might well seem superfluous, if not contrived. True, perhaps the cup has not changed substantially, nonetheless, quantifiable alterations have occurred. For example, the hygiene of the cup is nothing what it was prior to consumption. After use, the cup is no longer sterilized, its germ-count having increased, which means it has become a possible hazard. The consumer does not buy the cup for itself, but rather for the value it has as a commodity. Part of this value is safety. When consumption removes this value, the commodity as such no longer remains intact, and its object changes. Simple economics speaks succinctly where philosophy would seem fated to wander in circumlocution.

That we value objects for their function is nothing new. Novel, however, is the tendency of the value of modern commodities to depart from their function. Jean Baudrillard has argued this extensively:

outside the field of its denotation, the object becomes substitutable in a more or less unlimited way within the field of connotations where it assumes sign-value. Thus the washing machine *serves* as an appliance and *acts* as an element of prestige, comfort, etc. It is strictly this latter field which is the field of consumption. All kinds of other objects may be substituted here for the washing machine as "signifying" element. In the logic of signs, as in that of symbols, objects are no longer linked in any sense to a *definite* function or need.[6]

In themselves, signs have no meaning. They rely on whatever signification their users bestow on them. Thus, a kind of emptiness or void conditions their being. The extraction of function and especially of need, we shall see, also evacuates the being of things that previously had a certain independent meaning. As mere signs, objects become disposable, with no greater claim on durability than an uttered syllable.

The question still outstanding asks how historically physical, worldly things became mere signs—that is, how beings became insignificant in themselves and prey to substitution and finally to disposal. Without an ontology of disposables, their universal mutation from valued commodity to trash must come across as a kind of witchcraft or reverse alchemy. In itself there is no good reason why the perfectly functional cup must be thrown out upon its being emptied. Nor can we attribute the mystery to mere convention, to the irrational mores of consumer society. Something extraordinary, despite its everydayness, is at work that demands interpretation and elucidation. We must ask what is it about the being of commodities as such that they so readily turn to trash. At the same time, we must also ask what it is about ourselves that we so easily trash the increasing majority of beings that we encounter in the world.

Ontology has several millennia of philosophical legitimacy behind it, but not so trash. In fact, the very word is philosophically objectionable, academically indecent. But precisely its distasteful connotations make trash the mandatory subject of modern ontology. For "trash" connotes violence. We sometimes apply the word to people as a particularly venomous pejorative. As a verb it can be used synonymously with "to destroy," as in "the thugs trashed the place." In this sense, "trash" means a manner of physically relating to other beings. It is a mode of comportment, treating things without care, negatively, and destructively. By calling disposables trash, I wish to draw attention to the way in which we exist as consumers in the throwaway society. We exist, for the most part, in a way that violently negates beings rather than takes care of them. The question as to our role in the phenomenon of disposable commodities is answered succinctly in the single word: "trash." The ontology of trash, therefore, is the study of our modern technological mode of being—a kind of philosophical biography of our life as consumers.

Despite appearances, trash is not a phenomenon consequent to consumption. That once heard adage: "it's not waste until you waste it," no longer applies. The ontology will show that the being of technological commodities includes, a priori, their disposal. This means that the being of commodities is always already trashed. The only possible way to make sense of this is in the recollection that trash, first and foremost, is our active mode of existing with and among entities. Because, in other words, we comport ourselves negatively and destructively toward things, we necessarily disclose them as deficient in being, as disposable. Trash is, at one and the same time, the being of disposables as well as the being of "predisposed" commodities because at bottom it is also our disclosive mode of being as consumers of technology.

The attuned reader will have already detected familiar strains of Heidegger's thought. This study relies heavily on the great body of ontological insight that he formed throughout his life. It does not, however, seek to be carried along by this body, but rather to quicken and strengthen it. For one of the weaknesses of Heidegger's ontology and his analyses of human being is the absence of a thorough and explicit interpretation of embodiment. This absence is all the more conspicuous and problematic given the pragmatic and worldly nature of Heidegger's investigations. For example, Heidegger makes much of the disclosive power of specific moods or attunements. Particular things, he demonstrates, and the world in general reveal themselves through different ontological modes of being according to the various attunements in which we humans find ourselves. Among others, boredom, fear, angst, and concentrated involvement in a manual task are treated by Heidegger as ontologically significant aspects of our existence. Yet Heidegger remains strangely silent on the bodily basis of all attunements. He neglects to mention that boredom is not simply some kind of mental indolence, but equally a feeling of lassitude and inertia in our bones, a sense of heaviness and fatigue that burdens our bodies. Likewise, the tightened muscles in the neck, the clenched jaw, the scowl and balled fists cannot be separated from anger, as if these were merely accidental physical symptoms of an essentially mental occurrence. Hunger, sickness, sexual desire, and countless other "physiological" conditions all have as broad and profound an ontological import as those seemingly disembodied attunements which Heidegger treats.

The upshot of Heidegger's reticence concerning our essentially embodied being-in-the-world is that his critical interpretation of metaphysics retains a slightly metaphysical hue. It approaches at times the fantastical because it fails to articulate explicitly the history of metaphysics as it is written in the flesh of physicality. By not including the evidence of concrete changes in our embodied being-in-the-world, his grand history of metaphysics tends to appear as at best a probable fiction. I believe that trash becomes the natural subject for an ontology that examines metaphysics in relation to the human body because it is the metaphysical, scientific disinterest in things that allows us to disclose them negatively. The old metaphysical quest for transcendence, when technologically pursued, descends into trash.

The ontology of trash thus works out to be the history of human embodied being-in-the-world that takes seriously the physiological changes wrought by technology on our embodiment. In this respect, the present study departs quite markedly from Heidegger, even while helping itself to several of the categories, some of the terminology, and many of the insights found in his ontological project. Such a departure, although radical enough, remains true to Heidegger because it carries closer to the point of resolution certain problems and tensions implicit in his physiologically decontextualized construal of the history of metaphysics. It offers an often critical and, I would like to think, corrective supplement to this yet ongoing history.

Since change permits us to perceive the passage of time, the history must first clearly distinguish what was from what is. Consequently, the first chapter examines the phenomenon of waste, something not at all new, in order to contrast more sharply the uniqueness of the modern phenomenon of trash. Waste, we learn, stinks of the body, making it metaphysically aversive. To transcend physicality, metaphysics must rid itself of not only the body, but also of its souvenir: waste. Chapter two deals with the effacement of the lived human body effected by metaphysics by means of technology. The third chapter handles food and begins to show how technological devices, by disengaging the body from the physical world that sustains it, transforms waste into trash.

In chapter four the denaturalization of food is set into the wider context of the often physically inhospitable environment of modern urbanity. In the city, human dependence on commodities is nearly total. Out of reach of its natural needs and the ability to satisfy them, the urbanized body consumes what it neither produces nor comprehends. Its commodities appear opaque to it due, in large part, to the emasculation of its sensitive capacities. While not discounting its success in overcoming much of the isolation and parochialism that can plague rural regions, we also know that modern city-life, in another sense, is a way of being in the world quite removed from other beings. Most city-dwellers, for example, have not even a passing acquaintance with the miraculous diversity of nature.

This disconnection based on separation and insensitivity promotes a destructive manner of taking care of things. It makes trash ontologically possible. Chapter five systematically delineates the ontology of trash. It shows how the technological manner of taking care of things, as our modern mode of being, signifies our failure to be truly human. The delineation, in other words, concludes with the exposure of this dilemma: the phenomenon of trash exists as long as we fail to exist as humans.

Such an understanding of trash leads incontrovertibly to its counterpart, the phenomenon of human extinction. We know that the accumulating trash of our abandonment to consumption puts our continued survival at risk. We might also reflect that the possibility of the imminent termination of humanity would predispose us to a reckless production and consumption of disposables. Why would we bother to produce products likely to outlive all of us? The circular causal relation between disposables that expedite our potential doom and between the fear of our global demise that accelerates the expansion of disposables directs us to a deeper intimacy between trash and human extinction. The same behavior that engenders trash also endangers humanity. Trash represents a desecration of beings that contradicts our role as stewards and preservers of Being. Human extinction, our own annihilation, thus already takes place to the extent that we trash what has been entrusted to our essence. Essentially depriving us, trash threatens our existence.

For all that, however, the real significance of trash is affirmative, not negative. A proper understanding of the phenomenon encourages hope rather than despair. Therefore, this study emerges finally on the far side of extinction's shadow, cleansed of trash through the worldly practice of careful thinking.

The ultimate optimism of this work, I hope, will ameliorate any perceived excess in its critical approach. It is neither my business nor my desire to write a condemnation of the modern world. We all well know its benefits, but our gratitude for these must not leave us permissive of its remediable ills. Any age so satisfied with its situation that it succumbs to philosophical indolence and moral indifference has thus announced its decline. Moreover, any comparison between ages that does not contribute to greater understanding and concern for our own is odious. A philosophical treatment of trash in no manner insults our modern way of being, but rather enlightens it to the real dangers it faces. Wisdom, thankfulness, and change follow upon understanding.

CHAPTER ONE

Waste

Throughout their long cohabitation, waste has dogged humanity with a pack of woes ranging from embarrassment to pestilence. Yet the real problem behind these varying troubles is the ambiguity of waste. Anything and everything can become waste. We waste time, hot water, opportunity, money, potential, food, life, love, electricity, kindness and so on. None of these cases would be ambiguous were it not for the trite fact that what one person discards, some other person likely covets. Is watching television game-shows wasteful sloth or recreation? Like beauty, it appears that the phenomenon of waste belongs to the eye of the beholder. Radical subjectivism of this sort raises an inevitable question: if one and the same thing can simultaneously be both waste and not waste, does waste, per se, exist at all?

The ontology of trash commences here because it hypothesizes that trash is a uniquely modern species of waste. If the existence of waste cannot be firmly established, or its essence at least provisionally outlined, the study of trash stalls before it starts. Fortunately, by probing its layers of ambiguity, we can reach a functional, albeit incomplete, understanding of waste. We shall see that the uniqueness of trash lies in its repudiation of the subjective nature of waste. Trash takes on the aspect of a monstrosity, a species whose defining features contradict its genus. Trash signifies an attempt to render absolute the essential relativity of waste and thereby answer its central problem of intrinsic ambiguity.

This ambiguity revolves around the multiple revaluations of the distinction between natural and unnatural. This chapter will proceed by breaking down the complex judgments concerning the nature of waste into their constitutive parts. Waste is often bemoaned, but also sometimes celebrated according to respective evaluations of nature. When we encounter nature as the fecund source of prosperity, we want to emulate

1

its unstinting liberality. We blithely become prodigals. When, on the other hand, we feel dwarfed or bound by nature's constraints, we tend to regard our unfulfilled ideals as wasted on account of our biological inadequacies. So alternating between shame, censure, and celebration, we attribute waste to nature or to ourselves, depending on our current understanding of our relation to nature. Amid this conceptual confusion a single, solid fact stands out: that waste does in truth exist. So long as we continue to distinguish between positive and negative, we will always face waste. For all wastes result from the inveterate human habit of evaluation.

The Value of Waste

Our responsibility for the phenomenal existence of waste must be stressed because it sometimes vanishes in the surrounding fog of ambiguity. If we take nature as a domain indifferent to value, one on which values can only supervene, waste will appear utterly foreign to it. Ecology teaches that on the macro level nature wastes nothing. There death gets absorbed into life through an incessant, all-encompassing cycle impenetrable to the micro level judgments of positive and negative. Now, when we deign to situate ourselves within this cycle, we would seem to lose the distinguishing marks of judgment in the vastness of cosmic indiscrimination.

> Certainly humans, and other intelligent forms of life, are natural products, owing their existence to natural processes which determine their capacities and structures. On this, the broadest, view of the natural, everything that goes on in the universe is natural. When a tree grows and flourishes nothing non-natural is occurring; when a species becomes extinct, even as a result of degradation of wild areas by humans, nothing non-natural is occurring; when humans clear wilderness and build cities nothing non-natural is occurring. All of these processes occur because the laws of nature are as they are. Nothing that happens can, in this sense, be non-natural. Nothing that anyone ever does can be, in this sense, non-natural.[1]

Nature's universality, being absolute, without value and judgment, leaves no room for the distinctions that generate waste. In the cosmic scheme of things, the concept of waste falls from sight.

At this cosmological level it costs but little effort to brush aside the otherwise disturbing problem of waste. From nature's perspective, the phenomenon of waste appears a conceptual fabrication born of ignorance.

Something like this God's-eye view inspires former Executive Vice President of the American Can Company, Alexander Judd, in his *In Defense of Garbage*. Judd is convinced that "the garbage problem is not a physical crisis, a resource crisis, or a financial crisis. It is a political and informational problem which needs to be addressed as such."[2] By this Judd means that the problem boils down to the overactive imaginations and narrow understanding of pessimists and environmentalists. The reason why the problem is not physical, and, by implication, not real, could not be more elementary. As long as we have ground in which to dig holes, we need never worry about our refuse:

> The public perceives that the garbage crisis is caused by the runaway growth of disposables, packaging, and discards in general. The real problem, of course, is not the growth of garbage or the quantity of garbage; it is the closing of landfills and the failure to provide replacement sites or alternate ways to handle the discards of towns and cities.
>
> The production of garbage responds to growth in population, household formations, affluence, and commercial activity, but the capacity for the disposal of waste depends more on the availability of land—space—than any other factor. Table 2-1 compares MSW [municipal solid waste] discards, population, and area in the forty-eight contiguous states to similar figures for three other industrialized nations. Those countries discard an average of 22 percent less garbage per person, but we discard 85 percent less garbage per acre than they.[3]

The garbage-per-acre index takes full advantage of the astronomical blessings of an ever-expanding universe. Garbage will become a problem only on the day space begins to contract. Meanwhile, for Judd, the production of garbage could not be more natural. He proves this by demonstrating the neat cyclical nature of industrial production. The great pits in the earth, created by such production during the extraction of raw resources, are perfectly suited to be filled with the effluent of consumption.

Although breathtaking in its scope and ingeniousness, Judd's argument lacks phenomenological subtlety. While waste may not pose problems to humans in a cosmic state of nature, it undeniably disturbs our little, everyday life as lived in a world permeated with value. We might temporarily refrain from assigning values to what we come across, but we cannot so easily will away our evaluative character. Perhaps nothing humans do, not even their judging, is non-natural; yet our very nature makes us feel a kind of separation from the valueless order of the cosmos.

Willy-nilly we confront waste as a phenomenon of our world, and the fact that from some transcendental vantage point it appears an illusion does not help us in the least as we grope forward through imminence. Living in the world, we cannot look down on it disillusioned. Even while dismissing the problem of garbage, Judd clings to a certain notion of waste. Any large stretch of empty space vacant of our junk seems to strike him as reprehensibly wasteful.

What, then, characterizes the phenomenon of waste, whether illusion or not? Kevin Lynch provides a good, phenomenological description:

> Waste is what is worthless or unused for human purpose. It is a lessening of something without any apparently useful result; it is loss and abandonment, decline, separation, and death. . . . The dictionary definitions are centred on man. . . . The term is applied to a resource not in use, but potentially useful, wasted time, a wasted life, an empty building or machine. . . . Resources in use that are losing their usefulness unnecessarily are also thought to be wasted. The loss may be unnecessary, brought about by too rapid or inefficient an expenditure, or by lack of normal maintenance. . . . But if the loss is due to normal wear, then it is not waste but expected cost. . . . Moreover, if the loss is due to some uncontrollable event such as a tidal wave or a hurricane, the event is not a waste, since it could not have been prevented. *Thus we multiply our opportunities for waste as we improve our control and prediction of events. Waste implies negligence or human failure.*[4]

Waste embarrasses and shames us because it confronts us with a reflection of our own shortcomings.

On the strength of this, we could make two plausible hypotheses. First, any society, such as our own, that generates gross amounts of waste must have correspondingly gross inadequacies. Where the average person creates nearly five pounds of garbage per day, the human failure must also be proportionately massive. Second, a society preoccupied with concealing its wastes must have, so to speak, something important to hide from itself. Rather than countenance its own negligence, a wastrel society might take Herculean pains to sweep its waste under the carpet. Beneath the strain of this impossible task a society can grow inured to its increasing absurdity. Our exports in garbage destined for an exotic Third-World disposal increase yearly.

Waste offends us to the extent that it reflects back our own shortcomings, our failure to preserve the value that we originally invested in an object. While evaluating is an active rational process, waste-making involves a certain passivity. It follows on a withdrawal of our direct participation with things. When things degrade beyond our control, we think it unfortunate, but do not feel responsible. Our conscience is pricked when we neglect to intervene, when we fail to give of ourselves to the maintenance of our own projected values. Waste occurs only with a subtraction of worth; an already worthless object cannot be wasted. Since values are our investment into things, their subtraction marks our divestment from or indifference to things.

What this points to is the importance of care regarding the phenomenon of waste. When, despite, or even due to our earnest effort to the contrary, we end up destroying a valuable object, we feel more inclined to treat it as an accident than a waste. If, on the other hand, indolence, absentmindedness, or plain indifference were the cause, the ensuing destruction strikes us as an offensive waste. Even when in both cases the loss could have been avoided, the latter counts more as waste. It seems, then, that waste results from carelessness—that is, from a neglect or failure to care for the things we have valued.

Given that values are human projections, the process of devaluation in fact turns out to be more basically one of dehumanization. "'Waste comes from the Latin *vastus*, meaning unoccupied or desolate, akin to the Latin *vanus* (empty or vain), and to the Sanskrit word for wanting or deficient."[5] The prime deficiency is our own insofar as waste implies our failure and shortcomings. Thus, the privation that characterizes waste results from our own inadequate response to the obligations intrinsic to the worth we attribute to the valued thing. Wasting unsettles us because it involves a contradiction between our judgment and our conduct. When our actions confirm the value we project, we do not waste. When, on the contrary, we refuse to comport ourselves in accordance with our projections, we contradict them and in the clash of contradiction the thing has its value knocked out of it. We retract our values, leaving an emptiness in the thing. This, however, is preceded by a more basic and pragmatic retraction of our care and practical concern with the thing.

The dehumanization of wasted things occurs at a deeper level than the mere aesthetic faculty that subjectively regards one thing as trash and another treasure. True, the determination of wastes does involve a certain subjective imposition on the being of the entity in question. To this extent, waste-making resembles all other types of projection, and, moreover, a loose and arbitrary one at that. Anything valued can look like junk from some vantage point. Despite this subjective relativity, it is still most instructive to understand this supervening projection as more profoundly privative. Rather than seeing waste as an expression of an essential human activity—projecting negative values—we might better regard it first as a matter of human withdrawal and deprivation.

A case can be made for this on epistemological grounds. In her classic study on the sociological meaning of rites surrounding pollution and impurity, Mary Douglas writes:

> If we can abstract pathogenicity and hygiene from our notion of dirt, we are left with the old definition of dirt as matter out of place. This is a very suggestive approach. It implies two conditions: a set of ordered relations and a contravention of that order. . . . Dirt is the by-product of a systematic ordering and classification of matter, in so far as ordering involves rejecting inappropriate elements. . . . In short, our pollution behaviour is the reaction which condemns any object or idea likely to confuse or contradict cherished classifications.[6]

A sufficient kinship exists between the notions of dirt and waste to justify thinking about the latter in a similar fashion. Dirt is what settles outside the ruled lines of our conceptual schema. In other words, it eludes or resists our everyday conceptualizations. The use of concepts, of course, is the privileged province of reason, which is presumed, at least in the metaphysical tradition, to be the endowment unique to, and definitive of, human beings. What reason cannot conceptually work with, it relegates to the negative classification of dirt or pollution. But the unworkable elusiveness and incomprehensibility of its contents make this classification a kind of anticlassification that repulses reason. Reason cannot help categorizing things, and so it employs 'dirt' as the default category that appears in the absence of rational comprehension. Thus, the concept of dirt and waste is where, so to speak, reason loses its grip and where this definitively human faculty malfunctions.

Douglas begins to explain how this operates by arguing that the dichotomy between the pure and the impure serves traditional societies as the foundation for their cultural superstructure. Although this dichotomy matches more or less that between the sacred and the profane, it remains distinct and primary, for it results directly from the invariable epistemological makeup of human consciousness. As beings who function mentally by means of definite concepts, we inevitably encounter objects and circumstances within our wide range of experience that transgress our clean conceptual boundaries. These transgressional experiences threaten the order that consciousness constructs out of its concepts and are thus perceived as dangerous. Whatever conforms to our concepts and helps entrench them is experienced as safe, unambiguous—in a word, pure.

On this account, pollution originates with ambiguity. Dependent on a peculiarity of the human mind, it is more an epistemological entity than a material one. Wherever consciousness uncovers something unclassifiable, something against the weave of its conceptual patterns, there it finds a source of danger, able to contaminate its requisite order with chaos. That which consciousness cannot precisely situate repels it. So it happens that taboos develop around such things as feces and menstrual fluids. These are matter out of place; they are both of the body, but no longer contained within it. So with waste in general; it always dwells at the margins of our concepts. Wasteland is the scrub between city and country. Garbage is all that anonymous stuff falling between valued objects and simple dust.

Owing to the malleability of conceptual structures, their patterns can assume any number of variations. Cultural relativity arises partly from the fact that different patterns expose different sources of purity and pollution. This implies that no object in itself is immune to becoming waste, while, on the other hand, no object is in essence waste, given a more accommodating pattern. The conceptual constitution of reason conditions the existence of values. Concepts are, by definition, finite, otherwise they could not have any meaningful application. The finitude of conceptual consciousness, generating its particular pattern of finite concepts, renders this consciousness essentially perspectival. What secures and strengthens its sense of order and control attracts it. What disrupts this sense repels reason and is evaluated accordingly. Values serve to reinforce the concepts from which they derive. Although the projection of values is a conceptual activity, the platform from which all values are launched remains ultimately physical. We value those things that we perceive to bring us pleasure, health, and happiness, for these promote the physical security on which reason builds its conceptual order.

Since waste is, most simply put, our failure to preserve our values concretely, it, too, has a practical fundament. Waste, like dirt, is what our reason can no longer usefully comprehend and categorize in terms of our pragmatic encounter with the world. Yet reason arrives at this loss only after, so to speak, our hands no longer work to maintain the thing's former value. So here reason follows the physical withdrawal of our active concern with our projections. Our initial rational values formed "a set of ordered relations," while our physical behavior enacts "a contravention of that order." Only following this practical contravention does the object become devalued. It no longer accords with the ordered relations of reason because it has ceased to fit into the primordial world of our practical concern. Waste, then, is not just matter out of place; it is matter without place.

Natural Wastes?

If what has been said about waste has any bearing, it would seem to apply only to artifacts, that is, to objects invested not only with human value but also with some degree of human ingenuity and industry. But there exists an entirely different and prototypical variety of waste that never began as valued. Excrement provides our first experience of waste, on which all related experiences are ordered. I have suggested that wastage through devaluation results from a failure somehow to live up to our uniquely human capacities. Excrement, on the other hand, seems like a waste that directly expresses our humanity. Man, as Ernest Becker has colorfully put it, is the god who shits—a bizarre and fabulous combination of spiritual and rational aspirations and physical, corruptible matter. Becker writes: "Excreting is the curse that threatens madness because it shows man his abject finitude, his physicalness, the likely unreality of his hopes and dreams. But even more immediately, it represents man's utter bafflement at the sheer *non-sense* of creation."[7] Thus our fecal wastes instantiate our essential nature. They are redolent of our mortality. Ambiguity asserts itself here, because now waste seems like a wholly natural occurrence in opposition to the transcendental status of reason. It is easy to see why this type of waste would be inherently problematic, for it is emblematic of the crucial problems of our radically absurd human condition—that we are half divine (reason) and half bestial (nature). Bodily waste repulses us for the same reason that death does. They signify our finiteness, that which makes us human, all too human, and not gods.

How does this fit consistently with the claim that devalued wasting of objects represents an absence of our humanness, when our most basic wastes partially embody our peculiar nature? What does devaluation have to do with finitude? From the metaphysical point of view, finitude has always implied negativity or lack. When, for example, Descartes inquires into the cause of his errors, he notices

> that passing before me is not only a real and positive idea of God (that is, of a supremely perfect being) but also, as it were, a certain negative idea of nothingness (that is, what is the greatest possible distance from any perfection), and that I have been so constituted as a kind of middle ground between God and nothingness, or between supreme being and non-being. Thus insofar as I have been created by the supreme being, there is nothing in me by means of which I might be deceived or led into error: but insofar as I participate in nothingness or non-being, that is,

insofar as I am not the supreme being and lack a great many things, it is not surprising that I make mistakes.[8]

I have said that wasting valuable objects involves privation, but this must not be restricted to the kind of metaphysical privation mentioned here. The more primary privation is an existential one. The failure implied in this kind of wasting stems from a rejection of the truth of our insufficiencies. To be finite means, in addition to erring, not to be self-sufficient, to be reliant on other beings to preserve our being. Neglecting to care for the things that help sustain our fragile existence amounts to a denial of our finite nature. It is a mendacious assertion of our supernatural divinity and a wishful disavowal of our animality.

Waste, then, can imply failure at two very different levels: the metaphysical and the existential. With respect to metaphysics, bodily wastes symbolize the obstinacy of our "lower" animal nature and the latter's pitiable inability to live up to the directives and imperatives of pure reason. Yet, on the existential level, this rational flagellation of the body, which refuses to acknowledge and accept our physical dependencies, lapses readily into the negligence concerning things that leads to their wasteful devaluation. In other words, metaphysical denial of the flesh often leads to a dismissal of the world. So while metaphysics defines waste as privative when measured against an absolute transcendental order of being, an existential phenomenology of waste understands this metaphysical definition itself as the original withdrawal of our own active embeddedness the world.

Keeping these two opposing perspectives distinct is crucial for any degree of clarity on the issue of waste. Metaphysics, with its supernatural ambitions and affinities, treats nature as wasteful of the rational elements putatively imprisoned within it. The opposite perspective, what I have called, for lack of better terms, existential and phenomenological, regards the neglect of our worldly needy nature brought about by our carelessness toward things as ultimately the waste of our own complex human being. The present study adopts this latter perspective. For only in the view of this perspective does the overwhelming phenomenon of technological disposables—trash—appear in a meaningful and edifying way. Otherwise the sight of it must continue to dumbfound and dehumanize us.

Waste, however, is not yet trash. What this study must recount is the history of how the metaphysical perspective on waste has become technologically instituted as trash. Such a recounting will explicate the absurd position of certain technophiles, like Judd, who find no reasonable cause for concern in the mounting debris of the consumer culture. On the contrary, the magnitude of modern trash seems to convince such enthusiasts of modernity's unrivaled economic success and technological prowess. This can only make sense given a view that finds nature wasteful and the technological transformation of the natural as productive. Technology, we shall see, dissolves the problem of waste by fixating and absolutizing its inherent ambiguity. Technology replaces waste, a creature of value, with trash. Whereas waste results from a relative, subjective devaluation, technological objectification, that is, unconditional, absolute devaluation, engenders trash.

"Positive Waste"

Before moving out onto the concrete absoluteness of trash, we must traverse a final ambiguous slough of waste. For there remains a kind of waste that, having none of the negative implications previously dealt with, might well pass with the title of "positive waste." Guilt and shame do not burden all instances of wasting. Often relief and even festive celebration accompany certain acts of discarding. The ritual of potlatch, for example, not infrequently included the intentional destruction of highly valuable objects, even homes. Rituals (perhaps more than scientific modernity wishes to acknowledge) serve profoundly personal needs. To the extent that rituals humanize us, ritualistic wasting could not, as my argument would seem compelled to say, dehumanize us. In that case, waste would not imply human failure. It would bring about human fulfillment.

How does waste, the essence of which contains loss and negation, take on positive value? Baudrillard begins to puzzle out this paradox with his observation that "all societies have always wasted, expended and consumed beyond what is strictly necessary for the simple reason that it is in the consumption of a surplus, a superfluity that the individual—and society—feel not merely that they exist, but that they are alive."[9] Far from posing a problem and implying failure, waste in this case seems to offer a solution, or a salve, as it were, for the abrasions of physical finitude. Waste, Baudrillard implies, need not suggest death and privation. It can equally symbolize the life process, the abundance and exuberance of nature. By emulating this abundance, humans have submerged, to use Nietzsche's distinction, their discriminative Apollinian elements in a Dionysian participation in the valueless holism of nature. This "primitive" solution to waste is the antithesis of the metaphysical solution. Whereas metaphysics finds nature prodigiously wasteful and attempts to overcome the problem of waste by becoming supernatural, the "primitive" experiences freedom from the conceptual constraints of reason by joining in the undifferentiated flow of natural growth and decay. Both responses attain at best only partial success, for both leave one of the dual aspects of our physical–rational nature dissatisfied. Yet the primitive solution does have at least one advantage over metaphysics, in that, though it fails to satisfy reason, neither does it frustrate or deny it. Metaphysics, however, generally intends to break asunder the bands of human bondage, conceived as our specifically physical fallibility. Its tenor is more aggressive. Furthermore, in its disposal of nature, it refuses the core truth of nature as well as our own mortality. This truth is finitude.

Rough empirical evidence for this claim can be found by comparing the respective success met with by these two responses. If positive wasting is indeed unproblematic, this means its success can be measured according to how clean it is of human failure and neglect. As it turns out, authentic ritualistic wasting does not, strictly speaking, create waste at all, due to the care and attention it involves. Rituals cultivate mental concentration and heighten an awareness for details. They lose their point and power when performed distractedly, carelessly, hurriedly; thus, they are incommensurate with negligence and indifference. It is important to distinguish waste from ritualized attempts at surpassing necessity.

The Feast

The ritual of feasting provides the most obvious and basic example of the phenomenon of "positive wastage" ascribed by Baudrillard to all societies. An objective definition of feasting might run: consuming more than basic physical requirements of the body demand. However, as a ritualistic celebration of abundance, the traditional feast carves out a piece of nature's plenitude and offers the celebrant direct participation in the vitality and bounty of life. The feast inundates mere survival with abundance, thereby sublimating it. Survival ceases to be a concern within the special boundaries marked off by the feast because these boundaries concentrate the universal copiousness of nature, making it amenable to direct human participation and some measure of human control. The feast clears a space for humans to play at immortality by offering not mere excessive consumption, but rather the physical incorporation of abundance itself. When feasting, the celebrant consciously reenacts the unconscious law of nature. Or, more precisely, the celebrant personifies, both literally and symbolically, the essence of life.

As with all types of ritual, the feast accomplishes this nearly magical transcendence by setting limits. In this case, the most basic boundaries are temporal. Feasts occur at special times and have definite durations. A temporally undefined feast loses all of its symbolic force and efficacy. Without the concentration of abundance created by the delimitation of time, the feast distends, becoming undifferentiated from normal consumption. For its part, normal consumption always has more or less to do with mere survival, with satisfying the mortal needs of the body. So long as man remains in essence a mortal, ineluctably finite being, normal needy consumption cannot be done away with. This hangs as the backdrop on which the ritual of feast is meaningfully projected. In other words, the feast derives its power and meaning only in contrast to ordinary consumption characterzed by leaner necessity.

With the erasure of the feast's temporal borders, the ritualized concentration of abundance dissipates into mere excess. Since excess is defined relative to a given purpose, it must be called unnatural insofar as nature lacks any sort of express *telos*. The meaning of the feast depends on its symbolic power to rarefy base survival through a special concentration of the natural life force. This meaning disappears to the same extent as do the ritualized limits on which it depends. The absence of the feast's transcendent meaning consequently gets filled by the purpose of normal consumption, that is, the maintenance of the physical body. Since the human body consists of nothing but limits all the way down to its very spatial extension, its maintenance has very definite requirements. Whatever exceeds these said requirements is excessive. So, while the symbolic significance of the feast preserves it in the abundance of nature, the loss of this significance leaves room for the deluges of excess. Indefinitely prolonged feasting must end in mere gluttony—the excessive consumption that defies the body's limited needs as well as the brief taste of immortality offered to the spirit enthralled within the limits of the feast.

Being finite, humans can cope with abundance only under special conditions instituted by ritual. We cope by making sense of James's "blooming, buzzing confusion." Excessive consumption, however, because unconditioned, reopens bounded meaning to the kind of chaos that the institutions of ritual were built to contain. The consumer society, with its bottomless cornucopia of commodities, lays out a perpetual feast lacking beginning and end. It obliterates all meaningful temporal differentiations. As its advertisements vaunt, the consumer society permanently strives to replace the normal consumption associated with the needy body, with the extraordinary, transcendent consumption accomplished by reason, that faculty of ours nearest to the infinite. Even so basic a good as food is never advertised as a necessity. Rather it is sold—and bought—as simply another component among others that constitute a certain lifestyle inhabited by a specific persona of consumer. Semantic and symbolic significance—properties of our linguistic reason—take precedence over the pragmatic significance of the objects we desire and seek. Consumption becomes a kind of interminable chatter, a speaking in tongues that can no longer meaningfully address the real limits of the body. Excess thus enters the new discourse of consumption when the delimiting body is forced from its role as interlocutor.

Anyone who has ever overeaten knows the dull, heavy, and deathlike feelings that follow excessive consumption. Gluttony blunts the keenness of the senses; the experience of excess brings about sensations closer to the inertness of death than to the vibrant animation of life. Similarly, the technological supply for the unbounded celebration of lifestyle ends up destroying the meaningful vitality of the traditionally circumscribed feast of the lifeforce.

It remains to be seen whether the difference between the traditional and the modern forms of feasting entails a real ontological distinction between natural and technological abundance. While it does hint at such a distinction, mere insinuation does not permit decisive conclusions. The feast exists as a cultural response to a brute, inexplicable fact confronting man—the overabundance of nature—and any natural phenomena of this kind can elicit a wide variety of responses. It will prove helpful to point out some other essential features of the traditional feast in contrast to modern rituals of consumption. If sharpened sufficiently, the contrast may show an underlying difference between sources of these incommensurable forms of ritual.

Baudrillard draws attention to the first feature when he admonishes that:

> we have to distinguish individual or collective waste as a sym-
> bolic act of expenditure, as a festive ritual and an exalted form of
> socialization, from its gloomy, bureaucratic caricature in our
> societies, where wasteful consumption has become a daily obli-
> gation, a forced and often unconscious institution like indirect
> taxation, a cool participation in the constraints of the economic
> order. [10]

As a meaningful ritual, the traditional feast must also be culturally instituted, but, as an institution, it cannot obligate. As soon as one is compelled to feast, the possibility of genuine feasting vanishes. For a feast to
function truly its participants must enter into it voluntarily, otherwise it
amounts to a kind of forced-feeding—the very antithesis of the celebratory incorporation of abundance. The ritual of the feast serves temporarily to transcend the exigencies of the needy body. Any obligation with
respect to feasting simply substitutes one set of necessities for another.

Obligation subordinates the feast to the very thing it was designed to overcome.

Tightly bound to its voluntary nature is the celebratory essence of the feast. A ritualized affirmation of abundance, the feast allows its celebrants to appropriate the overwhelming fullness of nature, mitigating its awesome grandeur for a set period of time. Through this appropriation, the celebrant directly participates in the inexhaustible life force. A kind of spontaneous merger thus ensues between the person and her celebrated source of abundance, which traditionally has been nature. There results from this a feeling of limitless expansion, although conditioned, of course, by the all-important limits of ritual. Elative joy attends every authentic feast. Without this distinguished guest, the feast quickly deflates into a lifeless masquerade of mundane consumption.

The celebratory aspect of the feast reflects not only its content, but equally its form. Because a cultural response, the feast is also a collective one: it has to be shared to attain meaning. The feast involves other celebrants no less than it does abundance. It taxes the imagination to picture a solitary feast, which can be nothing more than a sumptuous feed. In short, the phenomenon of the feast is crowded with people, laughter, and edible plenty. It has a voluntary, celebratory, and communal structure.

A final essential feature of the feast remains. Although not to be attempted here, it could be plausibly argued that the ritual of the feast developed out of the ritual of sacrifice. In any case, the feast retains a sacrificial element in its receptive and grateful acknowledgment and celebration of abundance. For its part, the ritual of sacrifice performs a kind of dialectic exchange by offering back what has been received. Strictly speaking, the sacrifice is not a giving, but a returning. Moreover, it involves what looks like another example of positive wastage. In sacrificing, a person places something of utility outside the sphere of possible human use. Thus, the sacrificed object gains value to the extent that it escapes its use-function. With respect to utility, its value corresponds inversely to its being consumed. Like the feast, sacrifice transcends, by this means, the exigencies of survival. Feast and sacrifice seem to overlap, for there can be little joy without gratitude; and gratitude without joy is a grudging contradiction.

If we care to listen to Baudrillard, as well as to our own experience of disappointment and dissatisfaction, the modern consumerist feast lacks the primary qualities of its traditional antecedents. A gloomy obligation to excessively consume hardly qualifies as feasting. Add to this the typical attitude of the participant—characterized by an insistence on the inviolable right of the consumer rather than by receptive gratitude—and the notion of feast mutates beyond recognition. The dissolution of the necessary temporal limits has left modernity with an exceeding capacity to consume. The result is that the ritual of the feast, once the primary vehicle for making sense of and bringing order to the brute fact of nature, has grown almost irreparably ineffectual. It has lost its font of meaning. The extinguishment of the feast, however, does not mean the disappearance of the problem to which it originally responded. Douglas observes: "As a social animal, man is a ritual animal. If ritual is suppressed in one form, it crops up in others, more strongly the more intense the social interaction. . . . It is impossible to have social relations without symbolic acts."[11] A culture left with a mere husk of ritual must develop a substitute to handle the experiences no longer controlled by the moribund cultural institution.

Conspicuous Consumption

In lieu of the feast, technological society has developed its own codified behavior that mimics positive wastage in order to superimpose its own metaphysical excesses onto natural abundance. Metaphysics deals in excess because its very essence drives toward surpassing limits. This excess gets ordered, or, more accurately, gets ranked in what Thorstein Veblen called emulative wastage. In a manner reminiscent of the feast, emulative wasting attempts to impose order on the chaos of superabundance by introducing into it limits and distinctions. However, the attempt fails and falls short of meaningful ritual because these limits are manufactured by reason alone. Extrinsic to the phenomenon, they have an arbitrary and physically groundless character.

Written at the turn of the twentieth century, Veblen's *Theory of the Leisure Class* predates the completed construction of the modern monoliths of advertising and mass media. Nonetheless, the industrial revolution by that point had matured sufficiently to show all the most prominent features of its older age. Veblen's famous theory demonstrates how the nature of abundance is inoculated with cultural meaning through the needle of social status.

The theory claims that human community transformed from a primeval state of peaceable and egalitarian coexistence into a "consistently warlike habit of life."[12] Under belligerent conditions that threaten the security and survival of a person or a people, physical prowess assumes supreme value, thanks to its unrivaled utility. In war, as on the hunt, strength and power secure both the physical—for example, food—and the social—for example, stability—goods of life. In other words, power brings home the spoils and the kill. Through characteristic confusion, people began to equate material wealth—the product of power—with power itself. So it happened that the "possession of wealth, which was at the outset valued simply as an evidence of efficiency, becomes, in popular apprehension, itself a meritorious act."[13] More than merely reflecting power, wealth comes to materialize it, physically manifesting the possessor's importance to the community. Standing as indubitable proof of social worth, wealth thus becomes the surest determinant of social status.

The wealth produced through power and predation has an almost magical quality. What otherwise would require long periods of labor to procure is taken possession of with sudden celerity. A concentrated burst of energy fells the prey, bringing immediate material plenty, while prolonged hours of manual toil, or industry as Veblen calls it, fail to produce equivalent quantity. The conflation of power and wealth severs any connection that may have bound prosperity to work. Work thereby suffers a double debasement: because it falls short of wealth, it has always to labor on necessity, and because work does not require physical prowess, only the weak find it necessary. The occupation of the inferior, productive work comes to occupy a position of inferiority below power.

It follows from this that to work means to reveal one's low status. Conversely, to display through idleness the absence of the need to work means to enjoy the appropriated fruits of power. Ostensible uselessness on the productive level translates into great utility by the measure of prosperity. The activity of leisure thus manifests the possession of wealth and power. The more conspicuously one practices this activity in the sight of the community, the more stable one's elevated position of rank.

Conspicuous leisure functions well to establish order in communities small enough that most members may witness and understand the claims to status asserted by it. In the anonymity of larger groups, however, the efficacy of leisure as evidence of power decreases. To properly convey meaning, leisure requires a certain degree of familiarity among neighbors as to how they spend their time. Conspicuous consumption, on the other hand, can immediately convince even a complete stranger of the consumer's social rank. Fashion, for instance, enables the consumer of luxuries quite literally to wear his worth. Expensive, coveted garments and jewelery proclaim at once, through a kind of *lingua franca*, the disposable wealth possessed by the wearer.

"From the foregoing survey of the growth of conspicuous leisure and consumption," to quote Veblen, "it appears that the utility of both alike for the purposes of reputability lies in their element of waste that is common to both. In the one case it is a waste of time and effort, in the other it is a waste of goods."[14] For either leisure or consumption to persuasively demonstrate wealth, they must involve excess. With this, Veblen discovers meaning within the meaningless excesses of industrial society. Waste is ascribed a purpose: to make patent the wealth and power of the wastrel in question. What is naturally meaningless consequently becomes the very determinant and defender of social order. As in the case of feasting and sacrifice, waste sheds its repellent nature when it is purposively placed within the human project of meaning.

Veblen further bends the nature of abundance to the incipient consumer culture's requirement for meaning in the absence of traditional ritual when he writes:

> With the exception of the instinct of self-preservation, the propensity for emulation is probably the strongest and most alert and persistent of the economic motives proper. In an industrial community this propensity for emulation expresses itself in pecuniary emulation; and this, so far as regards the Western civilized communities of the present, is virtually equivalent to saying that it expresses itself in some form of conspicuous *waste*. The need of conspicuous waste, therefore, stands ready to absorb any increase in the community's industrial efficiency or output of goods, after the most elementary physical wants have been provided for.[15]

The ritual of conspicuous consumption gives some sense, albeit absurd, to the seeming pointlessness of industrialization's overproductivity, whose overwhelming aspect relents somewhat, just as the awesomeness of natural abundance relents through the feast within the signifying confines of ritual.

Veblen's prose, as the previous quotation witnesses, echoes with catches of a sophisticated social Darwinism, which is itself a cultural by-product of an industrialization that postdates the decline of ritual feasting. Emulative wastage opposes festive wastage in its most basic features. Conspicuous consumption is, by definition, competitive rather then communal; its very function is to stratify individuals into antagonistic classes. This competitive essence imbues the ritual with a feeling of compulsion, which can appropriate even a refusal to participate. Because the entire society operates on the principle of emulative wasting, every member of this society necessarily performs in its codified consumption. An individual can, of course, assume a greater or lesser role in the performance, but cannot completely exit the stage while remaining a part of the cultural play. In this way the "ritual" is personally manipulative.

The manipulation, furthermore, does not stop at the participants; it penetrates with even greater force into the objects of consumption. A tendency toward violence marks conspicuous consumption. Whereas the traditional feast sets up consumption as the grateful reception of natural power, emulative wastage seizes objects as a willful assertion of human power. The possibility of sacrifice in this latter "ritual" is completely foreclosed. Its mandatory consumption has no need for the integrity of its objects; it consumes them as mere empty symbols of its power. The feast, contrariwise, relies on the integrity of its objects, for they have not only to symbolize abundance, but also must instantiate it. Feasting evokes gratitude because it functions only insofar as its objects are received in the spirit in which they were given. The gift of natural abundance is not an interchangeable, metaphorical prop for the human subject's self-aggrandizement.

Scarcity and Abundance

These fundamental differences rest on a still deeper difference. Uncovering this difference means breaking ontological ground. It became clear earlier that the feast primarily enacts an affirmation of natural abundance. It expresses a human acceptance of the amazing fullness of nature that helps finite man find his bearings, howsoever briefly, amid the plenitude. Strictly speaking, feasting cannot waste. For just as the life force of nature, having neither purpose nor the values that purposes impose, cannot exceed itself, so its symbolic consumption cannot become excessive or wasteful. The feast recreates the immense fecundity of nature on a human scale, transferring the wastelessness of the original to the recreation. A feast cannot have too much. What the human celebrants do not consume, of this the presiding, though unseen, gods will partake.

The modern form of 'positive wastage' could not contradict this more starkly. Emulative wasting is predicated not at all on abundance; its real source is scarcity. From this source flow its competitive, compelling, violent, and ungrateful qualities. Because the codified consumption seeks to order experience and secure cultural meaning through the hierarchical establishment of rank or status, it necessarily trades in a scarce commodity. By definition, status cannot be abundant. It presupposes a hierarchy, the top of which remains forever exclusive. Should every member of a group possess like status, then the very notion of it would dissolve into vacuity. Emulative wastage thus flies in the face of what Baudrillard attributed to all human societies, namely, the festive rituals that celebrate the exuberance of life.

Marshall Sahlins's provocative essay, "The Original Affluent Society," exposes the economic mechanisms driving the consumer society. There he writes:

The market-industrial system institutes scarcity, in a manner completely unparalleled and to a degree nowhere else approximated. Where production and distribution are arranged through the behaviour of prices, and all livelihoods depend on getting and spending, insufficiency of material means becomes the explicitly, calculable starting point of all economic activity.[16]

Sahlin argues that true affluence belongs to unsophisticated hunter-gatherer societies, rather than to the materially excessive, though structurally impoverishing affluence of industrial systems. This does not mean that we must immediately start fashioning spearheads out of our credit cards. But it does mean countenancing the serious faults of a culture that presumes to have overtopped all limitation. The culture fails to see that its lofty achievements sit on a mountain of suffering and denial: "This is the era of hunger unprecedented. Now in the time of the greatest technical power, is starvation an institution. Reverse another venerable formula: the amount of hunger increases relatively and absolutely with the evolution of culture."[17]

A most fascinating conclusion issues from this. Technological excess, presumably the sublimated analogue to nature's abundance, grounds itself on scarcity. A significant difference between natural abundance and technological excess has come to light. The first stems out of a natural fullness, the second from scarcity, that is, from a lack, a nullity. This means that only the latter truly involves waste. Only the latter takes place within the desolate emptiness of failure and neglect that waste implies.

For all its excesses, then, consumer culture remains rooted in finitude. This accounts for its unlimited trash; for wastes in general implicate human finitude. Despite its abundance, the essence of nature is finite. The finiteness of matter, embodied in our physicality, is what the metaphysical perspective sees as wasteful in nature. Rationality is deemed wasted on the bodily animal. The technological quest to escape the waste of nature aims at dominating nature and breaking its essential limits on matter. The limitless material of this destructive initiative is trash.

This explains the unproblematic nature of trash from the phenomenological point of view. The phenomenon of trash appears within the metaphysical denial of finitude. The fact that such copious material cannot cut its roots to finitude, no matter what level of technology is employed, points to a fundamental truth of nature and of being. It indicates that the finitude of human being—its physical mortality—not only conditions phenomena, but relates eradicably to Being. Whereas waste implies human neglect and failure, trash forcefully declares the marriage between Being and finitude. It does this by showing that the metaphysical neglect for the needs of our finite nature results in a flood of material failure. Reportedly only two manmade structures are visible to the naked eye from outer space. The first is the Great Wall of China; the second, New York City's Fresh Kills landfill site. When properly perceived, trash signals the waste of our true being. There hides in all of modernity's *rejecta* unrecognized potential for edification.

Ontology is the study of being. An ontology of trash will focus on the mode of being unique to the technological era: disposability. Yet if the perception is to be edifying, as opposed to simply dismal and despairing, the insight must look through the being of trash to how it relates to our own current mode of human being. Trash can act as a lens that brings to clear sight the matrimonial bond between human being and what Martin Heidegger calls Being as such. Heidegger himself questioned Being with such unflagging devotion that no ontological pursuit coming after him can overlook his contribution. This study will lean greatly on the strength of Heidegger's thought. If it uses trash a lens to investigate human existence, then Heidegger's thinking of Being provides the frame that keeps the lens in place.

By no means does Heidegger have a monopoly on ontology. In fact, he even repudiated the term as his thinking matured. And other philosophers too have had just as much and more to say about technological modernity as he. This study's reliance on Heidegger is not for, as the saying goes, lack of options. On the contrary, I appeal to Heidegger's thought for what it shares with the wisdom of great spiritual traditions. For example, many commentators have noted the affinities between Buddhist and Heideggerean ontologies.

> Both Heidegger and the Zen master would say that Western humanity's technological will to power over nature arises from an inadequate understanding of what it means to be human. So long as we regard ourselves as ego-subjects who are the measure of all things, we will plunder the planet in an endless quest for security and control. Needed is a shift from our present understanding of all things as objects whose value lies solely in what they can contribute to some human purpose. Such a shift, which would be an epochal historical event, would reveal to us that our true aim in life is not to exploit things, but instead to let them manifest themselves as they are. The highest possibility of human existence, then, is to love and to serve: we become ourselves when we let beings be. Heidegger's notion of releasement seems very close to the Buddhist doctrine of compassion for all beings.[18]

To love and to serve is also the core teaching of Christianity and Hinduism. For me the spiritual sympathies shared among Heidegger's philosophy and venerable religious traditions lend credibility to the former.

This study, however, is not a theological work, but an ontological one. My concern is to demonstrate that indeed the "highest possibility of human existence" is the ontological service of "letting beings be." The prime reason I must turn to Heidegger and thus engage in philosophy rather than religion is for his historical insight. If acknowledged at all, history typically receives something of a crude interpretation from most religious traditions. Heidegger's thought is, on the other hand, explicitly and essentially historical.[19] If trash is to be properly understood and responded to, it must be approached in its peculiarity, which means in the context of its historical development. It does not help much to say our ancestors neither enjoyed nor suffered today's mass-produced disposables simply because they lacked the requisite technology. One could still intelligently ask why they lacked the technology. What made their world and their way of being so different that they likely could not have conceived what we now find commonplace? Heidegger's ontology marks a path that wends through such questions toward meaning.

Yet at spots the path grows quite obscure. Both his students and his critics have pointed to areas of trouble and grave concern in Heidegger's thought. His notorious silence on ethical, moral, and political issues does present a sizable, though not insurmountable, stumbling block to all who would follow him. So, too, the alleged traces of metaphysics that some believe to have turned up in his "history of Being."[20] His grand historical narrative itself might appear to some as a egregious example of metaphysical speculation gone awry. And, although masterfully adept at analyzing certain aspects of everyday existence, Heidegger at the same time refuses so much as to mention other equally, if not more important aspects such as our sexuality, our relationship to illness and aging, our quest for pleasure, and hope for corporeal immortality. He thus seems to dutifully follow the metaphysical tradition in its characteristic neglect of the lived human body. "Unfortunately," remarks Zimmerman, Heidegger's "discussions of embodiment are limited, perhaps because of his uncertainty about how to define the body without lapsing into naturalistic categories."[21] While caution here is indeed philosophically prudent, the omission is unfortunate because Heidegger's thought sympathizes with our inherited wisdom thanks to, and I know no better word for it, the spirit of humility running through it. In an age bent on surpassing all limits, Heidegger stresses the essential limitations of being, especially human being. From *Being and Time* on, human mortality plays a pivotal role in his philosophy. Our finitude defines our worldly being. But there is much more to it than just that. The mystery of our mortality is at once the bestowal and perfection of Being as such. For "man necessarily belongs and has his place in the openness (and at present in the forgottenness) of Being. But Being needs man as the there of its openness in order to open itself. . . . If Being needs man in this way in order to be, *a finitude of Being* must be assumed accordingly."[22] In this sense we are entrusted with mortality in our service to Being. The notion is not altogether foreign to Christianity. Eckhart says that "God needs me as much as I need him" and, more generally, Christian doctrine holds that our fallen existence is the means by which God's mercy, forgiveness, and love can be realized. The Buddhists have a similar idea that the dark realm of suffering and illusion (*samsara*) is the gift we receive that invites us to enlightenment. Whatever the details, these various ways of thinking accord in that we must find our salvation in the face of our limitation.

The heart of human mortality and finitude is our corporeality. For this reason, Catholics anticipate not just resurrection but specifically resurrection of the body. Similarly, the awakened one (the *Buddha*) exists incarnate in order to ease the sufferings of all beings and help them to enlightenment. Because of its inextricable tie to salvation, "the body phenomenon is the most difficult problem."[23] These words are Heidegger's, but the practical work of solving this problem he for the most part forgoes. Also, the lack of a solid physical basis to his philosophy of finitude makes Heidegger's thought susceptible to unwanted, perhaps unnoticed, metaphysical incursions.

Since Merleau-Ponty, Heidegger's phenomenology has received numerous "substantial" amendments that seek to flesh out a philosophy of embodiment missing in his thought. The ontology of trash hopes to make further amends by demonstrating how the junked material of our technological mode of being ultimately belies our metaphysical quest for the infinite and proves it to be irremediably flawed. It will do so by interpreting the bodily situation of modern humanity with a view to its ontological significance. Upon situating the modern body in a technological conurbation devoid of the nourishment of nature, this study will have arrived at a position at which it can show how trash wastes our mortal being through the looming phenomenon of human extinction.

CHAPTER TWO

The Body

What makes the body "the most difficult problem"? More to the point, what does this problem have to do with trash? I have suggested that trash materially manifests our failure at being human and that, when properly understood, this phenomenon unambiguously exhibits our existential shortcomings. Such an understanding reveals trash as a denial of our essential finitude. To put it otherwise, trash results from the attempted process of negating human finitude. Since the difficulty of the body lies in its finite nature—its mortality—the phenomenon of trash comes to appear as the negation or effacement of the human body. It would seem, then, that trash is unproblematic in itself because it represents the dissolution of the problem of embodiment.

This last is, however, a metaphysical conclusion. It explains the common unconcern on the part of the consumer society for the real physical perils of its pollution. Technological humanity, mistaking trash as the solution to the problem of physicality, continues to produce increasing amounts of it. The consumer of technology tacitly believes trash helps rather than hinders the fulfillment of her being. How could trash help metaphysical consumers? It distracts us from our bodies. If waste implies human failure and imperfection, and, furthermore, if waste bears close associations with our animal matter, then the predominance of trash over waste seems to signal reason's triumph over the body. Trash—objects presupposed as essentially disposable—results from a willful human determination concerning the being of the object. Trash flatters our delusive fantasy of omnipotence. Waste, on the other hand, affronts reason with the unhappy recognition of its own ultimate impotence in the face of physicality.

In this chapter, I begin the task of interpreting the paradoxical, unrecognized motivation that produces trash: we create trash to deny waste. Of course, as individual consumers going about our daily lives, we do not think of trash in this manner. In fact, qua consumers, we barely think about trash at all and feel quite at ease with this state of thoughtlessness. Because trash increases the GDP of industrialized nations it is considered productive. But this, as I will argue, dissembles the true educational nature of trash. The productive and the educative perspectives on trash clash irreconcilably. Existentially, trash is unproblematic to the extent that it calls attention to our own neglect of our proper embodied existence. Only when trash serves as the souvenir of our finitude does it pose no problems. This requires, however, a radical ontological interpretation of the phenomenon.

In the last chapter, two important quotes were cited without sufficient comment. Zimmerman let it be known that "we become ourselves when we let beings be."[1] If the being of trash is a sign of our own failure at being human, then this should be seen in a general inability to let beings be. I have just implied that trash itself is not allowed fully to be in the consumer society, where its essential didactic function succumbs to occlusion beneath unexamined habits of thought and action. Almost all other phenomena, however, share this fate of disappearance, which strikes first at our physicality. If "Being needs man as the there of its openness in order to open itself,"[2] that is, if finitude plays an essential role in the occurrence of Being, then the body must stand as the intermediary between Being and beings. This chapter, consequently, is a positive exploration of how the body relates to beings, human being, and Being as such. At the same time, it is a negative interpretation of the effacement of the body as the cause of trash.

Two demonstrations of these relationships are possible: one fashioned out of Heidegger's skeletal remarks on embodiment and the other gleaned from a critique launched against Heidegger's project of fundamental ontology. As the second is less involved, I will begin with it.

Needs of the Body

According to Emmanuel Levinas, Heidegger's preoccupation with ontology blinded him to the more radical fundamentality of ethics. Levinas argues that the true being of the Other encountering me as a human face eludes both ontic and ontological comprehension, which is a kind of possessive grasping, and instead elicits a receptive acknowledgment, which is a kind of caress. Each face is irreducible in its particularity and uniqueness, leaving the understanding, which operates with universals, empty-handed. This means that we do not, through our interpretative circumspection and comportment, disclose the Other or let the other be. Rather the Other confronts us with its sheer otherness.

Yet this most radical difference, and here I pass from exegesis to interpretation, is based on a still deeper identity between the Other and I. Shared between the two interlocutors is a common vulnerability, or sensitivity. I do not thereby project myself on the Other, which would negate the insurmountable difference between us. In fact, by recognizing in the Other that which individuates myself—my pain, my need, in a word, my finitude—I first meet the Other in his incomprehensible otherness. This meeting is irrevocably ethical: "Before the Other (*Autrui*), the I is infinitely responsible. The Other is the poor and destitute one, and nothing which concerns this Stranger can leave the I indifferent. It attains the apogee of its existence as I precisely when everything looks at it in the Other (*Autrui*)."[3] So our shared finitude makes me at once responsive to and responsible for the needs of the Other.

Whether or not Levinas's critique of Heidegger's ontological project actually hits its mark is beside the point here. Important is the priority he places on the neediness and fragility of human being. These quintessential features of our being are in the most literal sense pre-ontological because they condition not only the possibility of ontology, but also of Being as such. I use this metaphysical jargon with reluctance. If, as Heidegger maintains, "Being needs man," it must need his neediness because that is precisely what constitutes his receptive openness for beings. But Heidegger never acknowledges this; he does not consider that the fact that we thirst, hunger, require rest, shelter, and companionship solicits the beings that address these needs. Were we absolutely self-sufficient, we would not need beings to perpetuate our own being; self-enclosed, our existence would not be ecstatic in the sense that Heidegger uses this term. Not having to go beyond or to transcend ourselves in order to exist, our being could not clear an open dimension in which beings could manifest themselves. Levinas's insistence, in critical response to Heidegger, that the Other confronts us in poverty, destitution, and pain exposes the needy, vulnerable body as the very ground of Being.

Saying that Being needs humans in this way does not subordinate the former to the latter. This is not the pompous voice of anthropocentrism speaking. "More primordial than man," wrote Heidegger in 1925, "is the finitude of Dasein in him."[4] Finitude, understood now as bodily neediness, is the very thing that we most violently repudiate and ardently will to disown. Human mortality, in other words, is not our accomplishment; it is not even a matter of our choice. Although it determines the essence of human being, our needy finitude has nothing to do with us as autonomous, subjective agents. Being can depend on our finitude because our existence receives this willy-nilly from Being. Thus, Being's need for us evidences foremost our existential indebtedness, never fully repayable, to Being.

The Nature of the Body

The fragile body that needs beings in order to be incarnates the finitude requisite for Being. In this context, calling the body the ground of Being signifies something radically different from how metaphysics applies the term. This ground is more basic than sufficient reasons, and will not be uncovered by any purely rational effort. The body as ground is synonymous with the designation found in the *Bhagavadgita*, considered the jewel of ancient Hindu scripture. There the divine incarnation Krishna calls the body a field.[5] These geographical terms connoting earth and growth perfectly suit the naturalness of the body. Heidegger's later word for human being—*Lichtung*—meaning clearing, has multiple possible interpretations, though Heidegger himself favors the one with geographical connotations. A clearing in a forest is an opening amid the density of growth where light gathers and events occur. This empty yet pregnant space is best understood as yet another designation for the physicality of the human body.

Heidegger, of course, never himself said as much explicitly, but that his thought wandered in this direction becomes apparent in the seminar course he gave with Eugene Fink in 1966 on Heraclitus. Sparked by a fragment involving sleep and dreams, the discussion moves into themes of light and darkness, proximity and difference. Fink, trying to characterize the distinction of human being, says: "in so far as a human is a living being, he also has another character of being with which he reaches into the nightly ground. He has the double character: on the one hand, he is the one who places himself in the clearing, and on the other, he is the one who is tied to the underground of all clearing." Heidegger responds, "This would become intelligible first of all through the phenomenon of the body."[6] The implication here is that the clearing, or our pre-ontological understanding of Being, rests on some more basic enclosure, something incomprehensible. The underground of all clearing is the physical need, involuntary and unfathomable, for physicality. Just as the pioneers needed to clear land to support their corporeal being, so humans in general must stand as the clearing where beings can appear in response to our needy finitude. Being thus grounds itself on the fragility of our physical existence.

Heidegger subsequently clarifies his intention, aligning it with how "Nietzsche thought the body, even though it is obscure what he actually meant by it."

> FINK: In the section "Of the Despisers of the Body," Zarathustra says, "Body am I entirely, and nothing else . . . ." Through the body and the senses a human is nigh to the earth.

Then, after a brief exchange, Heidegger asks rhetorically:

> Can one isolate the dark understanding, which the bodily belonging to the earth determines, from being placed in the clearing?[7]

Indeed, the body itself places man in the clearing. This dark understanding clears or illuminates a space for the meaningful manifestation of beings. In one sense, we are right to think, as our metaphysical tradition has, of our physicality as foreign to us. For the physical belongs entirely to Being as such. This we cannot reduce or confine to our own needy being, which constitutes only one party in the communication of disclosure.

Physis to the ancient Greeks meant nature. It also meant Being. One can approach the paradoxical finitude of Being not only by way of our needy finiteness, but also in the latter's natural correlate—namely, the intrinsic limitations of nature. Science, of course, recognizes nature as a vast collection of limits that play themselves out in determinable laws. Yet, according to Heidegger, the ancients had no such conception. For them, the limits of nature were ontological in essence. Vincent Vycinas's description helps to show this:

> *Physis* in general means the rising or breaking through, unravelling and developing. Thus *physis* appears and comes forward and sojourns in this appearance; it *is* this appearance. . . . The breaking through and coming forward *is* Being, *is physis*. It is never a property of Being, but is Being itself. In breaking through, *physis* holds an order or a realm open within which it dominates all appearances. Such an order of dominating, *physis* gives unity and articulation and, as a result, the strength of being to everything. Anything whatsoever would not be thinkable, would disintegrate into nothing, if it were not for the power of *physis* which throws everything into its boundaries—waters, lands, animals, men, nations, and even gods.[8]

Throwing things into their boundaries, *physis* defines them. Every being exists as something definite, even if only as something definitely strange and obscure. Nature comes to pass through the limits within which phenomena appear.

"Meta," meaning beyond or above, signals the intrinsic dynamism of metaphysics, the essence of which is to surpass, exceed, and overcome the limits of physicality. Heidegger contends that history begins with metaphysics because the inability to rest within natural boundaries drives metaphysics to the incessant self-supersessions of historical change. Late industrial and "postindustrial" society has been dubbed by some commentators the "end of history." This becomes intelligible in light of what Thomas Tierney describes as the "trajectory of modernity": "to render everyone free not only from the limits which are imposed by the body, but even from the body itself."[9] Thus, the end of history and the end of metaphysics coincide in the negation of the possibility of their existence. That is, that the trajectory common to modernity and metaphysics is suicidal in that it seeks to destroy the limitations that make overcoming possible.

When we approach our essential finitude as "the bodily belonging to the earth," then the ontological aspects of physicality come into view. The Greek's dual understanding of *physis*—nature and Being—is, so to speak, most vitally alive in the nature of the body. According to Heidegger, Being occurs as the strife between revealing and concealing. In "The Origin of the Work of Art," he calls this interdependent pair world and earth.

> The world is the self-disclosing openness of the broad paths of the simple and essential decisions in the destiny of an historical people. The earth is the spontaneous forthcoming of that which is continually self-secluding and to that extent sheltering and concealing. . . . The world, in resting upon the earth, strives to surmount it. As self-opening it cannot endure anything closed. The earth, however, as sheltering and concealing, tends always to draw the world into itself and keep it there.[10]

So even while *physis* "appears and comes forward" into appearance, even as it throws beings into their limits of revelation, it also has a deeper counterpull toward concealment. Only something concealed can be unconcealed: "Earth is that whence the arising brings back and shelters everything that arises without violation. In the things that arise, earth is present as the sheltering agent."[11] The active strife between revealing and concealing that occurs as Being thus turns on the primacy of concealment.

Heidegger's poetic language is prone to remain metaphorical, making it easy to bandy about, but difficult to comprehend. This is remedied by understanding the earth, or concealing force, in terms of our "bodily belonging" to it. Quite simply, the body is the seat of all human experience. Every sensation, emotion, thought, desire, and intention occurs to an embodied agent. In Michael Zimmerman's words:

> Dasein is embodied openness to what is. A feeling is manifest to me just as much as is a friend. Although a feeling is different from a friend, both are manifest insofar as there is some temporal openness in which that manifesting can occur. A gnawing pain manifests itself in my stomach; as I open the refrigerator door, a turkey leg manifests itself. Seeing the turkey leg is not more "objective" than feeling the pain in my stomach. Of course, a turkey leg is not like a pain in any ontical way, but ontologically both turkey leg and pain are revealed through me.[12]

"Through me" means to the sensitive flesh that allows for temporal experience.

Leaving the discussion on temporality to chapter six, we can now begin to appreciate how well the name "field" fits the human body. Besides its associations with nature, a field gives rise to beings, while simultaneously becoming more concealed. The cover of flora hides the productive ground, and the thicker the cover the deeper the earth's concealment. With the body, the cover of manifest phenomena—perceptions, ideas, emotions—obscures their more basic and mysterious physical fundament. What goes on in my heart is completely inaccessible to me, yet I believe that, whatever may happen there, my existence relies on it. I wake up one morning feeling ill with a sharp pain in my neck and can make nothing intelligible of it. I exist as embodied, yet my body remains utterly remote and foreign to me. Without my body, I could not experience and hence would know nothing. However, when thematized, my body utterly baffles me and flees from my intellection. The body, the source of sensitivity, powerfully resists making sense.

Heidegger thought that Being as such withdraws as beings come into manifest presence. This perennial withdrawal accounts for our own perpetual conflation of Being and the phenomena that appear. We mistake Being as itself some kind of entity, thereby effacing for ourselves the so-called ontological difference between Being and beings. Without a careful maintenance of this difference, we become forgetful of the truth of Being. This typical state of modern human existence Heidegger labeled *Vergessenheit*—oblivion or forgetfulness. We might, without erring too grossly, also call it a kind of mindlessness and distraction. I can jostle through a crowd or hurry through a forest and see not a single human face or tree. Not only do I fail to allow the beings in my company to make themselves known, more regrettably, I fail to be struck by the astonishing mystery of which I am a vital part: that I am living amid a constantly renewing occasion for things to become manifest. Although it is not always clear whether forgetfulness is an inevitable feature of "fallen" human existence, Heidegger was convinced that the metaphysical history of the West had intensified it to an extremely dangerous degree.

Again, the ontological dynamic between retiring Being and manifest beings that so easily moves into oblivion is more accessible to interpretation and understanding via the flesh of the body. "The body conceals itself," Drew Leder observes,"precisely in the act of revealing what is Other. The very presencing of the world and of the body as an object within it is always correlative with this primordial absence."[13] Leder's *The Absent Body* can be read as an extended field study on the ontological nature of the body. The withdrawal of Being in the face of phenomena directly corresponds to the various levels of experiential absence that Leder investigates phenomenologically. For instance, "insofar as I perceive through an organ, it necessarily recedes from the perceptual field it discloses."[14] As with a geographical field, cognitive impenetrability deepens below the surface: "Buried within the bodily-depths, my viscera resists my reflective gaze and physical manipulation. To be in depth disappearance is ordinarily to recede from the arc of personal involvement as a whole, neither subject nor object of direct engagement"[15] The three ontological moments of withdrawal, manifestness, and forgetfulness thus physically transpire in the absence of the sensitive body that allows for perceptual openness. The impenetrability of absence and the openness of sensitivity together can slip into a kind of experiential disappearance of the lived reality of the body. Like *Vergessenheit*, this bodily disappearance has undergone historical development.

Although Leder does not explicitly draw out all the connections, his study provides the phenomenological wherewithal to understand the deep ontological nature of the body. Of preeminent interpretive importance is his history of the objectifying disappearance of the lived body because it retraces perfectly the metaphysical history of oblivion. Heidegger claims that the oblivion of Being brought about by the technological erasure of the ontological difference is itself a moment in the historical unfolding of Being. It is the destiny [*Geschick*] to which Being has destined metaphysical humanity.

> Since destining at any given time starts man on a way of revealing, man, thus underway, is continually approaching the brink of the possibility of pursuing and pushing forward nothing but

what is revealed in ordering, and of deriving all his standards on this basis. Through this the other possibility is blocked, that man might be admitted more and sooner and ever more primally to the essence of that which is unconcealed and to its unconcealment, in order that he might experience as his essence his needed belonging to revealing.[16]

Our needed belonging to revealing, I have argued, stems from our primordial bodily need for beings to be revealed. So at the same time the origin of human being—our fallenness into finite flesh—contains the fate of our own ontological undoing because it sends us out in heedless pursuit of things to satisfy our needs. Heidegger continues: "Placed between these possibilities, man is endangered from out of destining. The destining of revealing is as such, in every one of its modes, and therefore necessarily, *danger*."[17] Putting this together, the danger thus lies in the possibility that we become completely insensible to the neediness, which positions us as ontological servant to Being. Out of this numbness comes the absurd and fictitious feeling of omnipotence in which our technology enrobes us. In the end, Being, as the force of destiny, endangers itself.[18]

The essence of technology, according to Heidegger, constitutes the "supreme danger" because, to simplify somewhat, it hides from itself the fact that it is dangerous. But how does one come to understand a destiny bent on destroying itself? Leder's genealogy of metaphysics helps to make this clear. He shows that the striving to overcome the limits of nature embodied by our flesh burst forth from the very nature of the body itself. "It is precisely because the normal and healthy body largely disappears that direct experience of the body is skewed toward times of dysfunction."[19] Leder explains the result:

> The tendency to thematize the body particularly at times of disruption helps establish an association between corporeality and its dysfunctional modes. The body is seen not only as Other to the self, but as a definite threat to knowledge, virtue or continued life. Dualism thus reifies the absences and divergences that always haunt our embodied being.[20]

Of course, absences themselves resist reification, which can only falsify their true ontological status as no-thing. Thus, a naturally absent body, when reified, is a body misunderstood and falsified, one that can be experienced objectively only to the detriment of its own sensitive experience. A body that makes itself known only in its dysfunction makes itself undesirable and ultimately dispensable.

While the body is highlighted in deceptive modes, it tends to be taken for granted at times of accurate perception. The revelatory power of the body rests precisely upon its self-effacement. Moreover . . . this self-effacement is most marked in the case of abstract thought. Insofar as such thinking is regarded as the royal road to truth, this road seems to lead away from the body. When the body reclaims attention it is in the guise of an obstacle on the path: for example, the pain or fatigue that interferes with thought. Thus, for Descartes, as for Plato before him, a "disembodied state" is highly to be valued.[21]

The body gestates the same oblivion and devaluation of itself as does Being. Their shared destiny roots in the immovable givenness of physicality.

This is not to reduce Being to the body. Being is in no way a being itself, much less a material one. Rather the body embodies Being, that is, it presents the self-concealing finitude that opens up the need for beings to which Being responds. To put it otherwise, the nature of the body is always and everywhere at the behest of beings. While our bodily need seems to solicit beings into presence, it can do so only by virtue of an a priori covenant between need and presence, which in fact presses the need into service. When manifest, beings appropriate the sensitive body. But this body is not to be thought of as independent of its appropriation. Rather, it exists precisely and only as this ransom, sacrifice, or servant to beings. Physicality is the meadow across which Being blooms.

Consequently, the body suffers the same epochal transformations as Being and vice versa. Attending to the history of embodiment both illuminates and substantiates Heidegger's rather nebulous and at times tenuous history of Being. In *The Body's Recollection of Being*, David Levin reaches the same conclusion, though from a different direction:

> Just as Heidegger must tell the history of metaphysics as the history of the oblivion of Being, so we must tell the history of the human body as a history of its ontological affliction. In metaphysics as in life, the truth of the body, or the body in its truth, is kept in exile. We know it only in its *epoche*, its errancy, its objectification and automation, its crucifixion, its rituals of mortification. The oblivion of Being denies the human body an assuaging awareness of the primordial experience of its openness, its enriching depth-of-field, its inherence in the wholeness of Being. The history of the being of the human body is a crucial part of the history of Being.

"Overcoming" metaphysics means overcoming the metaphysical misunderstanding of the being of the human body. It means overcoming our historically deep-seated guilt and shame, flaming into terrible hatred of the body. The history of mind/body dualism and the history of the subject/object dualism are two symptomatic manifestations of a violent, nihilistic rage in the very heart of our metaphysics. But to overcome metaphysics, we must do more than formulate a conceptual critique. We must *retrieve* the ontological body.[22]

For Levin, this retrieval is preeminently practical. Calling the body not merely a field, but more specifically a "field of motility," Levin focuses on the motile capacities of the human body. Being, he argues, becomes manifest in our gestures, carriage, and stride. Our ability to move with meaning and awareness clears the space for the dynamism of Being to play itself out.

Although in agreement with Levin regarding the ontological importance of bodily engagement in the world, I feel that his singular emphasis on the abilities of the body also to an extent exiles the "body in its truth." The most fundamental truth of the body is its finitude, its mortality, its utter inability to sustain its own being by itself. It is our primary neediness that makes our active ability ontically and ontologically necessary. An infinite being is not moved to move.

To be sure, the Western metaphysical tradition has done its fair share of objectifying and mortifying the animate flesh. Nevertheless, the "deep-seated guilt and shame, flaming into terrible hatred of the body" is by no means the exclusive property of Plato's heirs. Leder shows convincingly that the body itself harbors the seeds of suspicion and animosity against corporeality. More to the point, guilt and shame go part and parcel with a finite being who has dark notions of his finitude and vague longings for the infinite. In his classic study of the mendacious human situation, Ernest Becker puts it well:

> Today we realize that all the talk about blood and excrement, sex and guilt is true not because of urges to patricide and incest and fears of actual castration, but because all these things reflect man's horror of his own basic animal condition, a condition that he cannot—especially as a child—understand and a condition that—as an adult—he cannot accept. The guilt that he feels over bodily processes and urges is "pure" guilt: guilt as inhibition, determinism, as smallness and boundness. It grows out of the constraint of the *basic animal condition*, the incomprehensible mystery of the body and the world.[23]

Attempting to overcome this guilt will only fan the flames that Levin would have extinguished. The guilt is pure because it expresses the knowledge of our facticity, our finitude, which is no metaphysical fabrication. "Pure guilt" simply glosses Heidegger's "formal existential idea of 'guilty' as being-the-ground for a being which is determined by a not—that is, *being-the-ground of a nullity*."[24] Overcoming this guilt is precisely the endeavor of metaphysics itself, which cannot abide the deficiencies and limitations of the mortal body. Overcoming metaphysics, then, must mean patiently accepting to abide with the pure guilt spawned by the body and the accompanying constraints of our animal condition.

While violence against the physical may penetrate the heart of metaphysics, it helps little, contra Levin, to think that rage motivates it. Were it merely rage, then the affective body would have to be held responsible for its self-immolation. Rather than rage, it seems that ignorance and forgetfulness of our own mortal nature have led us metaphysicians to neglect and devalue our own sensitive *res extensa*. Nor does dualism infest only the gardens of Western thought. Asceticism and mortifications of sundry kinds flourish in nearly every culture. This notwithstanding, something peculiar did occur in the Western philosophical scientific tradition that has now become planetary. Historical interpretation must be made in order to satisfy the understanding as to why industrialism and technological consumer culture developed where and how they have. What accounts for metaphysics' exceptional and exceptionally popular violence against the body? What does this violence signify?

The Bookish Body

If, as Levin maintains, the history of the body intertwines with the history of Being, transformations in the physiological situation of human being will coincide with wider ontological shifts. Observing the birth of Western metaphysics with an eye to the surrounding corporal reality proves illuminating. What one finds is that the history of the oblivion of Being is also the history of the deactivation of the lived body. Neither the body nor Being, of course, has gone away, but historically they have retreated into increasing concealment, covertness, and absence. This inherent destiny of Being is also alive in the nature of the body. "Only because the body has intrinsic tendencies toward self-concealment could such tendencies be exaggerated by linguistic and technological extensions."[25]

The exaggerations that occurred simultaneously with the establishment of Western metaphysics were epochal. In a fascinating article entitled "The Orality of Socrates and the Literacy of Plato," Eric Havelock demonstrates how the linguistic and technological extensions of the written word induced metaphysics.

> The Socratic *logos* was oral, the Platonic *eidos* is textual. As such, it is an unlikely candidate for inclusion in the original dialectic. It is the shape of a statement so final, so definite, so ultimate as to turn a reality beyond either linguistic or mental process, a reality which he who struggles to produce the required statement can see and contemplate. The metaphor of sight is central to Plato's epistemology. . . . The Greek alphabet had turned the Greek language into a visual thing; and the Platonic Theory of Forms was its creation; a necessary creation of Greek literacy. The formation of such a theory in the oral acoustic period of Greek culture would have been impossible.[26]

Heidegger usually, though not invariably, begins his interpretation of the history of Being (*Seinsgeschichte*) with Plato. The Theory of Forms, privileging the eternal and immutable over the transient and perishable nature of phenomenal existence, hypostasized the truth of Being—a temporal event—into the atemporal, unmoving ground of beings. Process thereby becomes product. Moreover, it is Plato who portrays death as a consummation devoutly to be wished by every philosopher. The tomb of our living bodies deadens us to the vivacity of the Forms. Biological death, liberation from physicality, is therefore the only genuine philosophical condition, worthy of zealous emulation by all philosophers suffering the misfortune of carnal life. Metaphysics is born of this will to death and physical destruction.

"Throughout the whole of history of philosophy, Plato's thinking remains decisive in changing forms. Metaphysics is Platonism."[27] According to Heidegger's interpretation of history, these first seeds eventually and inevitably grew into the present age of technological nihilism. Heidegger does not fault Plato for his pioneering role in the perilous history of Being, for he believes that great thinkers serve only as heralds who announce the unfolding of Being. Havelock's argument, which David Abram takes up and elaborates, provides the concrete means for understanding Heidegger's abstract apologetics by situating Plato himself in a historical context with respect to technology.

> Plato was teaching, then, precisely at the moment when the new technology of reading and writing was shedding its specialized

"craft" status and finally spreading, by means of the Greek cur-
riculum, into culture at large. . . . Plato, or rather the association
between literate Plato and his mostly non-literate teacher
Socrates (469?–399 B.C.E.), may be recognized as the hinge on
which the sensuous, profoundly embodied style of consciousness
proper to orality gave way to the more detached, abstract mode
of thinking engendered by alphabetic literacy. Indeed, it was
Plato who carefully developed and brought to term the collective thought-structures appropriate to the new technology.[28]

Plato's literacy decides his philosophy, and, insofar as Plato did not
develop the technology of writing and reading, the authorship of his philosophy does not belong to him alone. Plato's ontology expresses a new
way of being-in-the-world, made possible by the enhanced powers of
mind effectuated by literacy. The literary form externalizes memory, reifies speech, and fishes out immutable concepts from the ceaseless flow of
temporal change. The resultant amplification of the human intellect is
nothing short of astounding. All the same, it is not without its own dangers. The consummate dialectician, Socrates saw how the written word
"will produce forgetfulness in the minds of those who learn it, by causing
them to neglect their memory, inasmuch as, from their confidence in
writing, they will recollect by the external aid of foreign symbols, and not
by the internal use of their own faculties."[29] This will lead to the substitution of mere recollected fact for experiential knowledge. Without question, literacy has blessed humanity, but its tendency, intrinsic to the
essence of technology, toward totalization has mired the hyperliterate age
of postmodernity in a surfeit of senseless information.

   It does not do, then, either to praise or blame Plato as the conscious
creator of Western metaphysics. Like the rest of us, he was as much a
product as a producer of his times—a prototypical instance of Marshall
McLuhan's famous dictum: the medium is the message. For, as Havelock
and Abram argue, Plato simply gave philosophical voice to the technological innovations of his time. Metaphysics grew more out of the instruments
of literature than from the intellect of one particularly brilliant Athenian.

   Yet, despite appearances, this does not establish the truth of historical
materialism, which, even while providing a powerful explanative instrument, fails to countenance the grander mystery of historical change as
such. For even when we attribute transformations of ideology to alterations in the dominant means of production, we cannot thereby explain
why history operates through change in the first place. One technology
could be said to cause another and to initiate the corresponding system of
thought, but what motivates the entire causal series? Heidegger saves the

mystery of history from facile explanation by identifying technology as the expression of the historical movements of Being. And who can say what moves Being? As with the human body, Being has its own inscrutable pattern of growth, unfolding in accordance to an inherent logic deeper than our explanatory reason can penetrate. A philosophical genealogy that traces metaphysics back to the technology of the Greek alphabet is fascinating, though necessarily incomplete until the body and Being come to bear on it. In other words, we have to locate conceptual and technological change in the nexus of corporeal and ontological change. Abram nicely addresses the body, while Havelock speaks to Being.

> In multiple and diverse ways, taking . . . a unique form in each indigenous culture, spoken language seems to give voice to, and thus enhance and accentuate, the sensorial affinity between humans and the environing earth. . . . In indigenous, oral cultures, in other words, language seems to encourage and augment the participatory life of the senses, while in Western civilization language seems to deny or deaden that life, promoting a massive distrust of sensorial experience while valorizing an abstract realm of ideas hidden behind or beyond the sensory appearances.[30]

This general loss of the sensuous from alphabetic language takes its most acute and explicit form in specifically ontological terminology.

> One syntactical change is of a special significance and was soon recognized in Greece after the revolution (of literacy) got underway. The verb "to be" considered as the junction point in a veridical statement, began to come into its own both in the copulative and existential senses as a replacement for verbs of what the Greeks called "becoming and perishing." To quote an example . . . oral information is likely to be unfriendly to such a statement as: "the angles of a triangle are equal to two right angles." If, however, you said, "the triangle stood firm in battle astride and poised on its equal legs, fighting resolutely to protect its two right angles against the attack of the enemy," you would be casting Euclid backward into Homeric dress. You would be giving him his pre-literate form.[31]

The contrast between Havelock's corresponding statements speaks volumes. Not only does the preliterate form have a poetic and narrative style, it is also alive with imagery of the body. The subject of the Euclidian sentence is abstract and, insofar as no perfect triangle exists in nature, immaterial, whereas the Homeric triangle is a being engaged in the world and inseparable from it. "The new 'is'," Havelock writes, "required a new type of subject–impersonal, non-active, abstracted as we might say from any particular action or transient event. This called for and encouraged a use of vocabulary which could isolate this subject in its abstraction and its unchanging uniformity."[32]

Subjectivity, which Heidegger considers the essence of Western metaphysics,[33] first begins with this newly conceived subject, for previously the sharp subject/object distinction did not hold on account of the thorough interpenetration of the two. As soon as the subject appears to have acquired existence apart from the context, both syntactical and ontological, it assumes a kind of priority over that context. Meaning no longer arises from the reciprocal activity of a being-in-the-world, in which subject and object codetermine each other. Instead, the context attains meaning solely with respect to how it relates to the permanent, independent subject. The subject comes to enjoy the determining role, as if distanced from the object. In Heidegger's history of Being, the final outcome of this initial abstraction is the Nietzschean will to power, in which the subjective will claims creative authority over Being.

The decline of the narrative style marks the loss of the subject as embodied agent in the world. Curiously, while the Homeric subject is invariably personal regardless of its referent, the literary subject is far more anthropocentric. In Havelock's example, the Homeric triangle behaves as would a person; it is an entity defined and understood in humanistic terms, as a being-in-the-world. Through literacy's reifying powers, the being and the world take on distinct and autonomous existences. Since meaning pertains essentially to human being, and thus always has a personal origin, the original anthropomorphism of the holistic and temporal being-in-the-world gets concentrated into the first disjunct—being-in—which is obviously more personal than the "world." Anthropomorphic understanding thus becomes anthropocentrism as the world changes from appearing the interactive stage of human projection to the inert environment at the center of which rules the subject. Subjectivity implies subjugation; it introduces subordination into the primal partnership of being-in-the-world. The subject, of course, can subordinate the world only when abstracted and distanced from it, and this abstraction and distance come from a suppression of the physical body, the earthly, world-sheltering element of human being.

No historian would question the revolutionary nature of literacy. But it remains to be answered just how so basic and beneficial a technology could produce such epochal ontological transformations. The disembodiment of the literary subject that precipitated metaphysics had its cause in the antecedent disembodiment of the literate person. Reading and writing present a way of being-in-the-world completely novel to preliterate humanity. Together they offer the initiated a way of representing the world without their having to be physically there in it. The reader can experience things through the written word without actually sensing them. It may be here objected that all forms of language, and not just its written variant, accomplish this. Indeed they do, but not nearly so effectively and compellingly as literature.

Consider the physiology of reading. In order to maintain concentration on the page, typically the body must be stilled. At the earlier stages of literacy, it was not unusual for the reader to stand or pace, but, as time passed, these movements eventually ceased and reading became a sedentary activity. Also, for the greater part of literate history, most people vocalized what they read even when alone. Audibly verbalizing the written words aided comprehension in this as yet uncustomary behavior, as it still does to this day for children learning to read. Of course, the tongue, too, eventually grew quiet as the ability to read silently was culturally developed.

> It is important to realize that the now common experience of "silent" reading is a late development in the story of the alphabet, emerging only during the Middle Ages, when spaces were first inserted between the words in a written manuscript (along with various forms of punctuation), enabling readers to distinguish the words of a written sentence without necessarily sounding them out audibly. Before this innovation, to read was necessarily to read aloud, or at the very least to mumble quietly; after the twelfth century it became increasingly possible to internalize the sounds, to listen inwardly to phantom words (or the inward echo of words once uttered).[34]

Bodily effort became confined to the eyes and occasionally the hand. The rest of the body, meanwhile, was put in abeyance. This brief history outlines a tendency toward increasing physical inactivity, toward a more tenuous bodily engagement with the world.

The technology of literature produces metaphysics through the effects it works in and on the human body. Owing to the body's fundamental ontological and projective nature, any significant physiological change will alter the ontological atmosphere in which the body dwells. Metaphysics commences with literary technology because the latter provides the means to be-in-the-world with diminished physical presence and engagement. Leder describes quite well how this technology operates:

> The minimal materiality of linguistic signs demands only a minimal though intricate use of the body: small gestures of the writing hand, a swift scanning by the eyes, subtle movements of the lips and tongue. This serves an important function in the body economy allowing for maximal speed and combinatory number in exchange for little expenditure of energy. . . . The result is that language use is compatible with relegating most of the body to a merely supportive role. I forget my torso, the position of my legs, the panorama of the senses, as I concentrate here on my reading and writing. . . . Other bodily regions recede into a tacit background.[35]

These observations scratch at a basic relation between metaphysics, technology, and Being. Metaphysics and technology historically advance at the exact rate that Being recedes because advancing metaphysical technology pushes the physical–ontological body deeper into recession.

A working definition of technology may be gleaned from the above. I stipulate technology as whatsoever produces physiological effects of ontological import. This definition implicitly limits technology to humans; while, for example, a beaver's dam certainly has physiological effects on its maker, it does not, one must assume, have ontological significance, and for the simple reason that rodents, as far as we know, do not have an understanding of Being. The definition takes the essence of Heidegger's interpretation of technology and grounds it on the physical basis missing there. Heidegger denounced the popular notion of technology that construed it as a neutral assembly of instruments and techniques. Any such utilitarian definition dissembles technology's truth, that it is an ontological mode of disclosure whose chief characteristic is its intrinsic reductive exclusivity. As a mode of disclosure, technology is, for Heidegger, a way of being-in-the-world, an ontic condition of Dasein that shapes its ontological sensibilities and thus its possibilities. Since being-in-the-world is first and foremost a physical facticity—the crucial point overlooked by Heidegger—then technology, if essentially ontological, must function at the physiological level. A definition stressing the physical basis of technology at once reconciles Heidegger's ontological insight with the partially valid notions of everyday understanding.

The history of the oblivion of Being must be told by the technological eclipse of the active human body. As a general rule, the physiological effects of a new technology involve a reduction of the previous corporeal reality. The ontological import of such reductions depends on the extent to which the body's native capacities and needs are externalized into artifacts. The more that the ontological field of the body gets covered over by technological innovation, the less present the body becomes. "Farming out" the body's capacities can lead to perceptual desensitivity, and a leveling down of experience. As the field of experience yields less through lack of cultivation, the various possibilities for the manifestation of Being decrease. Being and the body retire in tandem. This is not to say that all instance of technology necessarily reduce bodily presence. Some devices, especially medical devices aimed at ameliorating physical defects that deviate from a general standard of human health and capacity, enhance perceptual and motile abilities. These we should want to distinguish from the much larger set of technology involved in everyday consumption that undoubtedly tends to disengage the body and objectify it in its detachment. The distinction, however, cannot change the fact that, simply by virtue of its ontological nature, any reification of the body brings with it a matching reification of Being.

Tools, of course, have long existed, but the technology of literature proved metaphysically decisive because of the physiological revolution it began. Suddenly language appeared outside the human body, cut off from the physical ground in which it had always been rooted. Leder makes the case most convincingly:

> [There are] structures of disappearance common to spoken and written language. Both involve an effacement of the body of the sign and the body of the subject engaged with language. . . . In speech, language remains closely wedded to its point of origin in the human body. Speech (excepting the question of recordings) happens in the immediate context of an embodied speaker and listener. Written language, on the other hand, brings with it a surplus detachment. For when written down, words and the ideas they express tend to develop a career independent of human bodies. Language, as concretized in the text, leaves behind its voice, to be instantiated unchanged in an indefinite number of locales.[36]

Metaphysics thus begins historically with the first major disposal of the body. For if it is true that "language is at once the house of Being and the home of human beings"[37]and, moreover, if the foundation of that house is the mortal body, then the disappearance of the latter can only have momentous ontological ramifications. The divorce between language and body destabilizes the entire structure that shelters Being. Needless to say, many novel and marvelous possibilities came to light with this destabilization; the written word also houses inestimable jewels. Nevertheless, the disappearance of the animate and sensitive element in language initiated the historical movement of ontological reductivity. The depth of the oblivion of Being is measured by the body's incapacity to sense and respond to the widest spectrum of present phenomena, which in speaking includes the ethical event that takes place wherever two or more speakers meet "in person."

The mechanically simple technology of literature directly evidences the physiological nature of this ontohistorical process. First, as was already seen, the written word over time increasingly subdued the active body formerly implicated in oral dialogue. As the technology of reading and writing penetrated culture more deeply, the literate body grew more passive, inert, and absent. The expanding absence of the body abetted the creation of more abstract and prosaic styles of expression, while rhythmic and poetic styles, which usually evoke somatic response and resonance, declined. Whatever public role and significance reading formerly had diminished as literacy progressed from being an exceptional ability reserved for the elite to a standard and universal practice. Thus, the democratization of literacy—undoubtedly a welcome process—also exacerbates its intrinsic tendency toward privatized experience. Obviously I am not advocating book-burnings as an antidote to metaphysical nihilism. I do, however, believe that it is salutary, prudent, and wise for us to become physically aware of the way that technology treats our ontological bodies.

On the side of composition, the muscular discipline and skill requisite to master early, cruder instruments atrophied as the technology of writing became increasingly refined. The keyboard, of course, has replaced the need for manual care and attention that make for artistic penmanship with sheer speed and very specialized dexterity. It confines bodily movement to an invariable digital template that predetermines the action of the fingers. Clearly, the technical–historical trend is one of decreasing corporeal engagement. Today voice-recognition technology allows us to dispense with our hands altogether. Having at last become "hands-free," we will no longer have to manipulate language in order to reify it.[38]

The steady physiological diminishment of literate humanity through history occurs in step with the diminishment of our literary objects.

Written language can "capture" the world more or less satisfactorily. But no matter how rich the representation, it necessarily flattens out the mountainous topography of the lived-world to a single dimension. The experience of the reader has only a minimal bodily component. The eyes are forced to stay focused for long periods of time at a fixed distance on a motionless page. The tools of literature effectively suspend the body because they necessarily restrict or even prohibit its native motility and sensibility. Advancements in paper production reduce and standardize the texture, weight, size, color and even odor of books. The printing press did away with the art of textual illumination and scriptural embellishment. Again, the obvious trend heads toward increasing sensory deprivation, as the diversity of stimuli and experience wanes.

A common argument against this conclusion objects that the trend is a function of imperfect technology rather than of technology per se. The computer is often trumpeted as perhaps the first successful enhancer of sensuality in the literary tradition (which is, in an unfortunate and perverse way, not altogether false, given the ubiquity of pornography in cyberspace). Real-life pictures and animation can accompany texts, as well as flawlessly recorded sound. Developers of virtual-reality technology are working to introduce olfaction into the "armchair" activity of reading. As communication technology matures, so the argument goes, it involves more capacities of our bodies and inches ever closer to real experience. Undeniably, high technology has begun to redress the neglect done to the human body by its lower forms. What I hope to prove, however, is that the rediscovered body of high-tech is an abstracted body, one that strays, with every technological leap forward, farther from the vital epistemological function that Merleau-Ponty attributes to the concrete body. In the weightlessness of virtual reality, the body itself becomes an abstraction; this basis of physicality is the ultimate object of technological consumption, where the body plays the part of wood, and technology fire.

In *The Phenomenology of Perception*, Merleau-Ponty picks the blind man's cane to explicate the extensive or telescopic power of the human body:

> The blind man's stick has ceased to be an object for him, and is no longer perceived for itself; its point has become an area of sensitivity, extending the scope and active radius of touch, and providing a parallel to sight. In the exploration of things, the length of the stick does not enter expressly as a middle term: the blind man is rather aware of it through the position of objects than of the position of objects through it. . . . To get used to a

hat, a car or a stick is to be transplanted into them, or conversely, to incorporate them into the bulk of our own body. Habit expresses our power of dilating our being in the world, or changing our existence by appropriating fresh instruments.[39]

The example demonstrates the body's capacity to extend its perceptual functions beyond the boundary demarcated by the individual's skin. Through repeated use and practice, the stick's point becomes an "area of sensitivity." This capacity for perceptual dilation into a seemingly alien world evinces the elemental unity of flesh, which integrates the objective world into the body of subjective experience. Of course, whatever degree of sensitivity the stick may come to attain depends fully on the living hand that plies it. Sensitivity always remains strictly an attribute of embodiment.

When we extend this attribute with tools we can often amplify its intensity, range, and clarity. We magnify our immediate sense organs with microscopes, televisions, stereos, and any number of other contrivances. Greater selective intensity, however, does not necessarily entail greater overall sensitivity. In fact, greater intensity is often bought at the price of a diminishment of overall sensitivity; the microscope is effective to the extent that it focuses the eye on a minuscule section of the visual field. We use implements and tools to enhance our native capacities, but we must also be aware of how these artifacts affect our overall corporeal facticity and our experience of this facticity. Every amplification of bodily power brings with it a correspondingly intensified occlusion of the lived body. Because limitation in its spatial, temporal, vulnerable multiplicity defines the essence of the body, artificially pressing beyond bodily limits always involves a movement away from the experiential core of the body as lived.

Habituation alone transforms the blind man's cane from a mere stick and potential tool to an actual and effective extension of his sensitivity. But, as Merleau-Ponty asks, "if habit is neither a form of knowledge nor an involuntary action, what then is it? It is knowledge in the hands, which is forthcoming only when bodily effort is made, and cannot be formulated in detachment from that effort."[40] It follows from this that as a tool minimizes the need or possibility for bodily effort, it reduces the lived body's sensitivity. For if "habit expresses our power of dilating our being in the world" and "is forthcoming only when bodily effort is made," then a body idled by implements gives up some of its native sensitivity.

The artificial extension of the body's absence turns out, in fact, to be an extension of artificial insensitivity. The absent body—the viscera, the brain and nervous system, even the sense organs themselves—function from a recessive position impenetrable to perceptual awareness. When looking, one never perceives the seeing eye itself, but only the object on which it is trained. Likewise, the blind man is not aware of the cane per se, but what it reveals about the world. Thus, the more of the world we "succeed in incorporating into the bulk of our body," the more of the world we effectively exclude from the field of our awareness. In the age of high technology, global communication systems have extended our senses universally: satellites allow us to observe every inch on the planet without effort. This very effortlessness, however, infects our perceptual omnipresence with bodily insensitivity. It does not permit us to form, through manual repetition, the bodily habits requisite for the coextensive corporeal awareness. Merleau-Ponty calls bodily habits knowledge because through them we learn to make sense or comprehend our tools and the world to which they and we belong. Such knowledge, to reiterate, "cannot be formulated in detachment from that (bodily) effort," and thus contrasts with the readily available but abstract information delivered by our telecommunication systems.

To the extent that technology minimizes bodily effort, it restricts the process of habituation needed to effectively extend sensitivity beyond the skin of the body. Bodily effort plays an equally vital role in forming sensitive habits in the unmediated body. If the body is never left alone with its native powers and capacities of perception and motility, its agility and awareness languish neglected and undeveloped. Insensate matter cannot feel and if it appropriates the sensuousness of the flesh, only a fragment of the perceptive ground of the lived body remains. Externalized and diffused, the experiential body becomes reified, materialized, and incapacitated with respect to its native sensitivity.

Physiologists have begun documenting what phenomenologist Merleau-Ponty emphasized as the somatic foundation of a great deal of human knowledge. A person achieves such knowledge through habitual physical effort. Each habit results from a specific repeated activity and develops certain types of knowledge by forging, current theory goes, specific neural pathways in the brain. The first problem with ostensibly stimulating computer literacy was pointed out some time ago by Jerry Mander with reference to television:

> Because so many of us were confusing television experience with direct experience of the world, we were not noticing that experience itself was being unified to the single behaviour of watching television. Switching from channel to channel, believing that a sports program was a significantly different experience from a police program or news of an African war, all 80 million viewers

were sitting separately in dark rooms engaged in exactly the same activity at the same time: watching television.[41]

Mander calls this the unification of experience and the term equally applies to those sensually heightened, "interactive" technologies that have followed television. While developers in virtual reality and other areas struggle to bring greater corporeal participation to their technologies, they necessarily exclude the primary ingredient: bodily effort. The technologies never demand the same level of physical work required of the mimicked activity when the latter is actually performed in the resistant world. This common lack unifies all their otherwise varied experiences. Whether "surfing the net" with surround sound, or e-mailing a friend, or word-processing a chapter of a doctoral dissertation, or playing a remarkably life like simulation, the basic experience remains identical: sitting down at a computer.

"At bottom," Levin reasons, "the problem with metaphysics lies in the tendency to *reify* experience and exclude fresh encounter."[42]In other words, the openness to Being embodied by our neediness for beings tends to narrow as we become less physical. As we grow less perceptive and observant of the beings present to us, we increasingly fail to esteem the full richness of reality. Our sensitivity to the wonder of Being, in both its present manifestations and its historical movements, suffers the same impoverishment. For, while the mystery called Being is certainly no-thing, we can approach it only through carefully attuned awareness of the things we immediately encounter. To the extent that the unification of experience dulls our sensitive awareness, it is ontologically deleterious. Physical labor of a very repetitive and strenuous nature can also deaden our sensitivity. If all one did was dig potatoes with a wooden spade for days on end, that person would likely become as perceptually numb as the typist chained to a full shift of data-entry. All unifed experience shares the problem of metaphysics in its tendency toward reification and exclusion of fresh encounter. Much of the appeal of new technologies stems from their promise to diversify our experience, by freeing us up from a limited set of physical tasks. This liberty, however, is often purchased at the expense of bodily activity and participation with the tangible world. Thus, one unified experience makes way for another, which likely ends up being yet more exclusionary due to its decreased somatic involvement. As our physical capacities weaken, the possibility for fresh experiential encounters also shrinks.

"Knowledge," Mander asserts, "results from personal experience and direct observation—seeing, hearing, touching, tasting, and smelling."[43] If this list exhausted the conditions for knowledge, then sophisticated technology that did not neglect the senses would suffice for the development of epistemological diversity. In that case, Mander's sharp distinction between direct experience, involving the human body in the natural world, and technologically mediated experience would break down. At best, he could maintain the distinction only prejudicially or perhaps on an aesthetic basis that would not prove conclusive or decisive. The distinction, however, does in fact rest on firmer ground, for direct experience is not composed simply of sensory stimulation, which, as scientists have long known, can be triggered by electrical or chemical manipulation of the brain. Motility, posture, effort, work, in short, full bodily engagement with the gravitational, physical, and frictional world engenders diverse personal experience. What we *cannot* do to or with a thing, what the limits of our strength and ability preclude, teach us as much about the beings we encounter as what we do, in fact, successfully accomplish. Moreover, resistance, together with our bodily effort against it, teaches us a great deal about ourselves. Yet precisely here we go wrong to rely on technology. To the extent that an object is technological, it necessarily excludes the aspect of physical difficulty requisite for learning. Tools have always helped to ease human toil. Since the scientific revolution, the express *telos* of science has been to make human life as easy, comfortable, and long as the current technology allowed. The essence of technological innovation, as conceived by scientific revolutionaries, principally Descartes and Francis Bacon, is the amelioration of our mortal, toilsome existence for the sake of human excellence as envisioned in the humanist tradition bequeathed to the West by the Greeks.

According to philosopher Albert Borgmann, at the heart of technology lies a promise "to bring the forces of nature and culture under control, to liberate us from misery and toil, and to enrich our lives."[44] Every human artifact, from the most primitive implements on, has made a similar promise, at least tacitly, otherwise it would never have known manufacture. With the Enlightenment, however, the utilitarian promise of general betterment acquires quasi-spiritual overtones. In Borgmann's words, "the Enlightenment was the original liberation movement of our time,"[45] that burst asunder the long prevailing political, superstitious, and, perhaps most significantly, religious strictures. Within the limitations imposed by such strictures, liberation was pursued as a personal project usually involving a soul and God. Truth, predominantly in the guise of religious revelation, set people free; tools merely helped to make their spiritual freedom more enjoyable and rewarding. The liquidation of social, intellectual, and religious strictures displaced the target of liberation. Religion could no longer promise freedom from the real suffering and hardships of mortal existence; its own dissolution voided its promise. The inextinguishable emancipatory urge toward transcendence transferred its object of hope from *deus* to the *machina*. Thomas Tierney explains the transference:

> Modern individuals have not become well, in the Nietzschean sense that they celebrate their mortality, their embodiment, their senses, both pleasurable and painful. All of these conditions still remain a source of anxiety to humans, but the projection of this anxiety into a supersensuous realm of immortality, access to which is determined by God, will no longer suffice to comfort most moderns. A new drug is needed; a new ascetic practice is required. My claim is that convenience is that drug, and the consumption of technology is that practice.[46]

At the risk of slight irreverence, one might sum this up by saying that the death of God put the Holy Ghost into the machine.

Tierney treats post-Enlightenment technology as a direct substitute for religion, as far as concerns the body. He argues that

> modernity is characterized by a certain revulsion against the body, mortality and necessity. The demands of the body, which were ignored or strictly regulated by Christian asceticism, in both its monastic and Puritanical forms, are no longer something to be neglected or restricted. Instead, they have become . . . limits imposed by the body. And the overcoming of these limits is the value of convenience, in the particularly modern sense of this word.[47]

While certainly characteristic of modernity, it is simply false to state that revulsion against the body distinguishes modernity from the past. Shame and guilt about our physicality are as old as Adam, that is, there are coeval with self-consciousness. The human condition itself begets a problematic relation with corporeality precisely because "man's body is a *problem* to him that has to be explained."[48] Every culture, every individual defines itself or herself through the peculiar manner of explanation employed. Thus, how it acts out the universal revulsion against bodily mortality, rather than the revulsion itself, characterizes modernity.

Since the scientific revolution, the metaphysical tradition of the West has reacted to the problem of the body technologically. Overcoming physical limits is the only way metaphysics can relate to corporeality. Technology is the singular force of overcoming, but it is not the sole solution. A nonmetaphysical response to the problem of embodiment would accept rather than deny the problematic nature of mortality. Traditions in this line—for example, *hatha yoga* and Buddhism—generally regard the body a means rather than an obstacle to human fulfillment.[49] Nor are they indigenous only to the East. Christianity, which has certainly bred brutal asceticisms, is also capable of handling the flesh with care. Thomas Merton, a brother of the austere Cistercian order, gives a spiritual interpretation of the body that is antithetical to metaphysics:

> The secret of this imperfection of all things, of their inconstancy, their fragility, their falling into nothingness, is that they are only a shadowy expression of the one Being from Whom they receive their being. If they were absolutely perfect in themselves, they would fail in their vocation, which is to give glory to God by their contingency. . . . As long as we are on the earth our vocation is precisely to be imperfect, incomplete, insufficient in ourselves, changing, hapless, destitute, and weak, hastening towards the grave.[50]

This vocation does not call us to despair. The reality of imperfection is, in Merton's language, the very condition of possibility of God's glory. The real divide, then, runs not between East and West, modern and ancient, but most precisely between the physical and the metaphysical, that is, between the human and the technological.

This is not to pit technology against humanity, a popular opposition in a certain genre of science fiction. It is, however, to assent with Heidegger in thinking that technology belongs more to the history of Being than it does to the genius and industry of persons. The deep underlying suspicion of machines, titillated by science fiction, comes from a vague understanding that under the rule of technology, in Heidegger's words, "man is threatened with the annihilation of his essence."[51] The science of genetics and cloning testifies to the restlessly transcendent impetus motivating technological change. Every person with basic moral intelligence must hold, at very least, serious reservations concerning the prospect of human cloning. Yet research is moved, as if inevitably, toward the realization of this stupendous potential. It is not, it seems to me, reactionary, phobic, or pessimistic to think that we are in some way the instrument of technology. It bespeaks an intelligent acknowledgment of our finitude, a humble understanding of the facticity of our worldly situation. But this by no means absolves us of responsibility or dissolves our freedom. Technology stands against the human and threatens human being to the extent that we forget our dependence on what presents itself historically. The danger of technology lies in the cloud of intoxication that descends on technological humanity; for this cloud obscures the fact of human receptivity. Within this cloud, we are too ready to believe that our existence is self-secured, invulnerable, and without debt, when in truth we exist always and essentially as helpless beneficiaries.

Though Merton interprets our vocation of imperfection and mortality in religious terms, this unique human calling is equally ontological. Our neediness opens up a world of beings that respond to the mortal cry of our existence. "We become ourselves when we let beings be" because the service of ontological disclosure always implies our essential finitude. To be human means to belong to the world through the necessity of physical limitation. It means to die. Technology opposes our humanness because the "trajectory of modernity is to render everyone free not only from the limits which are imposed by the body, but even from the body itself."[52] Thus, the real promise of technology lies deeper than the delivery of leisure, comfort, and security. These three are goods that our own definitive neediness naturally seeks. They go to provide the basis for the beneficial humanism that we have envisioned for millennia. However, the promise of emancipation from the body and its mortal limits is literally inhuman. Although we yearn for this kind of eternity, its actualization would contradict and destroy our very being. Technological emancipation as the elimination of finitude and mortality can only mean human extinction, if by human we understand all our manifold self-interpretations of this puzzling phenomenon throughout history. Without our bodily need we cannot let beings be. When we fail at this our foremost ontological task, we forfeit the possibility of becoming our true selves.

Technological metaphysics treats death, paradoxically, as unnatural and even as unnecessary. Apologist Christopher Dewdney prophecies "that the next few generations of humans will be among the last to die, and, if this is the case, future humans will regard the tragedy of death as an inconceivable horror and a cosmic waste."[53] The prophecy contains fragments of truth hopelessly confused with scraps of intellectual rubbish. First of all, whatsoever survives these generations "among the last to die" will not be human, a fact that Dewdney elsewhere apprehends when he speaks of a "post-human" era. Take away death and our entire human existence collapses. We would become beings-toward not an absence or nothing as Heidegger would have it. Instead, the absence of an absence or nothingness twice removed would supposedly direct and gather the essence of these technological immortals. In the case of such absolute absence, the presence always associated with being would disappear. So in truth humans would become nonbeings.

This waste of death would be cosmic indeed, for it would entail the negation of the cosmos. If there does not exist a mortal needy being to let beings be, then nothing can manifest itself. Dewdney rightly mentions waste in connection with death, only he gets it backwards. Since waste implies human failure, the end of death is the waste of humanity. This "cosmic waste" is the failure to be human, the ruinage of our mortal calling, our vocation of imperfection. This shadow of absolute negation appears to us today as the phenomenon of trash.

Trash, we will see, appears as the categorical denial to let beings be. It is the ontological arrogance of the consumer (itself an metaphysical fabrication) that pretends to have authority over the nothingness, hence also the Being of beings. The true nothingness, however, implicated in all unconcealing is the mortal imperfection of our temporal existence. Precisely this we cannot master, and the technological quest for its control, as was just seen, leads only to its destruction. Throwing things out is forcing beings to vanish. Disclosing beings as disposable deafens us to our mortal ontological calling.

We know that nature abhors a vacuum and does not waste. But neither does "man" in the proverbial "state of nature." Prefacing John Gregory Bourke's *Scatologic Rites of All Nations*, Freud writes:

> we can say that the principal discovery of psychoanalytic research lies in the fact that the child finds itself constrained to repeat during the first phase of its development the various attitudes of humanity regarding excremental materials, attitudes which began with the separation of *homo sapiens* from Mother Earth. In all the early years of childhood, there is no trace of shame about excremental functions, nor is there any disgust towards the anatomy associated with faeces. The infant shows a great interest in their faeces. . . . Excrement, considered as a part of the child's own body and a product of its own organism, has a part in the narcissistic overestimation, as we have called it, with which the child considers everything produced as an integral part of its person. Under the influence of education, the bodily functions and the tendencies of the child over time become distasteful; the child learns to keep these secret, to be ashamed of them, and to feel disgust for their objects.[54]

Just as bodily waste—the prototype of all other wastes—results from the ego's rational reaction to embodiment, so trash results from the technological confrontation with the same problem. "Technological culture," Zimmerman observes, "is egoism on a planetary scale."[55] Technology, the strong arm of reason, strives to efface the human body. It accomplishes this goal practically to the extent that it manages to suspend the native capacities and needs that define the body's physicality. In the suspension of the means of ontological receptivity and sensitivity, the openness of the body becomes closed off. Unable to experience the awesome manifoldness of beings, the physical ontological field grows infertile. Alternatively, the ontological clearing becomes overgrown, leaving no place open for beings to reveal themselves. The effacement of the body, in short, means the general disappearance of beings. At best they lead a wraithlike existence in the netherworld of "away" where we consumers throw stuff.

Technology effaces the body by externalizing its somatic functions and faculties, which technological devices often amplify. Two correlated consequences follow. The more apparent of the two is that the body's natural ability to evacuate spent substances is vastly extended and increased. Now the entire global industrial infrastructure acts as the digestive and eliminative systems of the consumer. What the flesh-and-blood body actually excretes in the average act of modern consumption amounts to nearly nothing compared to the excreta of the externalized technological systems. The calculus simply remains too complex to calculate the unseen sum of myriad energies and materials spent in a typical instance of modern consumption.[56] It is estimated that the average piece of food consumed in the United States has traveled 2000 kilometers. Every time we eat we consume not only the entire transportation network, but also the whole interconnected industrial web of production that created and maintains the former. When we discard a banana peel, for example, we throw away with it the tires, asphalt, spark plugs, workboots, fuels, pipelines, paper invoices, boxes, computer chips, television screens, newspaper flyers, and all the other countless objects required to produce, deliver, and market the commodity. The global effluent of each instance of consumption is the excrement of the technologically externalized body.

Of course, the bulk of this waste never comes to view in the everyday course of our consumption. Raw material extraction and production, together with the U.S. military create 95 to 98 percent of all wastes of the industrial system in this country. This characteristic covertness specifies the phenomenon as trash and makes it worthy of ontological attention. For phenomena by nature appear; their being is dependent on their meaningful presence within the signifying context of the world. Trash as a phenomenon, however, tends always to disappear—into black plastic bags, out-of-the-way landfills, incinerators, into the depths of the ocean and Third-World processing plants. Trash retreats into absence instead of breaking forth into presence. Items of industrial consumption are ringed round by concealment. They seem to lack all temporal integrity. Out of nowhere they magically materialize on the retailers' shelves and just as suddenly dematerialize after the brief act of consumption. Consumer goods lack ostensible origins and destinations. Their being is concentrated into the serial "now" of repeated consumption. They exist, therefore, only to the extent that they are consumed, which means they are a priori waste. An object that in its being is always already wasted, whose brief phenomenal appearance is preconditioned and predetermined by its immediate disappearance, has disposability as its essence. Trash is the paradoxical phenomenon of this unique ontological mode.

Conclusion

We need an ontology of trash for what it teaches about the ontological importance of the human body. I have argued that Being takes place in the field of the body because the openness or neediness of the latter clears space for the appearance of the world of beings. The body is the ground of Being and shares, both historically and viscerally, the latter's perpetual withdrawal. To use Heidegger's terminology, we can say that the body is the earthly striving, whereas our awareness, sensitivity, and understanding constitute the symbiotic worldly striving of Being. Symbiosis prevails because awareness, sensitivity, and understanding themselves arise out of the basis of the body. But I have also argued that technology tends to close off the body's natural capacity for experience or disclosure. Just as Being conceals itself behind the appearance of phenomena, so the lived body disappears in the presence of its perceptions. When technology externalizes the body, however, it casts the physical shroud of concealment across the very phenomena that the lived body discloses. That is, as we substitute for our own sensitive flesh unfeeling machinery, we become insensate to the world. "If absence lies at the heart of the lived body," concludes Leder, "then any extension of its sensorimotor powers must necessarily involve and extension of absence."[57] Thus, the more effectively technology externalizes the lived body, the more foreign, strange, and insensible the world becomes to us. The very element of manifestness and appearance goes into hiding. A world in which absence covers presence is a world in which phenomena—a word that "comes from the verb *phainesthai* meaning 'to show itself'" (BT 25)—disappear. Such a world is unworldly and no home for human being. It is a world of trash, fit to be deserted.

The externalized, insensate body produces trash because technology aims, howsoever indirectly, at the disposal of the world. In reality, technology disposes of the world by effacing its physical earthly counterpart: the body. This shows that the earth and world, or, if you will, body and spirit, rise and fall together. Trash is a wreckage of ontological paradox and deserves a careful ontology because it shows, although negatively, that finitude grounds Being and any willful leap above physicality throws us into the heady sphere of danger. Our failure to become ourselves, to be mortally human, embodies itself as trash. Therefore, understanding trash brings us closer to ourselves; it discloses our humanity.

Trash is not a problem. It rarely disturbs the course of our daily lives of consumption, yet at the same time it threatens our very essence. But if it does not disrupt, then how can it threaten? The reason is, as I hope to show, that the phenomenon of trash necessarily comes with a shadow. In fact, this shadow overshadows the phenomenon so completely that the latter disappears. Human extinction manifests itself in the phenomenal absence created by trash. In chapter six I intend to demonstrate how we inevitably find our own disposal in the phenomenon of trash.

To arrive at that point, I first must investigate the mechanisms by which technology externalizes the human body. In the next two chapters I will substantiate the claims made here concerning the ontological nature of the body. Once the covert technological body has been revealed, its waste will present itself for more detailed interpretation. The explicit ontology of trash must wait, then, until chapter five.

CHAPTER THREE

Food

Of all things, food most directly implicates our finitude. We experience hunger as a void, a lack that punches holes in any delusions of our self-sufficiency. Our need to eat reminds us ever and again of our visceral being-in-the-world dependent on innerworldly beings. From the perspective of developmental psychology, the unanswered cry for nourishment first awakens in the infant the distinction between self and not-self. The world, thus, unfolds from the infant's growing realization of the neediness and limitation of its existence brought on by the discomfort of hunger. Our worldly being is essentially gustatory. The infant puts every object within its grasp into its mouth because at this earliest of stages the world remains saturated in the hunger from which it originally arose. Ontologically speaking, food, which nourishes human being's mortal finitude, constitutes the world.

At its root, food is ontological, since as a phenomenon it always directly refers to our essentially constitutive finitude. This unusual interpretation of the significance of food resonates well with many religious interpretations. The Upanishads, for example, express the fundamental relation between Being and food:

> From food, verily, are produced whatsoever creatures dwell on the earth. Moreover, by food alone they live. And then also into it they pass at the end. Food, verily, is the eldest born of beings. Therefore, it is called the healing herb of all. Verily, those who worship *Brahman* as food obtain all food. For from food are beings born. When born they grow up by food. It is eaten and eats things. Therefore is it called food.[1]

Food gives birth to beings by virtue of its connetion to Being:

55

On this, my dear, understand that this (body) is an offshoot which has sprung up, for it could not be without a root. And what else could its root be than food? And in the same manner, my dear, with food as an offshoot, seek for water as the root; with water, my dear, as an offshoot, seek for heat as the root; with heat , my dear, as an offshoot, seek for Being as its root. All these creatures, my dear, have their root in Being. They have Being as their abode, Being as their support.[2]

Yet the partnership also runs in the reverse. Being has its abode in food, the most basic element of world. Being finds shelter in human hunger, for this primordial deficiency opens us up for the revelation of beings. In this sense, our eating nourishes Being.

Embodying finitude, food connects intimately with waste. Every meal, no matter how fine and dainty, eventually ends in excrement and all the fear and ambivalence that the latter so readily excites transfers easily to the former. For example, among the Trobriand Islanders off the eastern tip of New Guinea, food underlies the entire social, economic, and moral order. Individuals make ostentatious display of their food supply to announce their wealth, and they donate of it liberally to prove their virtue and largesse. Deficiency in food amounts to a social disgrace. Yet for all the societal significance placed on food by the Trobrianders, the actual consumption of food is far from convivial. They prefer to store up their food, to secure it, than to eat it. The "Trobrianders eat alone, retiring to their own hearths with their portions, turning their backs on one another and eating rapidly for fear of being observed."[3]

Compare this secretive behavior with the imperative placed on the adult males of the East African tribe of the Chaga. The initiation rite into manhood included the following commands:

Don't emit wind in the presence of women and uninitiated youths. If you do, the tribal elders will slaughter your cow. Beware lest you be surprised by women when you defecate. Always carry a stick with you, dig your faeces in, and scratch here and there, pretending that you are digging in some charm. Then if a women should have observed you, she will seek there and find nothing.[4]

The reason for this undue fastidiousness lies in "the myth of the power of retaining one's faeces [that] is employed by the men to justify their claim to ascendency over the female race."[5] Natural scatological functions are considered by the Chaga as signs of inferiority and weakness. They betray a lack of control over the body and prove that one is prey to its physicality. Food equally proves this. The fear of being seen eating is likely a symptom of the bedrock anxiety of being finite

Hoarding and showcasing food dissemble its phenomenal nature. For only the act of consuming allows food to be in its true being as that which sustains human finitude. Food not eaten is, strictly speaking, not food at all, as it denies food's essential transience in the relation to the evanescent, needy body. In an atmosphere of shameful rejection of mortal embodiment, food must appear a priori as waste. One then tries to "save" it by treating it other than it really is. The phenomenon of food is thus neglected, its essential affirmation of human finitude withheld.

If the body denaturalized a priori consumes waste, then the technologically denaturalized body will consume trash. The task of the present chapter is to evince this proposal. In so doing, the ontological nature of the body argued for in the preceding chapter will become more firmly established, while the physical–historical process of submerging or suppressing this nature will receive further interpretation. The technological occlusion of Being will reveal itself through the meaning of the modern meal.

Although municipal solid waste (MSW)—the collected discards of urban households and commercial enterprises—constitutes only two percent of all solid waste produced in the United States per year,[6] this minute fraction signifies the bulk of trash in our everyday lives. Most of us simply never have to confront the lion's share of waste generated by the industrial and military complexes. Of that 2 percent, discards somehow associated with food predominate our daily commerce with trash. Packaging plays perhaps the most egregious role in the diurnal drama of disposing, and 59 percent of it goes to encase food and beverages.[7] This, of course, does not include the orange rinds, banana peels, and other "natural packaging" subject to identical disposal as plastics and paper where municipal composting is not practiced. Although food scraps, which account for about one-quarter of the MSW, are not, by essence, disposable in the same sense as plastics, within the industrial system of agriculture, they become phenomenologically indistinguishable from trash in its technological form. Finally, food itself suffers the same ontological fate where "American families waste between ten and fifteen per cent of the food they buy."[8] The technological commodification of food transmutes food's being from mere wastage to trash.

Junk food provides the most convenient means to prove this. In common speech, the title generally refers to highly processed, highly packaged edibles consisting mostly of some combination of refined white sugar, corn syrup, white flour, salt, a variety of vegetable oils, and a plethora of artificial flavors and preservatives. Potato chips, candy bars, and canned soda are the most popular representatives. In the course of this chapter, however, junk food will be seen to extend its application to include nearly the totality of foodstuffs technologically procured for and by the industrial world. By analyzing junk food beneath the incisive lens of Borgmann's device paradigm, I will argue that the promise of technology necessarily cooks up junk, the ambivalent allure of which resides in the semblance of a fulfillment of this promise. Since food smacks so strongly of physicality, technology must dispose of it so that it may become metaphysically palatable. Junk food, that is, trash, constitutes the diet of metaphysics.

The Device

Borgmann's theory of technology revolves on the axis of what he calls the device paradigm. This paradigm establishes a very specific manner that humans "take up with the world." That is, it lays out certain definite patterns of engaging with the world, patterns mediated but equally constrained by the technological devices that inscribe them. Since all manner of our worldly engagement stem from our embodied neediness for beings, the paradigm and its patterns constitute a specific mode of letting those beings be in response to our mortality. These beings reveal themselves in this paradigm, as in all other modes, within certain fixed parameters. What, according to Borgmann, distinguishes the device paradigm from other modes of revealing is the tendency of the device to conceal the general context in which it functions. Its presence does not communicate a wider relational world. This lack of world-forming communication results, I hope to show, from the exaggerated absence to which the human body is relegated by the presence of a device.

Although in the last chapter I argued that the real promise of technology is immortality and transcendence of the body, the explicit and popular expression of this promise first voiced by Descartes and Francis Bacon spoke in terms of disburdenment and freedom, undoubtedly two worthy goals. To pursue freedom is to be human, and is no less essential to our being than our finitude is. In keeping with its object, the pursuit can course down any number of different avenues. The scientific revolution engineered a novel avenue, unique in the assessment that the successful attainment of these goals relied on harnessing the indifferent forces of nature to suit the self-interested human will. Once mastered, nature would serve humankind from its material fecundity, physically liberating us so that we could fully indulge our distinctive rationality. A kind of indigence imposed by the ostensibly mechanical needs of the body has kept us from claiming and spending the full wealth of our minds. Insofar as the metaphysical tradition perceived the superior mind as chained to the inferior body, freedom of the former entailed at least partial mitigation of the enslavement to the latter. The basic truth of this anyone who has strained for extended periods of hard physical labor will avow. The new approach to nature envisioned by Descartes advanced on the premise that these "notions of liberation and enrichment are joined in that of availability. Goods that are available to us enrich our lives and, if they are technologically available, they do so without imposing burdens on us. Something is available in this sense if it has been rendered instantaneous, ubiquitous, safe, and easy."[9]

These attributes compose the essence of the technological device because they uphold its public promise. Instantaneity alleviates the constraints of time. Ubiquity removes all spatial restrictions. Safety diminishes mortal vulnerability, while ease does all three; circumventing lengthy practice required for the development of skill, ease eliminates the effort involved in all work done in and through space. To argue against safety or ease would be neither fashionable nor intelligent. The combination of properties that produce availability does help us immensely. But a caveat must be borne in mind. Whatever freedom these properties grant is purely negative. No contributor to the scientific revolution esteemed physical inactivity as an end in itself. Rest was valued as a prerequisite to mental activity.

When technologically secured, availability applies to commodities rather than to things. The difference between the two is primarily semantic, that is, it involves meaning. For Borgmann, things inhere in a physical and social world, having a definite place in accordance with the myriad relations to other things and people that all beings bear. In other words, things are embedded in the world, and constantly refer beyond themselves in a way that makes them irreducible to a single meaning or function. The meaning and use of a thing will vary depending on which of its multiple worldly references takes precedence. Contrary to the contextual, multifaceted significance of a thing is the commodity's singularity of purpose. Technology achieves the fourfold essence of availability by extracting a single function from the web of social and physical relations that constitute the thing, and then devises the most efficient means for reaching this presupposed end. Through a disruption between function and the machinery that performs it, technology frees the function from the physical contingency of the machinery. It severs the material and social ties that bind most things to restricted availability. A commodity, then, is the unambiguous, unequivocal end loosened from the totality of relations that form the world. Its availability increases in inverse proportion to the number of its worldly relations.

By way of illustration, Borgmann contrasts the hearth—with all its familial and cultural significance—with the modern central heating system. This choice of example does illustrate well the immense semantic difference between the two phenomena. A hearth is a thing because it demands physical attention and effort and this demand gathers around the hearth a world of human significance. For "physical engagement is not simply physical contact but the experience of the world through the manifold sensibility of the body. That sensibility is sharpened and strengthened in skill. Skill is intensive and refined world engagement. Skill, in turn, is bound up with social engagement."[10] The device of the furnace does away with most of this.

> A device such as a central heating plant procures mere warmth and disburdens us of all other elements. These are taken over by the machinery of the device. The machinery makes no demands on our skill, strength, or attention, and it is less demanding the less it makes its presence felt. In the progress of technology, the machinery of a device has therefore a tendency to become concealed or to shrink. Of all the physical properties of a device, those alone are crucial and prominent which constitute the commodity that the device procures. Informally speaking, the commodity of a device is "what a device is for." In the case of the central heating plant it is warmth, with a telephone it is communication, a car provides transportation, frozen food makes up a meal, a stereo set furnishes music.[11]

By virtue of their physically and socially decontextualized and unworldly state, commodities do not fully engage the human being in its essential, careful finitude. Instead they invite "carefree" consumption, and hence assume a measure of the care needed for the perpetuation of our existence. This, of course, explains their desirability, for an existence overly occupied with exigencies of mere physical survival strikes us as something less than entirely human. The question is: how much care for our essential physicality can we hand over to devices before we begin to undermine our own existential structure?

Borgmann lists frozen food as merely one instance among others of the technological device. What I would like to suggest is that the modern industrial system of food production, also known as agribusiness, is itself paradigmatic of the device paradigm. Junk food, it will be seen, is the single-faceted commodity of this global device. In general, owing to its

ontological significance as both the support and consequence of our finitude, food has a unique and immediate relation to technology, which
itself stands for a peculiar way of being-in-the-world.

Certain historians have put forward the claim that food has acted as
the catalyst for technological invention. Lewis Mumford argues that the
danger and complexity involved in bringing down large game thrust early
man into the creation and use of language, the forerunner of all subsequent technologies. A small band of hunters could not hope to fell an
animal many times the size and strength of an individual man without
precise coordination made possible only by the quick means of unambiguous and direct spoken commands and replies.[12] After speech came
the weapons and implements needed to kill and prepare the quarry for
consumption. Fire, too, may have functioned first in cooking and only
later as a source of warmth.

While the connection between food and primitive technology is
basic and obvious, as technology advances, the connection appears to
grow tenuous. In the age of modern technology—the technology that
Heidegger felt dire need to question and understand—the most exciting
innovations no longer seem directed at food. Microcomputers, artificial
intelligence, virtual reality, and space exploration, though perhaps all tan-
gentially amenable in some degree to alimentary applications, are developed mainly for epistemological, military, and entertainment purposes.
High technology, so it seems, caters to the cerebral rather than the
abdominal region of humans. However, as Tierney points out, even the
most heady of current technologies has spun out of the nineteenth-
century agricultural revolution wrought by mechanized farming.

[A] discussion of nineteenth century agricultural technology
may seem irrelevant to an understanding of the techno-
fetishism of the late twentieth century, since in technologically
advanced countries relatively few people are engaged in agricultural activity. But that is the peculiar nature of agricultural technology; the more successful this technology was in freeing up
the time involved in the production of food, the less visible and
prevalent this technology became, as fewer people were
required to spend their time in agricultural production. Nevertheless, the nineteenth century advances in agricultural technology are important for understanding the role convenience plays
in modern techno-fetishism. It was the success of agricultural
technology in reducing the time that had to be spent in agricultural production which enabled technology to further establish
itself in the modern household.[13]

Further establishment in the household, of course, meant deeper entrenchment in the modern way of life, such that technology has become a closed and nearly exclusive manner of taking up with the world.

Tierney, in the passage just cited, attributes the tendency toward invisibility and retirement in the industrial food production to the "peculiar nature of agricultural technology." That Tierney would link mechanical concealment especially to agricultural technology further bolsters the claim that food is the paradigmatic commodity. For the concealment of its means is quintessential to the technological device in general. Borgmann explains:

> The concealment of the machinery and the disburdening character of the device go hand in hand. If the machinery were forcefully present, it would *eo ipso* make claims on our faculties. If claims are felt to be onerous and are therefore removed, then so is the machinery. A commodity is truly available when it can be enjoyed as a mere end, unencumbered by means.[14]

The articulation of the promise of technology announces the disappearance of all things that elicit physical effort. From the perspective of modern technological urban populations, food production has effectually vanished. Not only cultivating, but also cooking has succumbed to the eraser of convenience. As a commodity, food comes in excessive abundance because its astounding quantity conceals its essence.

Food as Commodity

"Food," writes Marc David, a self-styled food psychologist, "is not something we eat. It is a ceaseless reminder that we are mortal, earthbound, hungry and in need. We are bound by a biological imperative that forever keeps returning us to the soil, plants, animals, and running water for replenishment. Eating is life."[15] This last sentence is equivalent to the ontological statement: "Eating is Being," for eating nurtures human finitude, which is the field where Being occurs. Thus, we relate to Being primarily through food. The advent of the industrial system of agriculture marked a seismic disturbance in that primordial relationship. It meant that, "farming had become less the satisfaction of a demand of the body than the practice of overcoming limits which hinder the production of food as a commodity."[16]

As a commodity, food becomes available in the fourfold manner that Borgmann describes. The consumption of food is an instantaneous, ubiq-

uitous, safe, and easy affair. Each of these qualities, in themselves beneficial, contrasts sharply with the common ways of eating prior to the Green
Revolution, precipitated by the wholesale mechanization of farming and
the introduction of petrochemicals. Steady advances in the sophistication
of food-processing methods and packaging have dispensed with the need
for personal participation in food preparation. Fewer and fewer people
have a hand in not only the growing of crops, but also the cooking of
meals. While this historical process has democratized the leisure formerly
enjoyed only by the wealthy, who could afford hired hands to stir their
pots, it does impose a certain price. This dissociation from, and the consequent ignorance concerning the most elementary of human activities,
creates the inhospitable atmosphere of alienation that surrounds all commodity production and consumption.

Thankfully, at least for most of us in the developed world, the ready
abundance of food has stilled the primal fear of hunger, and also opened
the door for women to exit the confines of the kitchen. Without depre-
cating these real gains, we nevertheless need to balance them against the
rarely acknowledged, though no less real, losses. The satisfying and creative potential of mindful cookery lies more or less dormant in the world
of commodities, despite the latter's astounding selection of ingredients. I
believe that our technological alienation from our food leaves us chronically, ontologically underfed.

Commodification detemporalizes food, making its consumption
instantaneous. Given the fundamental relation between food and Being, it
should come as no surprise as to how thoroughly and essentially time saturates the former as well as the latter. In many ways, food actually demar-
cates time. Seasons of the year divide into periods of sowing, cultivating,
harvesting, and storing. Meals structure the otherwise amorphous shape
of the day. Feast days punctuate the calendar. Food represents the passage
of time and equally its continuity from one moment to the next. In other
words, food is temporal extension in material form. Not only does a piece
of food contain the duration of its growth and maturation in the process
of nature, its preparation and consumption entail the span of cultural
development that instituted the diversity of mores, manners, skills, and
knowledge inseparable from a people's foodways. With commodities,
food's temporal breadth narrows to a point of atemporal consumption.
Commodified food does not reveal its temporal contents, which run
through the seasons, phases of the moon, and the hours of preparation.
Because instantaneous, food has no history and its consumption can take
place unhindered by temporal restrictions. The appeal, of course, of fast
food is that it saves time. However, part of the reason that we desperately
feel that time needs to be saved while eating is that the very food that

ought to measure and preserve time in fact compromises time's natural integrity and meaning.

As it disassembles temporal limitations, technology also removes the spatial barriers that have traditionally contained food. In manifold ways, food has become ubiquitous. Packaging and chemical preservatives allow for the transportation and storage of food to and from any location. This has multiplied nearly beyond belief not only the array of available food-stuffs from all corners of the globe, but, far more important, also the pos-sibilities of careers available to women, the traditional nurturers. The globalization of the kitchen, though, has left the convivial meal in rather a sad state of dereliction. Where formerly food was prepared and eaten in areas dedicated to these activities, now one can effortlessly "grab a bite" just about anywhere, including libraries and bookstores. Another aspect of ubiquity is spatial nondifferentiation, which goes along with temporal contraction. Supermarkets illustrate this vividly. Architecturally, they tend to be nondescript and uniform, having little to no connection to their immediate geographical surroundings. Inside, they offer an eclectic, one might say chaotic, collection of foodstuffs that presumes to sample every culture of the world and in its entirety ends up being foreign to them all (the fate of all so-called fusion foods). Canadians reportedly ingest more bananas per capita than they do apples, despite the obvious fact that not a single banana has ever been harvested from Canadian soils. Ubiquity finds food everywhere, ready at hand. Yet it involves an enormous paradox: the scene of ubiquitous food is the technological, inorganic, and sterile "urban jungle" where nothing grows. A veritable desert surrounds the cornucopia of technologically available food.

The third element of availability magnifies the paradox. Food safety begins with food security, which, from any sane and natural point of view, is tenuous at best wherever nothing edible grows. Nevertheless, the vast industrial system of agriculture manages, once more in the First World, to make the infertile cityscape the proprietor and chief beneficiary of its global fecundity. Urban North Americans typically have access to more abundant and less expensive tropical cash crops than the southern peas-ants who tended and harvested them. Structural adjustment programs imposed by international economic organizations such as the World Bank and the International Monetary Fund guarantee that the industrialized northern cities are fed before the rural poor of the producing nation. This inequity ought to unsettle us. If the express promise of technology is supposedly humanitarian in spirit, then immoral consequences of its ful-fillment point to profound problems in the conception of its promise. The hungry will continue to feed the sated until their hunger becomes unbearable. At that point, technologically won food security will have to recognize its perilous dependence on an apparently incorrigibly unjust and unstable system.

The safety associated with commodified food has for the most part only a cosmetic nature. Commodities exhaust themselves fully in consumption and ought to bear no trace of their production, which remains forever the domain of the concealed machinery. Technology can and does employ any number of hazards to produce food, but so long as its consumption appears safe and hygenic to the consumer there is little public concern. These hazards include lethal chemicals, intensive factory farms for the mass manufacture of livestock, feeding offal to strict herbivores as cheap fodder, bioengineering, and biological patents. Conventional chemical agriculture presents its labor force with one of the highest risks of poisoning of all occupations. Meat-packing has "turned into the most dangerous job in the United States, performed by armies of poor, transient immigrants whose injuries often go unrecorded and uncompensated."[17]

It is tempting to take these unfortunate circumstances as accidental to the technological commodification of food, but the perils of the process actually worsen with the increasingly safe availability of the product. If so many perils plague the industrial process of food production, what kind of safety accompanies the product? Purely a metaphysical safety. Because food itself threatens the will for physical transcendence that is the hidden impetus of technology, the safe consumption of commodious food must minimize all associations of finitude that natural food carries.

First, technologically produced food is stripped of all its natural qualities. Of course, nature's primary quality is ephemerality, its permanent state of continual change. Thus, safe consumption requires the stabilization of the impermanence of food. Technology, through packaging, preservatives, freezing, and chemical and genetic alteration makes food virtually imperishable. Food that does not decay, that overcomes temporal limitation, furnishes the fit diet for mortals who do not care to die, who strive to wade out of the stream of flux known to Heraclitus as Becoming. In this sense, processed food best models the general technological reification of Being. Technology fixes the impermanence of nature (*physis*) in a form that best suits a will to mastery that first arises in its own unacceptable experience of distance and difference from nature.

Technology reifies Being in its own image. Having arrogated the powers of the process of Being, technology processes food in a manner that will safely conceal its naturalness, that is, its limitedness. Meat products best exemplify the phenomenon. Meat for consumption, even when traditionally prepared, generally bears little resemblance to its previous incarnation as a living animal. Processing effectively renders the source completely inscrutable. Hamburgers, hot dogs, bologna, fish sticks, and innumerable other products seem to have no conceivable biological origin. "Each Chicken McNugget is a copy of a copy; no original Chicken McNugget ever existed. The original, the chicken is hardly recognizable in the McNugget. The Chicken McNugget is 'fake chicken'."[18] Safe food, food that does not smack of human mortality, must not look like food. Nor may it smell of the earth. Supermarkets sell their safe commodities in a sealed, air-conditioned environment devoid of odor. Smell is the most animalistic and uncontrollable of all human senses, and so must be enervated as much as metaphysically possible. The technologically available abundance of supermarkets asserts its independence from nature by suppressing all its scents.

The denaturing of food initiated by technological processing culminates in disposable packaging. Whatever natural remnant that may have chanced to survive the rigors of processing is suffocated, usually within a tomb of plastic. In the age of commodification, plastic becomes nearly inseparable from food. To seal a piece of food in plastic means to sever all remaining relations it has with living nature. The modern marriage between plastic and food extends far beyond utilitarian concerns of storage and preservation. Plastic is a substance completely inert and lifeless. Technology favors it for its outstanding malleability; plastic, unlike natural materials such as wood and stone, offers no substantial resistance to its manipulation. The natural aspects of food remain recalcitrant to the technological will to mastery, but, when enclosed in lifeless matter, these aspects lose the vitality of resistance. Technology masters substance in the form of plastic, and then uses the latter to master food, the very substrate of substance. Hermetically sealed off from its natural cycle of growth and decay, packaged food, despite its toxic encasement, appears safely disconnected from finitude.

George Ritzer makes a similar observation regarding packaging and predictability. Safety comes from a sense of control, which in turn relies on an agent's ability to predict the effects of her actions. "Packaging is another important component of predictability in the fast-food restaurant. In spite of the fast-food restaurants' best efforts, unpredictability can creep in because the nature of the materials. . . . Whatever the (slight) unpredictabilities in the food, packaging . . . can always be the same and imply that the food will be too."[19] The nature of food materials is, of course, natural, that is, essentially bound to the unpredictable sequence of becoming and passing away, of emerging and receding. Where technological food-processing fails to fully fix this Heraclitean flux, technological packaging succeeds. It arrests food artificially in its natural ontological passage and suspends it in a kind of eternal, immutable realm. The

Chicken McNugget, remember, exists first and foremost in the ideal. Packaging is literally the material proof of the reification of Being. An ontological interpretation of packaging must not ignore the real salutary benefits the latter bestows. Without doubt, plastic packaging has saved food, stemmed the spread of communicable diseases and introduced an unprecedented variety into everyday cuisine. Yet the conatus motivating the multibillion dollar packaging industry, which melds seamlessly into the multibillion dollar advertising industry, draws its strength from a concern deeper than that of mere public health. Now "conatus" is a deliberate term, the same that Leibniz employed to designate the monad's individual will to subjective perfection. A metaphysical entity par excellence, the monad strives after perfect metaphysical freedom, which means absolute independence from all other beings (monads have no windows) and ultimately from Being as such. The monad is self-contained, packaged, as it were, in its own self-sufficiency. Other monads can only represent at best a philosophical problem, if not a threat to this sufficiency.

Before the late nineteenth century's discovery of germs and the subsequent formulation of the germ theory of disease, people generally lived less monadic existences. The very impulse toward forming human society, as Aristotle pointed out long ago in his *Politics*, springs from the individual's recognized need for others for security and assistance. The ancient *polis* was built on the belief that mutual dependence contributed to the flourishing and excellence of each human life inhabiting it. Various social institutions reflected this belief, from grand public works to ancestor veneration, which acknowledged the indebtedness of each generation to its predecessors. Public parks and festivals, common grazing and agricultural lands provided the geographical structures for these communal institutions. The history of the West, however, both economically and technologically, has tended toward increasing privatization. The loss of the commons was industrial capitalism's gain; with each technological innovation in communications, the possibility of direct personal contact and *tête-à-tête* dialogue becomes ever more remote.

The germ theory, which attributes disease and infection to invisible and ubiquitous organisms, created the conditions for a scientific privatization that paved the way for many of the twentieth century's strange technological novelties, in particular disposable items. Prior to the germ theory, explanations of sickness centered on the patient's bodily constitution, diet, environment, even her moral behavior. The immediate precursor to the germ theory, called the miasmic theory, blamed the malodorous vapors expelled from rotting matter for causing disease. Novel to the germ theory is its singular attack on life itself. Germs, and later bacteria, were thought to be living creatures; hence, the modern conception of cleanliness goes beyond the mere absence of dirt. It entails sterility, which means the absence of life. Although science provides sound empirical evidence in its defense, the germ theory, especially in its technological application in mass society (witness Lysol and its extended family of disinfectants), contains a good measure of metaphysics.

The projection of disease onto an alien and threatening nature gives license for the complete technological subjugation of the latter. Illness, frailty, indeed mortality, come to be seen as extraneous impositions on us rather than being accepted as our inescapable condition. While alleviation from these natural burdens is a healthy and intelligent goal, the pretense of complete emancipation from them is asinine. It implies the absolute removal of nature. Thus, precautions reasonable in light of evidence brought forward by the germ theory get trampled by absurd obsessions and neuroses. Ironically, our very drive for security compromises our natural health. Since all living things, germs included, exist in and of nature, metaphysical freedom demands their evacuation from the world. Only from this metaphysical point of view does the modern enthusiasm for sterilization show some plausibility through the cracks of its absurdity. In the name of health, we moderns saturate our homes and bodies with an ungodly host of toxic poisons, most potentially lethal in any sizable quantity. However, when sickness becomes equated with life, presumed human flourishing in the shape of rational metaphysical progress has to take place in a lifeless, sterile environment under complete human control and determination.

The germ theory also lends its strength to the defense of the folly of overpackaging. Technologically speaking, the nature of food makes it highly susceptible to germs. Indeed, modernity experiences eating as one of its most hazardous activities. Packaging caters to this experience by sterilizing the food it encloses. A packaged product is a denatured product, one thoroughly humanized and therefore safe from the inhuman presence of germs, provided that the item does not stay unwrapped for any length of time. According to the metaphysical mind, an unpackaged product cannot be clean, for germs, the nefarious remnants of nature, will surely infest it. The lifelessness of plastic must smother the liveliness of germs or else food might likely bring down Transcendent Man. Packaging individualizes food, stealing it away from the grand natural nexus and locking it safely in its own monadic container.

The commodification of food privatizes it economically, socially, and, as just now seen, ontologically. These three aspects work in unison. The metaphysical danger of food that creates the need for increasingly individualized packaging also promotes individualized consumption. In the case of other eaters, the technological solution to germs, namely, processing and packaging, cannot as yet be legally employed. The only way to avoid sure contamination from others polluted, perhaps by unclean food, is to consume packaged food as quickly as possible in the safety of isolation. Drawn out communal consumption carries weighty and irrational risks. If they absolutely must eat, monads should eat alone. Swanson TV dinners did a superlative job in the 1950s of cleaning up the unhygienic family meal. Televisions host far fewer germs than brothers, sisters, fathers, and mothers. For this one reason alone, they are welcome dinner guests. Now add to their hygiene their extra feature of controllable volume and one could not imagine more congenial company. The founding fathers of today's fast-food empires were fastidious, perhaps neurotically so.[20] This characteristic made them model metaphysicians. They developed an intricate technological system that hustles customers through the rapid consumption of highly processed, individually wrapped food items. Thanks to drive-thrus, the monadic consumer need not even abandon the safely sealed cocoon of one's automobile.

Taken to its obsessive extreme, the germ theory proscribes companionship. The Latin root for this word, *cum pani*, literally means to share bread. But insofar as each eater harbors untold numbers of hazardous germs, it is safest to keep one's food strictly to one's self. Safety in a world of bacteria implies isolation. Packaging successfully isolates both food and consumer within a structure of sterile control. In essence, it encloses the commons. Susan Strasser narrates part of the history of this enclosure through the career of the disposable drinking cup, which appeared in the early years of the twentieth century.

> While the sanitary advantages of toilet paper might have been obvious, those of the paper cup required a belief in germs. The widespread use of paper cups was a direct result of a public health crusade educating people about the invisible organisms spread by the common drinking cups once standard in public places, especially trains and railroad stations. Manufacturers of paper cups teamed up with public health authorities to campaign for federal and state regulations banning common drinking cups from use in interstate traffic. Succeeding in 1912, they competed for the business of the railroads and train stations. . . .
>
> Disposable paper cups met significant resistance. Most public places offered them in coin-operated dispensers, and some people were not willing to pay for what had once been free. Respectable travellers carried their own cups, available in metal and celluloid in a variety of collapsable and folding designs. Others reused paper cups from the trash or drank out

of the public tanks, putting their lips to the faucet or using the cover of the tank as a cup. Some people protested against the vending machines: soldiers smashed paper cup dispensers in Washington's Union Station during President Wilson's inauguration in 1913. And some public places installed drinking fountains instead of paper cups dispensers, although at first these, too, were attacked as unsanitary because people could touch the nozzle with their lips.[21]

The resistance, we well know, soon yielded and disposable cups began to pour voluminously into the world. For us today, the idea of a public common cup is nearly unthinkable. Secretly, we are so accustomed to regarding others as menaces to our unnatural health and monadic freedom that we can no longer imagine anything shared in common with filthy humanity at large. We already take in commodified water in bottles and commodified oxygen in tanks. The commodities of food and drink must be safe, sterile, and private.

Ease is the fourth element of availability and encompasses the other three. A ubiquitous, instantaneous, and safe commodity makes few demands on its consumers. Ideally, the perfect commodity would make no demands at all, quietly consuming itself outside the awareness of the consumer. The more attention that a commodity solicits, the more care it involves in its consumption, then the more crude and imperfect remains its availability. The very telos of a commodity is to render the consumer "carefree." At its basis this has to do with the notion of saving time. I will examine the ontological import of these two crucial aspects of the commodity fully in chapters five and six. For now, I need only indicate that ease, as a technological end, is at heart a metaphysical property. Ease loosens the physical bonds that bind mortals to their worldly condition. In other words, ease alleviates the essential gravity of being-in-the-world.

In Borgmann's example of the device, a flick of a switch or the turn of a dial on the thermostat replaces the many physical tasks and skills demanded by the hearth. In contrast to the latter, a central heating system delivers warmth easily to the consumer. Commodified food is above all else easily consumed (though more often than not digested with difficulty). Ease has permeated everything associated with modern food, from the field to the mouth. The first and most decisive step is to free the majority, and ideally the totality, of humanity from the necessity of participation in the production of food. Globally, the shift from a land-based, agrarian population to an urbanized, industrial one accelerates daily. In industrialized countries, only a threatened minority of agriculturalists survives. The fact that the "United States now has more prison inmates than full-time farmers"[22] puts their numbers into perspective. This, of course, marks a complete historical reversal, as before the nineteenth century, only a slim—figuratively, not literally—elite had the luxury to eat without having to contribute their sweat to the production of what was eaten. The positive aspects of this reversal include the immense expansion of "life options" available to women and the underclasses. The negative aspects include a wholesale surrender of knowledge, skill, and even enjoyment of the consumer to the technological apparatuses of industrial agriculture.

As explained earlier, a technological device functions precisely by separating production from consumption. Commodities belong exclusively on the side of consumption. The device of modern food, however, not only relegates production to its hidden machinery, but also lumps domestic preparation in with agribusiness. If present trends continue, the skill and joy of cooking will soon become as rare as the art of farming is now. One author boasts that since World War II the time spent by average Americans for food acquisition, preparation, and cleanup has decreased by 80 percent.[23] He congratulates processed food made available through innumerable innovations in packaging for accomplishing this truly extraordinary feat. This is, of course, the view of popular technological enthusiasm, or "techno-fetishism," to borrow Tierney's phrase. Whether or not it is clear-sighted enough remains to be seen in light of contradicting evidence: "One (study) even indicated that the amount of time middle class urban housewives spent on food preparation actually increased slightly from 1931 to 1965. Processors and appliance makers seemed to inadvertently admit this by portraying cooking less as a labour of love and expression of creativity and more as a part of kitchen drudgery."[24] Perhaps the introduction of so many unfamiliar gadgets and processed products can account for this contradiction because, over all, the active and personal involvement in food preparation has indubitably declined over the long run. Preparation has increasingly become part of the production of commodified food, which removes it from the consumer. The restaurant industry constitutes a growing portion of the technological machinery of modern life. In the United States, despite war rationing and supposedly "lean" times, "from 1939 to 1946 restaurant sales almost quadrupled."[25] At the end of the century, according to one statistic, American "people spend 46 cents of every food dollar on meals and snacks away from home."[26] Restaurants, especially the fast-food variety, are now ubiquitous and serve up apparently safe food instantly. In short, they make eating preeminently easy.

The domestic scene is hardly any more onerous. "When Gallup asked a sampling of (American) people eating at home in September 1989 what they were eating, almost half were sitting down to frozen, packaged or take-out meals."[27] Freezers, microwave ovens, and plastic packaging have together succeeded in importing the ease of restaurants or hired hands into every modern kitchen. Indeed, today this trio could easily substitute for all other domestic culinary implements, as they effectively eliminate possible participation in food production, meal preparation, and utensil cleaning. The consumer simply ingests, a task the ease of which roughly equals the disposal of the accompanying packaging.[28]

Because a metaphysical urge drives commodification, the process has no inherent terminus short of absolute transcendence beyond all physical limitation, which is tantamount to incorporeal disembodiment. Tierney reminds us that:

> The need to continually reduce the amount of time and energy people spend upon bodily necessity has become an end in itself. . . . [Yet] such assaults on the limits of the body, especially temporal limits, are never ending. It is no wonder that modern ascetics have little time for the "development of human power as an end in itself." They are too busy trying to be rid of their bodies and the limits those bodies impose upon their freedom.[29]

Tierney thinks the automobile best exemplifies this interminable drive. We are constantly developing faster and more powerful cars to overcome distance more effectively. Our use and development of computers are perhaps even more revealing. Even the slightest of delays in loading or processing data strikes us as tedious, if not unbearable. Perfect availability, the goal of technological devices, exists outside of time and space. A truly metaphysical consumer dispenses with her body.

Commodified food illustrates this more forcefully than computers and cars because its ease aims directly at minimizing bodily engagement and presence. Freed from both production and preparation, the modern consumer is also offered ease from the travails of consumption itself. Energy bars and other "meal replacement" products trade off maximum calories for minimal chewing. In general, processed food requires minimal mastication. Protein shakes and "booster gels," not to mention the stupefying selection of soy drinks, leave the consumer's jaw slack with idleness. It is estimated that the average American teen acquires 9 percent of his daily caloric intake through the easy consumption of carbonated soft drinks.[30] The one-time science fiction fantasy of total human sustenance contained in a pill or two has entered into the sights of legitimate scientific research. Technology progresses only so long as it diminishes our stubborn physicality. Soon the most consumable food will not have to be eaten.

Eating Reason

We saw that the hoarding behavior of the Trobriand Islanders dissembles the phenomenon of food. Their preference for displaying food over actually eating it does violence to the ontological essence of food. Food not eaten is not food at all, since it denies food's essential transience in its relation to the changeable, needy body. The technological perspective also envisions the ideal food as inedible. What seemed a superstitious fear among primitives ends up becoming rational scientific endeavor. The common cause behind them both is the will to transcend the impermanence of Being incarnated as the mortal human body. Both seem to me doomed to failure. If the behavior of the Trobrianders appears somewhat more laughable than the goings-on of sophisticated modern consumers, it is only because the doom surrounding our failure is too dark to provoke much laughter.

The metaphysical definition of human being—the rational animal—exalts the species' difference at the expense of the entire genus. Reason, supposedly eternally abiding and unchanging, constitutes the real metaphysical essence of man, whereas his needy animal nature only disturbs and detracts from his primary perfection. Escape from the prison of the body leads directly into the boundless realm of reason, of the incorruptible Ideas, of pure contemplation disengaged from the physical world. Here mathematics and pure scientific speculation also reside. I have shown how technological processing and packaging cover over food, preventing the phenomenal truth that reflects its ontological nature, that is, its essential relation to Being. Covered over in this manner, the phenomenon of food itself undergoes phenomenal changes that further obscure its ontological nature. Even apart from its packaging, food appears always coated with metaphysical impositions. Such impositions reduce food to a number of safe and calculable scientific rationalizations.

Rationalized food is first and foremost mathematical. Every piece of food, whether processed or not, has been translated into a flavorless numeric code of calories, fats, proteins, carbohydrates, and oils. Packaging, of course, clarifies the mathematical appearance of food by displaying the precise scientific breakdown of its contents. Even unpackaged food, however, like an apple, emerges out of nature into the technological world as merely a sum of calories, vitamins, and sugars. The real substance of the apple, that is, its truly wondrous ability to support our finite neediness, lies hidden behind these concepts. Rationalized food primarily sustains reason; it feeds our scientific ideas about eating. Whatever nourishment it actually gives to the body we take as happy coincidence.

In the technological world, people calculate rather than eat their food and the complexity of these calculations bespeaks the level that popular metaphysics has reached. This fundamental transformation in the relation between humans and food results from the latter's commodification. The calculation begins with assessing the price and market value of a chosen item and ends with tallying up the amount of potential energy gained against the number of grams of fat potentially incorporated. Amid this calculating and concocting of concepts the physical food is hurriedly, absent-mindedly, and perhaps even grudgingly consumed. For not only is the substantial side of food inherently unsafe with respect to the metaphysical subject, it is also unsightly. Wherever technologically secured abundance flourishes, food, whatever else its physical effects, does one critical thing: it makes people fat. This ought not concern a transcendent rationality, but it does disturb the metaphysical will to power that wants to fully dominate, control, and form to its own preconceptions the physical body. A fat body signifies rebellious physicality not yet subdued by reason. A fat body errs dangerously close to nature: "Traditional societies, which have not been involved in the modernization associated with the industrial revolution tend to appreciate and value at least moderate, if not larger, amounts of fat. Traditional societies viewed stored body fat as a sign of health and wealth, particularly for women."[31] In opposition to this, the consumer society regards fat as a failure, and its prejudice has less to do with health than with reason's mania for control. Consumers are admonished to consume everything as voraciously as possible, including the lucrative commodity of fad diets. Drugs, cosmetic surgery, and pseudo-foods are all considered legitimate ways to stay slender. These unnatural and often pernicious techniques make sense only to an insensitive rationality itself consumed by the vision of an inhuman ideal of the perfect body.

Commodification is the process of rationalization applied to inner-worldly beings. As Borgmann explains, the process reduces a multifaceted, world-embedded thing to a single of its functions, which is then set up as an end in itself. This determines the direction of technological progress along the straight line of refined efficiency of means toward the presupposed end. As the independent and dislocated function gains precedence over the holistic, interrelated original, the thing as such recedes from worldly presence. Thus, commodification in a way evacuates nature, replacing its physical phenomena with rationalized reductions of them. Consequently, the physical world becomes phenomenal in the specifically metaphysical sense of this term. That is, it seems to conceal more than it reveals. It becomes illusory, or, in the most current metaphysical lingo, virtual. Nowhere in nature do carbohydrates, proteins, and fatty acids grow, yet these phenomena appear to the exclusion of grains, beans, and nuts in the technological world. Their presence usually relies on the absence of worldly things.

Nevertheless, the metaphysical substitution of the physical for the conceptual, the process now recognized as commodification, is itself fundamentally illusory. Being is so inextricably related to physical beings that all phenomenal occurrences necessarily have physical effects. This basic truth makes trash a fit being for ontological study. By emptying the world of physical things and filling it with seemingly immaterial concepts, commodification creates trash, that is, beings whose disposal supposedly leaves no physical consequence or remainder. But the costs and woes resulting from unchecked consumption of disposables have forced the consumer society to acknowledge the paradox that plagues it: the greater the number of rationalized commodities it deals with, the more massive the material debris it leaves behind. The very same paradox plays havoc with the rationalized human body. The more we conceptualize and commodify the food we eat, the greater the incidence of obesity among us. We grow physically fat on our metaphysical concepts.[32] This paradox will become more clear in due time. For now, the following statistic suggests the hidden reality of rationalization: "The United States devotes about 4 percent of its energy to packaging food, almost as much as American agriculture uses to grow the food."[33]

The Fast-Food Device

To further fortify my claim that food is the paradigmatic device, I will briefly compare George Ritzer's analysis of Western rationalization with Borgmann's theory of the commodity. Ritzer's study helps immensely in that it takes as its subject the fast-food restaurant's own paradigm: McDonald's:

> The fast-food restaurant has become the model of rationality. Although it has adopted elements of rationality pioneered by its predecessors, it also represents a quantum leap in the process of rationalization. What we have today is sufficiently more extreme than previous forms of rationalization to legitimize the use of a distinct label—McDonaldization—to describe the most contemporary aspects of the rationalization process.[34]

Working from Max Weber's critique of Western formal rationality, Ritzer finds that the fast food industry, of all modern industrial systems, has done the most to perfect and socially entrench the four cornerstones of every bureaucracy: efficiency, calculability, predictability, and control through nonhuman technology. The very fact that the name of a single restaurant can garner universal recognition while instantly evoking a very specific set of images and concepts proves the validity of Ritzer's coinage.

The four elements of formal rationalization cited by Ritzer relate intimately to the four elements of availability that Borgmann regards as necessary to commodification. I have already touched on the important role that predictability plays in safe consumption. Calculability is made possible by the wholesale quantification of all phenomena that fall within the compass of the rationalization process. Prices, weights, and, in general, precise measurements of all kinds remove the contingency and uniqueness of each individual being. The more that measurements of quantity substitute for conditions of quality, the easier it becomes to provide ubiquity in consumption. Numbers are universally standard; they admit of no local peculiarity. To be ubiquitous a commodity must share this global uniformity, appearing everywhere the same. The quantification essential to calculability also abets temporal uniformity. Calculations always operate in a kind of fictitious future state projected beyond the present situation. When we pose to ourselves a mathematical problem, we always anticipate the answer: "when two is added to two, then it will make four." Nonetheless, this unchanging mathematical future can exert causal influence on the present, which allows for instantaneity in consumption. Calculability gives a commodity a phenomenal existence prior to its substantial existence. Because this preexistence can be reckoned with in advance, the consumption of its substance can occur immediately without delay. The calculated commodity, a product of sophisticated mathematical forethought, appears instantaneously in the present consumer world. The fairly recent stock market innovation, enabled by computers, of trading in unreal future commodities, which may or may not eventually manifest in reality, wholly depends on the instantaneity implied by calculability.

Control through nonhuman technology is, of course, prerequisite for any commodification and the prime function of the device. "A *human technology*," Ritzer stipulates "(a screwdriver, for example), is controlled by people, a *nonhuman technology* (the order window at the drive-through window, for instance) controls people."[35] It is not difficult to see how the safe and easy technologically produced commodities exert control over consumers. A customer of McDonald's, say, not only has no choice as to how her meat gets cooked (computerized broilers strictly regulate the cooking time); she also has no choice about the methods of cattle raising used by modern agribusiness. To buy any item at McDonald's is to consume the entire industrial complex that supports it. The very ease and safety essential to commodity-availability demands the surrender of human control to nonhuman technology. Availability subtracts the consumer's skill and physical participation from the process of production and even to a large extent, from consumption. Without a knowledge of a device that the prolonged, skillful handling of it calls forth, the consumer is powerless in the face of its commodity. Her consumption of it is compelled and channeled by the structure of the device.

If control is the prime function of the device, efficiency is its raison d' être. Here all the elements of commodification combine, and since ease contains ubiquity, instantaneity, and safety, efficiency bears special relation to ease. Efficiency has absolute value because it supposedly achieves convenience and saves time: "Although the fast-food restaurant certainly did not create the yearning for efficiency, it has helped turn efficiency into an increasingly universal reality. Many sectors of society have had to change to operate in the efficient manner demanded by those accustomed to life in the drive-through lane of the fast-food restaurant."[36] Just two of the many sectors that Ritzer enumerates are franchising and the deskilling of work.

The perceived efficiency of chain outlets like McDonald's depends on the economies of scale made possible by the throughput of standardized products. Variety and regional irregularities complicate, if not prohibit, the buying and selling of the massive quantities of commodities that allow the company to keep down its production costs. By franchising its business, a company can control the uniformity of its product, thereby maintaining its large economic scale, while the franchisee alone assumes all the financial risks of opening a chain branch in a new location. Although, in the words of Eric Schlosser, "franchising schemes have been around in one form or another since the nineteenth century . . . it was the fast food industry that turned franchising into a business model soon emulated by retail chains throughout the United States."[37] The upshot, of course, has been the homogenization of culture and decimation of place. The Big Mac is a global phenomenon as are now thousands of commodities and stores. The ubiquity of these commodities supports the efficiency of their production, while, at the same time, the perceived efficiency of their consumption contributes to their ubiquitous demand.

Uniform products result most efficiently from uniform methods of production. In general, industrialization advances to the detriment of skilled craftsmanship. Recognizing the intrinsic incompatibility between temporal efficiency and careful craftsmanship, Henry Ford invented the assembly line to maximize uniformity and speed. The invention constrained workers to simple repetitive tasks that neither required much initial skill to master, nor provided opportunity to develop new skills.

Many of the early fast-food innovators consciously modeled their restaurants on Ford's invention, although they ignored his more progressive labor policies.[38] As a result, the fast-food industry, whose principles the larger service industry religiously follows, has successfully eliminated skill from its production. Attracted by the high corporate profits of fast-food chains and to keep pace with them, a widening range of businesses have adopted their aggressive deskilling techniques. For instance, "at the dawn of the fast food era, IBP (Iowa Beef Packers) became a meat-packing company with a fast food mentality, obsessed with throughput, efficiency, centralization and control. 'We've taken the skill out of every step', A. D. Anderson (one of IBP's owners) later boasted."[39] Ritzer's list of other enterprises outside the food industry includes hospitals, funeral parlors, and even—believe it or not—universities. As work becomes increasingly mechanized in the name of efficiency, the tasks still performed by humans grow more mechanical. Efficiency calls for the surrender of human skill to technology.

Standardization of places and commodities along with the decrement of bodily skill share more than an economic connection. At a more basic level, they relate to each other physiologically. Uniform environments typically leave the body disoriented due to their dearth of outstanding sensory stimuli. Standardized commodities, naked of nuance and difference, likewise deny the senses the necessary diversity of stimulation that fully exercises them. This occurs on the side of consumption. On the opposite side, that of production, mechanization in general deadens and steels the living flesh so that it better meshes with the tempo and constitution of the machine. One need not be a trained phenomenologist to observe the profound physiological effects that factory-styled labor, whether in an automobile plant or a largely automated fast-food restaurant, inflict on the body. The stress and exhaustion practically shut the senses down so as to protect the beleaguered organism from sensory overload. Forced to replicate the rhythm of the machine, the body comes to assume its inanimate insensitivity. In terms of speed and precision, the machine is indeed superlatively efficient, yet it lacks sensory awareness. The ghost within it does not feel. The body becomes similarly haunted when pressed to surrender skills learned and practiced through its innate physicality.

The mechanization of the body, brought about in the service of commodities, reinforces the physical desire for commodities. Mechanized senses begin to seek the precise regularity of uniform commodities. A disembodied appetite craves rationalized victuals. The body is experienced objectively, as if it were itself another robotic appendage to the vast assembly-line of the technological world. This explains Ritzer's comment that "people do not go to McDonald's for a delicious, pleasurable meal but, rather, to refuel. McDonald's is a place to fill their stomachs with lots of calories and carbohydrates so that they can move on to the next rationally organized activity. Eating to refuel is far more efficient than eating to enjoy a culinary experience."[40] Here Ritzer very deftly breaks down the secret recipe of fast food: it is equal parts rationality, commodification, and the objectification of the experiential body.

The rationalization, not yet so perfect that it can dispense with the physiology of taste, must therefore transform it. The excessive flavors of fast food overwhelm the body even as they fuel reason. Among the many ingredients and additives stuffed into a Big Mac, subtlety, in any form, is not one. When consumed in quantity, salt and sugars—the staples of fast food—desensitize the palate and habituate it to excess. Cravings soon ensue. While this happens on the physiological level, one floor up, so to speak, at the psychological level, advertising inculcates mental habits and yearnings. McDonald's owes much of its international success to the unprecedented advertising campaign it aimed at children, a demographic sector previously ignored by advertisers as supposedly innocent and penniless. But a child's uncultured palate, impressionable mind, and innate genius for manipulating parents makes for a lucrative combination. Furthermore, the rationalization of a child, a creature that ranks one rung up from primates on the ladder of reason, marks a special achievement for metaphysics.

Eating to refuel may indeed be efficient, but it is not, ontologically speaking, true eating. Food, it does no harm to repeat, "is a ceaseless reminder that we are mortal, earthbound, hungry and in need."[41] Food's inherent reference to our finitude constitutes a major element of, to borrow from Levin, "the body's recollection of Being." Recollective eating is a participation in the play of Being that arises out of need. Machines, although they require fuel, do not need food because they do not die. Neither do mechanized human bodies, or at least that is the metaphysical hope. Fuel does not awaken the senses; it is supposed simply to maintain them in functional order for "the next rational activity" that will end up leaving them further disconnected. Food, on the other hand, in keeping with its ontological nature, always quickens the senses, flooding the body with the stream of sensations where the process of Being takes place. Rather than fill the insatiable mind with reified concepts of substance (e.g., calories and carbohydrates), food, when it actively draws the body into present sensory awareness, in fact empties the body of concepts. To taste with awareness is to tarry in the openness of the sensuous. Food teaches the process of phenomenal revelation common to all things. From concealment, a being passes into the presence of sensitive lived experience, only to lapse again into internal absence—the great mystery known as digestion. But even this concealment is not final, for it, too, gives way to consequent manifestation. The natural succession of appearance and disappearance rehearses on the physiological level the grander play of Being on the historical level. Finally, refueling has nothing to do with the companionship that accompanies true eating. The being-with-others of mortal human being can only get in the way of maximum efficiency.

Food can suffer the gastronomic abominations perpetrated by the fast-food industry because the latter fails to encounter its essence, which takes root eradicably in the sensorial, experiential body. The dissembling objectification of food goes in tandem with the technological objectification of the lived body. Which objectification happened first cannot be answered. For the body, so the Upanishads tell, is itself its food, while, phenomenologically, food always already refers to the mortal body that needs to incorporate it. Food not eaten, which means food not tasted and not experienced by the senses, is not food, but rather fuel. The composition of fuel includes calories, proteins, and the many other concepts that feed rationality. As Ritzer notes, consumers of fast food trade quality for quantity. Quantity is a mathematical reality of reason, whereas quality belongs to the affective life of the senses. When these senses have been ossified beneath a crush of concepts and overwhelming flavors, they lose their sensitivity to quality. Now, conceptual reification itself marches in step with the physical and social disengagement from innerworldly beings, whose care nurtures skill and sensorial acuteness. Again, whether the reification precedes the vitiating of physical engagement and skill or vice versa is a question wholly moot. A reified mind bars sensorial awareness and an insensitive body will scrounge for its sustenance in rational concepts.

We can now fully appreciate the perspicuity of Ritzer for having seen the fast food industry as the protagonist in the historical drama of formal rationalization. However, Ritzer's predominantly sociological analysis lacks the ontological basis that our study of the commodity provides. The reason that fast food is at once the protagonist of rationalization and paradigm commodity is that it, of all other commodities, succeeds best in obscuring and objectifying the experiential body. During production, fast food mechanizes the skillful body, even as the consumption of fast food offends the sensitive needy body. Given the essential ontological physicality of food, metaphysics has an imperative to rationalize it. Without the unconditional commodification of food accomplished through McDonaldization, the metaphysical will would remain stunted at a relatively low level of maturity. The physicality of food, its complicity, if not identity with the mortal body, towers as the most formidable obstacle to the unfolding of Western metaphysics. Its commodification was a metaphysical necessity before it became a technological triumph for the first time in the twentieth century. To make eating a mathematical exercise and food a substance of rational efficiency is to veil the sensitive temporality of the needy body. It marks the enclosure of the body, the loss of the physical commons as the receptive clearing for Being.

Junk Food

The successful rationalization of food accomplished by the likes of McDonald's and its competitors has helped to create a global appetite for junk food. Although the meaning of the latter term can vary widely depending on the tastes of the speaker, it generally includes all highly processed, overpackaged foods featuring large sugar or salt content and low nutritional value. Phenomenologically, the term has a broader application; it applies to all food that essentially denies the needs of the body. To reiterate, these needs are fundamentally ontological; because "the body is my very means of entering into relation with all things,"[42] it clears the space through which Being comes to pass. Phenomena appear within the overarching relational network of the world that exists only in conjunction with our experiential bodies. Experience requires vitality and health. Defects in the senses, by narrowing the body's possible relations to things, diminish the phenomenal fecundity of the world. Food, then, when truly eaten in sensitive awareness, directly nourishes our ontological understanding by keeping our body of experience receptive and expansive.

Junk food thus doubly denies the body. First, it coarsens the subtlety of the senses by patenting overly strong, uniform tastes. In the absence of diversity and variety, experience tends to dull and atrophy, sinking into a false sense of permanence, which is the antithesis to the true impermanence of Being. Second, junk food denies the body by withholding from it the proper nourishment that keeps it vitally keen and capable of physically engaging in the world. The widespread consumption of junk food has raised a coextensive problem of obesity, which experts warn has reached epidemic proportions in North America. An obese body sadly forfeits much of its native motility and worldly capacities. The greater this forfeiture, the more undifferentiated the experience of the obese body. The sedentary lifestyle that comes prepackaged with junk-food diets severely stifles the natural expressiveness of the body through its movements and work. Most of the modern world confines the mobile body to two static positions: seated in chairs and supine. Richness of experience dwindles with the foreclosure of different possibilities of posture, carriage, and motion. Thus, junk food standardizes, in addition to sensual experience, bodily experience in general.

As for taste, its standardization bears a more overt mark of its underlying metaphysical will. Eric Schlosser writes that,

> About 90 percent of the money that Americans spend on food is used to buy processed food. But the canning, freezing and dehydrating techniques used to process food destroy most of its flavour. Since the end of World War II, a vast industry has arisen in the United States to make processed food palatable. Without this flavour industry, today's fast food industry could not exist.[43]

Having destroyed the natural link between food and the human senses, commodification technologically replicates it according to its own dictates of availability. The resultant uniform flavor, however, has no natural counterpart because nature does not contain identity and permanence. No apple tastes identical to any other, yet to a body bred on junk food the technologically concocted flavor of, for example, McDonald's deep-fried "apple pies" tastes better and more "apple-y" than any untampered fruit. In part this has to do with the blunted senses of the technological body that require the overstimulation of artificial enhancers. More radically, manmade flavors cater to the metaphysical appetite for transcendence and control over nature. The impermanence of Being is, so to speak, too bitter for the palate of everyday existence. Food processing leeches out this impermanence, injects the food with its own objectified and conceptual surrogate, and then hermetically seals it off in plastic so that the natural impermanence cannot reenter. Inevitably, as with all things metaphysical, flavors come to occupy their own eternal space in the realm of immutable Forms, in which each individual jar of Cheez Whiz or bottle of Coca-Cola participates. Metaphysical taste buds will invariably find purple Kool-Aid more appealing and more real-tasting than vine-ripened grapes.

A disquieting ambivalence saturates the phenomenon of junk food and colors the term itself. For the most part, junk, contrary to food, is not something that humans have traditionally savored. Junk connotes worthlessness, filth, and potential harm—all qualities seemingly incommensurable with the salubrious benefits of food. However, when viewed metaphysically, the essential physicality of food takes on these very characteristics. In the context of metaphysics, which devalues the sensuous realm, "junk food" sounds more like a redundancy than an oxymoron. Yet the residual human reaction to this phenomenon betrays an existential unease with the hegemony of the metaphysical will. Junk food is caked with an invisible layer of guilt thicker than its layers of salt, sugar, and plastic. Although we readily consume junk food when it is present and often crave it in its absence, a tinge of shame usually taints the consumption and cravings. Often we must convince ourselves that we can indulge in junk food as a reward for some kind of perceived hardship endured or chore terminated. Despite this, the conviction not infrequently collapses at the time of consumption, which typically rapidly occurs in a state either of distraction (commonly in front of a television) or of emotional turmoil. Few people can linger over and genuinely relish junk food with epicurean delight.

The same ambivalence that contaminates junk food also associates food with trash proper, and gives further evidence of their more than metaphorical kinship. Having distractedly consumed an item of junk food, the consumer proceeds to rid himself of its mandatory trash while lost in the same perceptual oblivion. The act of disposal most commonly occurs as a blank in the stream of conscious experience, executed thoughtlessly and hurriedly. A consumer rarely has qualms or second thoughts about creating and disposing the trash of his consumption. There is at times, moreover, a certain uncanny pleasure in this production of trash that is parallel to the consumption of junk food. This pleasure is, I believe, something other than the satisfaction of the sated hunter regarding the remains of the kill. I have observed smiling picnickers deposit sizable mountains of trash in park refuse containers with a kind of artistic flourish, insinuating that their contribution of dirty plastic plates, forks, bottles, and bags enhanced the beauty of the natural surroundings. Sometimes also a sense of civic pride rewards instances of legitimate disposal when citizens takes the small effort of using designated municipal receptacles rather than municipal streets for their disposables. Here neither quantity nor quality of trash matters a moral jot compared to the fact that it gets thrown away in keeping with the by-laws. Metaphysical consumers find much more merit in keeping their cities and highways clean than they do in keeping their landfills empty or their ecological inheritance intact. Nevertheless, despite these exceptional occasions, a mainly ignored unease also accompanies consumption's production of trash. Trash evokes anxiety, as if our relation to its being were somehow askew and not as it should be. A vague ineffable intuition insinuates that a more careful and sensitive existence would not have to handle the stuff.

The by now fairly widespread public recycling campaigns and programs can be interpreted as a collective response to this oblique call of conscience. Unfortunately, its popularity situates it in the everyday world of business, distraction, and convenience. Stating this, I by no means wish to belittle the necessity and real benefits of industrialized public recycling. Without doubt, it helps to save virgin natural resources. But for all intents and purposes, there is negligible phenomenological difference between throwing a soda can, or a polystyrene takeout container, or a Tetra-pak into a blue recycling box rather than into a black garbage bag. Such actions equally represent the denial of the integrity of the trashed being. The ontological reason for the popularity of public recycling is that consumers, feeling vaguely uneasy with having defaulted in their guardianship of Being through their carelessness toward beings, hope at least to preserve the substance of the latter. In truth, however, technological consumers conceive of substance in a kind of disembodied Cartesian sense. For Descartes, the truth and essence of any material thing involve its mathematic properties, accessible only to reason: "Let us focus our attention on this and see what remains after we have removed everything that does not belong to the wax: only that it is something extended, flexible and mutable."[44] Substance with just such essential mathematical properties is perfectly suited for the constant manipulation and transformation of its accidental physical properties wrought upon it by reason's technology. A *res cogitans* has neither need nor ability to grasp physical beings because the necessary means to do so, to wit, a finite, physical body, does not belong to it. To the extent that the metaphysical consumer also doubts away the fundamentality of her physicality, she, too, is forced to conceive of physical things strictly in the reductive terms of insensible substance. Furthermore, since Aristotle, most philosophers have held that substance without form cannot phenomenally exist. Industrialized recycling, which requires of the consumer only the slightest degree of discretion in the act of disposal, essentially subtracts the form from the substance of the beings it endlessly reprocesses. It thereby treats them as trash, albeit of marginal value insofar as they help perpetuate the technological system. In this way, industrialized recycling is a metaphysical solution to a metaphysical problem. As such it fails ontologically.

Processed food requires packaging because packaging perfects the metaphysical transformation of food initiated by technological processing. The convenience of industrialized recycling is credited for the latter's popularity as an "environmental action." Tierney has brought to light the deep philosophical complexity of this modern ultimate value, whose supremacy rests on the metaphysical will. With respect to metaphysics, the convenience of public recycling has to do with the significant phenomenal substitution that such programs enact. Essential to the phenomenon of food is its perishability, its evanescence, whereas reliability, as Heidegger memorably portrays in his study of the peasant's shoes, is the essence of thingly beings.[45] Reliability implies a certain kind of durability, a resistance to ephemerality. Together trash and recycling switch these phenomenological characteristics so that the thingly being (a plastic bottle, say) transfers its reliability or perdurance to its contents (the immutable taste of Coca-Cola) and receives in turn the latter's natural transience. Strangely enough, the bottle rather than the contents is the true object of consumption. The bottle loses its form and the integrity of its being, while the commodity that it contains goes on forever unaltered as the transcendental, trademarked Form-ula of Coca-Cola.

Industrialized recycling, for all its many tangible environmental benefits, serves also as a convenient distraction, a kind of white noise to muffle out the vocational call of ontological care. It promotes increased commodity consumption, for the greater the number of beings negated through their deformation, the higher the quantity of raw (i.e., metaphysically dematerialized substance) stands available for technological use. Thus, recycling pulls off a double metaphysical coup: it acknowledges and abets the technological denaturing of food; by imposing the perishable nature of food onto enduring beings, it annihilates them even as it proclaims to save them.

Modern throwaway recycling bears no ontological resemblance to the careful preservation of things known to our predecessors. In her well-documented history of trash, Susan Strasser writes that, "throughout most of history, people of all classes and in all places have practised an everyday regard for objects, the labour involved in creating them, and the materials from which they were made."[46] This ontological regard for beings worked itself out in the physical practice of manually maintaining and repairing them. True preservation of things depends on a sensitive human intimacy with them that arises from a physical understanding of their innerworldly being, their situation within the inclusive context of the world. This intimacy embeds a thing inextricably into the world that gives it being. When so embedded, a being resists the metaphysical negation of trashing or industrial recycling. Because things express innerworldly being through the physical engagements they propose to people, the world of things, as Borgmann shows, is always physically engaging. It commands our physical presence and care. In contrast to our own throwaway industrialized version, former "recycling" measures involved personal and bodily participation: "The reuse of packaging (in the nineteenth century) expressed the fundamental principles of household bricolage and stewardship of materials. For most of the century, people paid for packaging: unless old bottles or sacks were brought in for reuse, new ones had to be purchased from the grocer, druggist or flour miller."[47] While perhaps explicitly motivated by economics, this kind of personal and manual participation had the far greater significance of preserving the things within a hospitable world of relations tailored to the human scale. Direct care for what to us today looks like expendable packaging helped infuse things with their own kind of physical personality, relating them more meaningfully to their human partners.

Conclusion

In this chapter I have tried to show the deep ontological significance of food. From our ineluctable need for nutrients and nourishment, the world of beings constitutes itself. The infant behaves as if all was edible and only later learns its first phenomenal distinction: the division between the edible and the inedible. Although a myriad of more complex distinctions will subsequently develop, the world remains rooted in the material of physical sustenance. Our hungry mortality, our bodily need to engage with and incorporate innerworldly beings, clears the ontological field wherein Being transpires. Thus, the world continues always to unfold in our dual physical need of its nurture and its nurturing. Beings grant themselves to our need in our involuntary, absolute dependence on them. It is hard not to think of this arresting mystery as the cooperation of some cosmic providence with faith.

Why this faith has faltered at this point in history is beyond the present scope of discussion. For whatever reason, first Western man and now humanity at large have reacted to the fearful insecurity of finite existence with a grasping will to control. Where once people sought to placate the cosmic source of their anxiety, now we strive to seize and break it. But there must lie a path between superstition and arrogance, a path open to the reception of Being through beings. One cannot steal a gift since theft essentially distorts the phenomenon of the gift into the phenomenon of possession. An analogous distortion takes place with Being when conceptually seized upon by a mind ill at ease with its needy mortality. The act of seizure crushes the appropriate human response to the gift of Being—our grateful wonder. Without this perceptive response, the original gift of Being recedes from presence and languishes unseen and forgotten. Something indeed takes its place, but this something, like the newly won possession, does not correspond with the original intention.

The primary gift of Being, food, must be mastered and objectified in a paradigmatic fashion. The metaphysical will for corporeal transcendence must first of all dispense with the physical beings that sustains human mortality. Traditional asceticism advocated denial and sometimes starvation to this end. Technology offers the consumer cake to eat and also to have. Through the process of commodification, food—the perishable and ever-changing—becomes hypostasized, or, more aptly, frozen. Branded foods, together with the doctored flavors that create them, rationalize the sensual experience of eating. Tastes become conceptual, their static, unvarying Forms appealing to the insensitive appetite of reason rather than to the living flesh. Rationalized, or call it, à la Ritzer, McDonaldized foods desensitize the consumer from tasting and thus discovering in any meaningful sense the essential impermanence of the truth of Being.

Both materially and ontologically, trash surrounds food. The metaphysical urgency to rationally reify food expresses itself in the sundry forms of packaging that commodify it. Plastics and foils may help to keep food "fresh," for the duration of its shelf life but, more important, they render it metaphysically innocuous. Along with its flavor and nutritional quality, food loses its essential nature when secured through commodification. As the processing of commodification proceeds with greater complexity and range, less is left to distinguish food from its packaging. Equal amounts of energy go to package the food as to grow it. Of even greater absurdity is the fact that most items of packaging contain much more energy spent in their production than the consumption of their contents can supply to the consumer. The one hundred and fifty or so calories available to the thirsty consumer in a can of Coke do not even begin to offset the thousands of kilojoules of energy wasted in the production of its aluminium container.

The coalescence of food and packaging into a single, uniform commodity ensures that food shares the fate of its encasing; it also gets trashed. In a commodified world a consumer throws away from 10 to 15 percent of all the food she buys. Because the estimated 1.2 billion chronically undernourished people barely surviving on this planet do not figure in this same world, their pitiable presence cannot repudiate this behavior. Trashing food is metaphysically defensible because it is, more important, metaphysically expedient.

If, as I have argued, food is the paradigm device, and consequently the model instantiation of trash, then, by investigating the process of its commodification, one may expect to reveal essential aspects of trash. In this chapter I have dealt with food primarily as an already commodified phenomenon ubiquitous in the world of consumption. To understand this present phenomenon and its trashy nature, we must now turn to its history in the world of production. My intention of keeping these two worlds methodically segregated takes its cue from "the things themselves." One of the key purposes and effects of the device is to distance and disengage consumption from production. This distance makes room for convenience, ease, carelessness (or, carefree-ness, as advertisers prefer) and, not incidentally, trash. The native soil of commodities is, of course, the city, that fascinating, unearthly region where trash flourishes and thrives.

CHAPTER FOUR

The City

First, refuse is primarily an urban blight. Agrarian societies throughout history have successfully avoided solid-waste pollution; cities and towns have faced the gravest dangers.

—Melosi, *Garbage in the Cities*

Garbage has befouled settlements since their inception. The price of stability and security in the form of permanent dwellings and fortifications was the relinquishment of the highly efficacious nomadic technique of waste management. When stifled by his waste, the nomad simply picks up and shifts on. Settlement implies accumulation, in numbers of people, their possessions, and also their waste. Accumulation, in turn, implies a concentration of matter, which beyond a certain point becomes problematic. The problems arise due to the exclusive nature of all excessive phenomena that tends to suppress the conditions of possibility of other phenomena. Historical records testify to the all-pervasive presence of refuse in premodern cities, the sight and stench of which could not be ignored. The same circumstances hold today for the reckoned one billion people worldwide who inhabit urban slums lacking sewer systems and organized waste collection. In terms of sheer quantity, more human beings now endure the allegedly inhuman conditions of cities prior to the twentieth century than at any other given time in history.

There can be no doubt that garbage posed a host of problems and even dangers to the premodern city. Householders of Rome and Troy, for instance, periodically had to raise their roofs to reclaim the headroom of their homes stolen by the steady accretion of refuse strewn underfoot. Although a problem for all cities, garbage did not become a crisis until it met the modern, industrial megalopolis. The Greek word *krisis* means decision, and its English equivalent connotes a moment of decisive import, a turning point of some sort or other. A revolution in garbage occurred with the scientific discovery of germs. Previous to the acceptance of the

89

germ theory, garbage was considered a nuisance, perhaps an offense, but it subsequently became a menace. The seeds of this revolution were already planted in the forerunner of germs: the miasmic theory of disease. This hypothesis linked human disease and, by extension, mortality to fetid collections of filth. If wastes were allowed to collect and fester, they would sooner or later begin to exhale gases noxious to human health. Waste per se was not yet held responsible for spreading disease, but rather its neglected decomposition. Sanitation—a word rooted in the Latin *sanus*, meaning health—still had fundamentally to do with apparent cleanliness and order. It still possessed an aesthetic element. Sanitation did not yet mean sterilization.

A healthy denizen of industrialized culture, I do not for a moment wish to dismiss the verifiable gains that modern scientific sanitation has won for human longevity, survival past infancy, and general well-being. Yet one can be both grateful for the gains and at the same time wary of the manner of their attainment, so long as this wariness aims at the amelioration, not the condemnation, of the situation. Science itself has begun to suspect that its obsession with sterilization, vaccination, and the constant manipulation of the biosphere may produce less than salubrious results. So-called super germs, super weeds, and super bacteria have burst onto the medical and agriculture scenes. These new strains have, thanks to our predilection for excess, developed resistance to the very chemicals originally created to combat their predecessors. Besides, it turns out that a certain level of exposure to dirt and germs keeps the human immune system strong. The critique here applies not per se to the modern attempt to improve our lot. It confines itself to the unthinking dogmatism, extremism, and even arrogance so often attached to it.

With the popular acceptance of the germ theory toward the end of the nineteenth century, waste itself, and not just its neglect, was implicated in crimes against humanity. The postulation of invisible germs transformed the perception of rejected articles. Now no matter what its size and apparent condition, waste was considered a hothouse teeming with potential diseases. As remarked with respect to food in the previous chapter, from our perspective of modern science, germs represent nature's last stand. They menace human health because they elude human control, and the metaphysical will to power dictates that whatsoever cannot be tamed must be destroyed. This dictate forced sterilization on sanitation; mere cleanliness and order fell short of the metaphysical aspiration for supernatural existence. Since waste harbored nature in the invisible form of germs, waste had to be effaced.

The technological solution to the metaphysical menace of waste was the "garbage destructor," later known as the incinerator. Its invention dates back to the 1870s, making it contemporaneous with the first widespread disposable paper products. Incineration, however, did not become common procedure until the early twentieth century, the decade of Gatling guns and germs. Of course, incinerators always addressed the material problem of waste, reducing its constantly expanding volume to a fraction of its original bulk. Yet the primary appeal of incinerators to the incipient science of sanitary engineering lay in their power to exterminate the nature of waste. No germ could survive the inferno of incineration, and continuous development of the procedure and its mechanism aimed at minimizing all residual physical substance that survived in the form of inert ash. This will to total mastery through wholesale destruction of matter suggests an underlying violence at work in the technological solution. It marks a crisis in humanity's relation to its waste. The novelty of this emerging technological stance is witnessed by the initial opposition and distrust it encountered. Strasser comments: "to those who held on to the traditional view that organic garbage and other refuse had value, burning it was profligate. One American discussion noted that a proposed incinerator in London had been opposed as a 'sinful extravagance' by neighborhood residents."[1] Such sinful extravagance was the price of sterility, which had become a synonym for security.

Since we value security for its promotion of ordered and peaceable life, some strange transmutation must have occurred to permit an alliance between it and sterility. The germ theory occasioned a new interpretation of waste. Formerly merely emblematic of human failure and mortality, germ-ridden waste becomes identified as the primary and efficient cause of death. The superlative metaphysical achievement of this change resides in the successful projection of the mortal essence of human being onto an objectified physical nature. Human being is needy and vulnerable only in its connection with foreign matter, that is, with nature. Whereas the humor theory of disease locates the source of illness, hence mortality, within the constitution of the body, first the miasmic, then, even more thoroughly, the germ theory externalized and disowned this inherence, and our inheritance of nature. Having laden waste with all the perceived chains of human bondage, the scientific (i.e., metaphysical) mind discovered liberation in the annihilation of all phenomena fraught with physicality. Sanitation, which sought to create the conditions for truly human, rational flourishing, now meant the controlled absence of nature.

This revolution in waste gave birth to trash. Trash signifies a being wholly denuded of nature. As such, it opposes waste, which implicates our imperfection and finiteness. Much of the initial resistance to disposable objects among the practical skeptics of the day was overcome by conclusive claims about the sanitary benefits of throwaways. This highlights once again the paradox of disposables; they are a priori waste, yet essentially unnatural. They emerge as phenomena only to disappear. Their substance has no physical presence in the manifest emergence of nature. Trash is, like the ash of the incinerator, sterilized waste, mere substance metaphysically overcome. While waste implies human neglect and failure, trash signifies reason's triumph over nature. From the elevated viewpoint of metaphysics, trash destroys waste.

This historical gloss begs further interpretation. The basic hypothesis to be tested in this chapter is this: if waste is an urban blight, then trash is a special invention of the modern megapolis. The phenomenon of trash first appears in a thoroughly urbanized world, where cities geographically contain the majority of the population and greatly influence the minority still residing outside their precincts. Although England's rural–urban population ratio tipped in favor of cities in the mid-nineteenth century, the rest of the world remained predominantly rurally based for another hundred or so years. As for historical significance, it is no exaggeration to say that the shift from country to town is earth-shattering. It marks the collapse of an ancient way of dwelling on the earth, a revolution in being-in-the-world whereby an important manner of interpreting, under-standing, and thus disclosing innerworldly beings gets overturned and buried. So momentous an overturning will of necessity have upsetting ontological ramifications. The indivisible unity of being-in-the-world means that man neither moves nor is moved independently of his world. Unprecedented phenomena will accompany each new disclosive mode of being-in-the-world. Trash is the unique associate, the metaphysical side-kick, as it were, of the urbanized humanity of late modernity.

In keeping with the first principle of this study, which affirms the deep ontological nature of the human body, the test for this hypothesis will be speculatively physical. This means that the changes in the manner in which humans physically take up residence in the urbanized world will provide the contextual basis on which an interpretation of trash will rest. Given the hypothesis in question, it will prove to be acceptable if the interpretation succeeds in making trash stand out in clear distinction from premodern waste.

Alienation

Much can be read into the English term that translates what Marx saw as a key consequence of capitalist production. No longer connected person-ally either to the means of production or its products, the alienated worker grows strange to them both. "The product of labor is labor which has been embodied in an object and turned into a physical thing; this product is an objectification of labor. The performance of work appears in the sphere of political economy as a *vitiation* of the worker, objectification as a *loss* and as *servitude* to the object, and appropriation as alienation."[2] The ambiguity here is fruitful. Because the product does not reflect the worker's personal skill, control, and ingenuity, it confronts her as a more or less inscrutable object. It is thus encountered as strange, remote, alien. Equally, having lost control and comprehension of the product of her labor, the worker herself feels strange and helpless in its presence. The more extensive her daily commerce with these strange, opaque objects, the more the worker feels herself alienated, not only in her workplace but everywhere in her world. This experience deflates the sense of belonging to a world that responds to skillful human attention and care.[3]

The English noun "alien" has also acquired the meaning of an otherworldly creature. Popular imagination, educated on science fiction, typically pictures extraterrestrials with corporeal proportions, features, organs, and capacities differing from our own. Frequently they are attributed with the possession of additional and marvelous sense organs. Due to this, the alien arrives out of place into a world attuned to the human body and its senses. The alienated worker experiences a similar dislocation. Because the surrounding objects that occupy her world do not engage or respond to her physical presence, needs, and capacities in a full and meaningful way, the worker can feel otherworldly while here on earth. Her alienation takes the shape, at the most basic level, of the rift between her bodily being and the technological world that houses it.

Capitalism, with its drive for optimal efficiency and productivity, set industrialization in motion, which has kept its momentum up thanks to the grease of surplus labor. Industrialism ultimately creates the conditions for its own flourishing. Its surplus labor must always be ready at hand in a concentrated form, able to fill cheaply and immediately any gap that might appear in the system of production. Providing this necessary concentration, the city gives birth to industrialism and is then bred by it. Subsistence farming and its ancillary cottage industries are the first victims of industrialization, whose mechanical innovations brand such traditional modes of production as unpardonably inefficient. Those pushed out of rural livelihoods trickle inevitably into the city, seeking work in some industry or other. In short, the process, though circular, has three distinguishable moments: mechanization creates unemployment; unemployment fattens the city; and the city prepares the field for increased mechanization.

At the heart of industry, there beats the city. Its pulse also quickens the life of culture, arts, and learning, which Descartes rightly treasured as the fruits of scientific industry. These fruits feed the cosmopolitan spirit alive in urban centers, where many of the parochial prejudices that can overrun the outlying country are challenged and corrected. But while the city offers its refined attractions to those in the fortunate position to enjoy them, here also the dispossessed and uprooted come in search of prosperity and often find themselves aliens in a world strangely at odds with their mortal needs. Although they gradually accept the techno-logical reduction of their person to mere worker, their productive labor fails to satisfy their existential concerns, their anxiety for their own passing being. Literally and at the most basic level, industrial labor fails to nourish the worker, who cannot eat her paycheck. In fact, industrial manufacture heightens the worker's natural hunger by bodily subordin-ating her to the tempo and idiosyncrasies of the machine. Through an appropriation parallel to industrialization's repossession of the subsist-ence farmer's land, the machine annexes the worker's body, setting it into motion at its own tireless speed. The experience of industrial labor is less of producing than of being forced to keep pace. The induced worker feels unable to attain any purchase of autonomy or responsibility in the incessant process of production. Consequently, the products of her labor confront her as not her own, as alien. This disturbs the traditional Lockean understanding of property, which bases ownership on the addition of personal effort and use into a portion of the natural common wealth.[4] No longer belonging to the worker by right of her role in its production, the industrial product must be purchased monetarily. Susie Orbach nicely sums up the entire dynamic:

> Westerners are experiencing an increasingly less physical relation to the wealth of the society in which they live. This alienation increases a general mystification as to how the available goods are produced. Quixotically, the avenue offered out of this particular alienation is the involvement of more intense consumption. A cycle of alienated buying is thus energized.[5]

Since the advent of globalized corporate economy this cycle of alienation has accelerated and diversified. Those Westerners still directly involved in factory labor, a dwindling population, assuage their sense of helplessness and disjuncture in a world of alien products by mastering them in the segregated realm of consumption. My own short stints in manufacturing plants have taught me the otherwise inexplicable mass appeal of beer, television, and potato chips. The exhaustion and physical inertness reached at the end of a day "on the line" leaves one with such feelings of hollowness that all one cares to do is to cram the cavity full with whatever readily presents itself. What is always available, of course, are commodities.

In the so-called post-industrialized sectors of the Western world, the alienation has an added dynamic. Sitting confined to a computer for a day of data-entry can severely exhaust and tax the body such that it numbly craves commodities. The high-tech proletariat, which now includes most of the middle class, has lost even the remotest physical connection to the production of the commodities they consume. The mystification surrounding commodities deepens as more productive work is exported overseas to countries still caught in the growing pains of rapid industrialization. Now most Westerners do not share even a ten-uous physical proximity, let alone any kind of ownership, with the means of production. The body cannot even begin to comprehend what does not physically present itself to its grasp. Thus, the alienation leading to commodity consumption described by Marx is only exacerbated as production literally grows more foreign, geographically and epistemo-logically, to the final consumer.

Although Marx does pay heed to the importance of transformations in human physicality, more basic than historical materialism is, so to speak, historical corporealism—the ontological interpretation of history as the changing relations of embodied being-in-the-world. According to this interpretation, the phenomenon of trash is the excretion of the technologically alienated body.

Bodily Capital

Relative to England and the United States, industrialism came late to Germany. Since it arrived already fairly mature (one might say "pre-fab"), the industrialization and simultaneous urbanization of the German population occurred more abruptly than elsewhere. Perhaps the violence of this transition from rural to urban made the German mind peculiarly susceptible to and aware of its import and influence. The pioneering German sociologists such as Max Weber, Georg Simmel, and later the Frankfurt School all have plumbed the soul of the city to uncover its social and philosophical meaning.

According to Weber, capitalism represents a historical rationalization of economic relations that permeates all aspects of life. It owes its pervasiveness to its insoluble ties to industry and the city, which bind to it the primary human occupations of work and dwelling. The fast food restaurant, as Ritzer has clearly shown,[6] epitomizes the chief characteristic of historical rationalization. The fast-food industry serves and is serviced by the alienated city populace. Its monolithic and expansive structure, made possible by huge capital investments in technology and advertising, concentrates profit at the highest levels. The industry is a kind of urban agriculture, whose workers are also its harvest. Fast food sells best among the less affluent and less educated segments of society, the very population that supplies the McDonaldized workforce, but rarely reaps the higher cultural fruits of its urban milieu. Analogous to the metaphysical body in its absence and suppression, the urban underclass suffers the most acutely from capitalism's process of rationalization.

The conditions of the possibility of the fast-food industry must be sought not merely in economic spheres but first of all in physiological ones. Here Simmel offers, in my opinion, his greatest contribution. Noting that the city is the "seat of the money economy," he writes that the "money economy and dominance of the intellect are intrinsically connected."[7] Monetary value, of course, is purely a rational abstraction, whose superimposition on objects requires a certain degree of distance and disassociation from them. To things personal and dear to us, we refuse to fix a price. Distance intervenes between ourselves and our goods when our bodies lose the sense of a physical partnership with them. Monetary value takes its seat in the city as a result of the unique physiological effects caused there.

> The psychological basis of the metropolitan type of individuality consists in the *intensification of nervous stimulation* which results from the swift and uninterrupted stream of outer and inner stimuli. . . . With each crossing of the street, with the tempo and multiplicity of economic, occupational and social life, the city sets up a deep contrast with small town and rural life with reference to the sensory foundation of psychic life. The metropolis exacts from man as a discriminating creature a different amount of consciousness than does rural life. Here the rhythm of life and sensory mental imagery flows more slowly, more habitually, more evenly. Precisely in this connection the sophisticated character of metropolitan psychic life becomes understandable—as over against small town life which rests more upon deeply felt and emotional relationships. . . . Metropolitan life, thus, underlies a heightened awareness and a predominance of intelligence in metropolitan man.[8]

Simmel's description depicts a vulnerable and sensuous body so besieged by stimuli that it abandons its more balanced native sensorial awareness, which enmeshes it with the world, and retreats to the insensate citadel of reason. The "heightened awareness" mentioned by Simmel is more intellectual than sensual, for it deals in quantity over quality. In the bustle of the city, the body must contend with an amount of stimuli too great for it to integrate. Its capacity of discriminating subtler sensorial differences decreases. This at once explains the uniformity and ambiguity of chemically enhanced seasoning in fast food. Uniformity appeals to the intellectual appetite for the immutable and eternal ideal. Excessive artificial flavors appeal to a sensual, somatic appetite battered to a state of indiscriminative dullness.

The urban scape, across which roams what Oswald Spengler colorfully calls the intellectual nomad, is, however, not completely assualtive; the other part of it is deprivational. Even as the city attacks the nervous system, it also neglects it. In its innate tendency to control and homogenize all environmental conditions, the city in effect establishes chronic sensory deprivation. Central heating and cooling systems—Borgmann's favorite example of the technological device—maintain unfluctuating temperatures regardless of climate and season. Electric light blots out the temporal cycle of night and day, thus depriving the musculature of the eye its natural exercise in accommodating to darkness and shades of luminosity. Concrete levels out geographic variation and contour. Urban smells are typically either offensive or unnoticed. Besides that of automobiles and crowds, there is little real movement to attract visual perception. Most of the city's motion is neither real nor relative, but virtual, occurring within the artificial domains of computer, television, and movie screens. This produces great tension in an essentially mobile being, for virtual motion is watched mostly from a sedentary position that puts the body out of action. In the words of Gerry Mander, "When we reduce an aspect of environment from varied and multidimensional to fixed, we also change the human being who lives within it. Humans give up the capacity to adjust, just as the person who only walks cannot so easily handle the experience of exercise."[9] In short, the same sensorial body that is assaulted by the city is at the same time neglected by it. Already injured, this body succumbs to further insult to its native capacities. Mander puts it squarely: "If people's senses were stimulated to experience anything approaching their potential range, it would be unlikely that people would sit for eight hours at a desk reading memoranda, typing documents, studying columns of figures or pondering sales strategies."[10] Notwithstanding the wry cynicism of Mander's tone, his comment does point to the incontrovertible fact that, in economic lingo, an urban accumulation of industrial and monetary capital comes at the direct expense of lived bodily capital.

While some of this cost is inevitable, it need not be great or terribly debilitating. When built with attention to the surrounding landscape and to the social, physical, and psychological needs of its citizens, a city can in many ways enliven rather than mortify the sensitive openness of the human body. One thinks immediately of old Vienna and other pedestrian hearts of ancient cities. Here, as opposed to the exaggeration of skyscrapers, the grandeur of the edifices seems more to elevate than to dwarf the bodies moving through and around them. A recollection of the human scale and speed has led some modern architects and urban planners to embrace construction that responds hospitably to the body rather than frustrating it. The critique does not extend to them, nor to those genuinely interested in creating "greener" urban neighborhoods. Unfortunately, however, most urban development continues to pander to the automobile, a device that seems bent on grinding the last remnants of the city's habitability into dust beneath its wheels. So long as the physical requirements of automobiles take precedence over the needs of people, our cities will continue to dehumanize us.

Nor, most regrettably, is our countryside exempt from these detrimental driving forces. In a kind of queer reversal of fate, it turns out that rural populations generally now exhibit higher rates of obesity and inactivity than bona-fide city slickers, who, faced with the implacable fiend called parking, tend more often to flee on foot or bicycle to their daily destinations. In the suburbs and beyond, on the contrary, where wide lawns and fields spread out, cars are given free rein, without any compensatory offering of activity made to the riders they carry. Suburban and rural folk rightfully appreciate the powers of the private automobile, which enables them to escape the sometimes baneful isolation of their locales, but for this they do pay a price in taxes on their bodies.

Although rooted in physical skill, sensorial acuteness, and motile capacities, the true wealth of bodily capital lies in its epistemological and ontological functions. A body is simply more physically present and capable of more diverse activities in a world that continually exercises its natural capacities. In *Being and Time*, Heidegger convincingly demonstrates that most beings are first disclosed as equipment ready to hand to an embodied agent. Only by subsequent abstraction does the essentially useful thing become disclosed in a mode of scientifically disinterested objective presence. The rational pursuit of science—recall Descartes' famous meditation on the piece of wax—tends to dematerialize beings by discounting the physical relation they have with the human body, the physical needs of which constitute its own essence. A general tendency results: the more deeply science penetrates the being of an object, the less amenable the latter becomes to bodily comprehension and handling. The reason is dialectical; as the body grows less able to grasp things, it experiences them in an increasingly abstract and distant fashion. When beyond the reach of the needy body, objects appear to possess an essential immateriality.

Bodily capital can be understood as the initial investment of Being into a world of beings. It ensures, to mix in one of Abram's metaphors, "that my body is a sort of open circuit that completes itself only in things, in others, in the encompassing earth."[11] This initial sensual investment guarantees the primordial disclosure of beings, or, alternatively, makes the world as such viable. All other possible modes of disclosure depend on it. Loss of bodily capital endangers the world because, by damaging the circuit, it prohibits the body's completion in worldly things. Modern science, a human pursuit indigenous to the intellectual tropics of the city, assumes as its ideal comportment vis-à-vis objects the same disinterest and disengagement that, according to Simmel, characterizes the "blasé attitude."

> There is perhaps no psychic phenomenon which has been so unconditionally reserved to the metropolis as the blasé attitude. The blasé attitude results from the rapidly changing and closely compressed contrasting stimulation of the nerves. . . . A life in boundless pursuit of pleasure makes one blasé because it agitates the nerves to their strongest reactivity for such a long time that they finally cease to react at all. . . . An incapacity thus emerges to react to new sensations with the appropriate energy.[12]

Such an incapacity signals a drastic loss of bodily capital, and at the same time aligns it with the scientific attitude, forever driving at the absolute reduction of all physical being: "The essence of the blasé attitude consists in the blunting of discrimination . . . the meaning and differing values of things, and thereby the things themselves are experienced as insubstantial."[13] The indiscriminate and insubstantial strike the blasé consumer only as readily disposable.

Bodily Losses, Wasteful Gains

Things experienced as mere empty substance, things of indistinguishable value, are typically known as waste. Nature, itself valueless and holistic, does not know waste, for nothing falls outside its material compass that could count as insubstantial. From one point of view, the urban blight of waste may serve those contending with it as another visible proof of their contradistinction from and supremacy over Nature. That waste could provide this affirmation of the human might explain the historical forbearance of city-dwellers to what seem like appallingly filthy conditions. In this case, waste would express what Spengler saw as the main intention of the city:

> The country town *confirms* the country, is an intensification of the picture of the country. It is the late city that first defies the land, contradicts Nature in the lines of its silhouette, denies all Nature. It wants to be something different from and higher than Nature. . . . And then begins the megatropolis, *the city-as-world*, which suffers nothing beside itself and sets about *annihilating* the country picture.[14]

The annihilation begins when the indifferent values of blasé consumerism overtake the creative and inclusive values of healthy cosmopolitanism. Through a process of absorbtion, consumerism and its accompanying refuse draw the countryside into its exclusively anthropocentric urban vortex.

Until the rise of capitalism and industrialism, the city remained, as it were, relatively provincial. Only the unprecedented global urbanization sparked by capital and industry could confer on the city the status of world. The problem with this status, however, is its successful comprehensiveness. As the possible expression of defiance, waste could make sense to a city that still had some surrounding nature to defy. Any such meaning vanishes into the acidic fumes of a totally urban world. But waste does not thereby go away, and not simply because it has no place left to go. As seen already, waste follows causally on the loss of bodily capital that inevitably follows urban industrialization. What the body loses in terms of physical presence transfers to the metaphysical concept of waste. In economics, for example, the transferences occur like this:

> Since World War II there has developed a more or less coherent, self-conscious, and until recently, effective solution to the problem of great and growing productive capacity in the capitalist [i.e., urbanized] world economy. The solution is *waste*. The waste is systematic and institutionalized, as measured by what is produced and how, and by what is withheld from use and/or is destroyed. . . . The waste of productive capacity, of human energy and skills, and of almost all natural resources

must be seen as systemic, as a principal way in which the system survives, in both war and peace.[15]

If the industrialized city-as-world were to survive on waste, the latter would have to be reinvested with some new kind of meaning. On a denatured urbanized globe, waste no longer expresses defiance toward Nature as it did in the provincial city. It now has to express the total domination of Nature explicit in the city-as-world. This reinvestment of meaning was afoot long before World War II. The germ theory, it will be recalled, transmuted waste, which went from being an offensive (to nature and to sensible bodies) by-product of civilization, to being a mortal hazard. The mutation called for the complete destruction, the total dematerialization, of waste. Long the co-occupant of the city street, waste was enjoined to disappear forever. In large metropolitan centers at the time, particularly New York City, armies of streetcleaners were rallied together to sweep clean the city. Incinerators (also called crematoriums) did their best to negate all vestiges of nature. Finally, the advent of the sanitary landfill in the 1930s made the ordinance for the disappearance of waste realizable.[16] The landfill differs from the old-style dumps in one key regard: it hides its contents. Whereas dumps allow their waste to reek and fume up to heaven, landfills conceal their contents daily beneath a layer of dirt.

Before its industrial transformation, waste was not absolute. Ever since cities began, a healthy economy of scavenging has built itself on refuse. What the scavenger passed over went on to fatten the local herd of swine that eventually turned up on citizens' plates. Much of what the swine would not stomach went to fertilize neighboring fields or urban gardens. Part of the history of cities is their constant negotiation with their waste, a negotiation that tried to reconcile the physical and symbolic aspects of waste that associate it with nature, together with the implications of human distinction from valueless nature that waste expresses.

The industrialized capitalist city-as-world cuts short this historical negotiation. Herein lies its mistake, for the suppression of dialogue usually ends in causalties of some sort. No less grateful for clean streets and good sanitation, we modern metropolitans must begin to question the sanity of design of our globalized city-as-world. The design insists on encountering waste in an unprecedented and unnegotiable manner, neither physically nor symbolically, but now metaphysically. The rationalization of the physical and the symbolic, which metaphysics brings quite literally to a head through the extreme loss of bodily capital sustained by modern humanity, has had the effect that we now actually experience nature in the abstract. Ultimately, the mortal threat of waste is that it embodies nature's vicissitudinous essence. At least since Descartes, metaphysics has understood nature abstractly as mere extended substance perceptible to reason alone. Embodying nature, even as it defies it, waste abstractly conceived must also disclose itself essentially as substance. Again, Cartesian metaphysics teaches that this bare substratum has no sensible qualities, and a fortiori, no value. But by withholding the essence of physical things from intercourse with the body, metaphysics effectively removes physicality from nature. Insensitive to the constitutive and primordial truth of physicality, reason produces out of itself the pure idea of extended substance, a being without description, much less utility. Waste as substance, therefore, is absolute waste. It is, in our technical sense, trash.

The historical mutation of waste from being a means of human defiance (which implies a position subordinate to nature) to one of domination (which signifies mastery) stems from its novel metaphysical disclosure. Metaphysical domination over nature means mastery over substance. From the point of view of reason, this equals the power to determine what does and does not exist, because, by metaphysical definition, whatever exists must either itself be a substance or else a property belonging to a substance. When waste becomes absolute and substantial, that is, trash, a momentous ontological transformation occurs. What formerly could be understood as the result of subjective valuation (one person's trash is another's treasure) suddenly appears essentially wasted. No longer do values merely supervene on an ontologically independent and neutral nature; they now inhere in and even constitute its essence and existence. The phenomenon of trash testifies to the fact that the evaluative subjectivity, that is, modern scientific humanity, has attained authority over the being of innerworldly objects. In essence, every disposable item is a priori wasted from the metaphysical point of view. From the ontological perspective, however, this absolutization of waste, which contradicts the conditioned and imperfect nature of human being exhibited by bodily waste, denies the phenomenal existence and implications of waste, all of which indicate human finitude. To avoid confusion, we must take care to keep these countervailing perspectives distinct.

Trash appears to confirm subjective authority by virtue, paradoxically, of its own disappearance. In contrast to the odiferous conspicuousness of premodern garbage, a chief characteristic of trash is its inherent bias toward concealment. Insofar as Being takes place through the disclosure of beings, any phenomenon that only appears as concealed is somehow deficient in Being. In creating trash, metaphysical humanity diminishes, in a way, Being by failing to practice, as will be seen, its own carefulness. As the phenomenon of trash engulfs more facets of the world, its ontological defacement grows more complete. To understand this adequately, our thought must return to the needy, that is, ontological body.

Leaving the Field

In a passage quoted earlier, Orbach draws a connection between physical alienation from the goods of industrial capitalism and increased consumption of commodities. She regards the connection as basically palliative. An urbanized body, already alienated from its own senses, is further mystified by the existence of products that do not respond helpfully to its needs, skills, scale, and care. Quixotically, says Orbach, greater consumption of these same alienating and somatically frustrating commodities, whose production remains incomprehensible, promises to alleviate the mystification. "A cycle of alienated buying is thus energized"[17] because the cure in fact exacerbates the complaint.

Within many cycles, the lines delineating cause and effect begin to blur. It would seem that alienated production would have to precede alienated consumption, insofar as consumption requires some product available to be consumed. Yet possibly a taste of alienated consumption first makes alienated production palatable and acceptable. Still a third possibility suggests itself: the hard-and-fast distinction between production and consumption, which translates into the incommensurable urban duality of work and leisure, may itself be indigenous to industrial capitalism. In that case, not only the alienation itself, but also the terminology of "alienation" arise from the very cycle they create. Here the most interesting question does not ask whether the chicken came before the egg or vice versa. Rather it inquires into the conditions that made possible such a knotted and self-reflexive problem.

The cycle of alienated production and consumption, with its coextensive trash, is more precisely a tight spiral that has spun out of the primeval cycle of nature. In the end, the spiral straightens out and destroys its cyclicity. Wendell Berry, who as a farmer has a practical inclination toward philosophy, makes the initial argument when he contrasts biological energy with the mechanical energy that propels industrialism:

> The moral order appropriate to the use of biological energy . . .
> requires the addition of a third term: production, consumption
> and return. It is this principle of return that complicates matters,
> for it requires responsibility, care, of a different and higher order
> than that required by production and consumption alone. . . . In

> an energy economy appropriate to the use of biological energy,
> all bodies, plant and animal and human, are joined in a kind of
> energy community. . . . They are indissolubly linked in complex
> patterns of energy exchange. They die into each other's life, live
> into each other's death. They do not consume in the sense of
> using up. They do not produce waste. What they take in they
> change.[18]

This principle of return in a sense implants production into consumption. Within the natural cycle, their distinction is arbitrary and artificial and can only apply to a narrow segment of its entirety.

Berry is not so naive to espouse a strict dualism between biological and mechanical energies, between natural law and human endeavor. The principle of return also functions within the human realms of practice and work. In the previous chapter it was shown how the technological device fulfills the promise of emancipation from practical, physical involvement with the world by means of the device's unique ability to segregate consumption from production. The device delivers commodities that eclipse their productive machinery behind consumption. When Borgmann writes about nontechnological things, such as the hearth, and the physically engaging practices that these require, he furnishes examples of human participation in the economy of biological energy. According to old rural economics, splitting firewood doubles one's investment of labor: first the physical work itself warms up the body, then later its fruits— burning dry logs—do, too. In this way, the presumed commodity— warmth—cannot be consumed independently from its production. Consumption and production happen both at the same time and at the same place; their relation is dialectical rather than dualistic.

The fusion of the production and consumption of human biological energy in this case occurs through skill. Skill answers to the natural imperative of return. Traditionally, to consume the heat of the hearth entailed a variety of practices of production: not only wood-splitting, but also starting and nursing the fire, maintaining the necessary tools involved, keeping aware of the changing meteorological conditions, and so on. In performing these tasks, one simultaneously secured the product of one's labors and, equally as important, grew more practiced in their efficient execution. Thus, every act of consumption necessarily involving productive work returns an increased capacity to activate the dialectic again. Skill, like the biological soil, builds up from the repetition of the production-consumption cycle, with its fertility increasing in proportion to its accumulating depth.

The cyclical workings of biological energy found in nontechnological practices are, as should be expected, most apparent in the practice of agriculture. Here the primary return is health, a much broader natural synthesis than skill and in fact inclusive of it. In nonindustrialized settings, the practice of agriculture returns in addition to skill, also exercise, appetite, and a vital understanding of the being of food through direct participation in its emergence into *physis*. Health makes production and consumption mutually enhancing. Berry, by grace of his practical vocation, states it more convincingly:

> Our system of agriculture, by modelling itself on economics rather than biology, thus removes food from the cycle of its production and puts it into a finite, linear process that in effect destroys it by transforming it into waste. That is, it transforms food into fuel, a form of energy that is usable only once, and in doing so it transforms the body into a consumptive machine. It is strange, but only apparently so, that this system of agriculture is institutionalized, not in any form of rural life or culture, but in what we call our "urban civilization." The cities subsist in competition with the country; they live upon a one-way move-ment of energies out of the countryside—food and fuel, manu-facturing materials, human labor, intelligence and talent. Very little of this energy is ever returned. Instead of gathering these energies up into coherence, a cultural consummation that would not only return to the countryside what belongs to it, but also give back generosities of learning and art, conviviality and order, the modern city dissipates and wastes them. Along with its glittering "consumer goods," the modern city produces an equally characteristic outpouring of garbage and pollution—just as it produces and/or collects unemployed, unemployable, and otherwise wasted people.[19]

In this passage, the major themes of the previous two chapters—the objectification of the body and the commodification of food—converge on the city. Berry lists a host of discontents afflicting "urban civilization," all of which ultimately terminate in waste. This waste is what I have specified as absolute, because the linear process by which it becomes waste is first of all ontological.

The roots of our current ecological and economic crises, Berry argues, reach down into a deeper crisis, which has resulted from our society's deracination from agriculture. The device paradigm, which ruptures the synthetic relation of production and consumption, putting all emphasis on the latter, now has nearly universal breadth, due to its successful commodification of food. If food literally embodies our mortal being, then any rupture in our ontological understanding of it will necessarily rock our existential foundations. Although human understanding, by its very structure, is essentially, and therefore always, disclosive, it can nevertheless be more or less truthful. The extent of a disclosure's truthfulness, we shall see, corresponds to its revelatory capacity, that is, its ability to reveal more than it conceals of a phenomenon's meaning. Truth speaks to our understanding, nourishing and satisfying it like a wholesome meal. We say that meaningful and truthfully exhibited phenomena make sense. A body in sensitive relation to the food that expresses its mortal being will make more sense of its food, will disclose it more truthfully, than a desensitized body bred on junk food.

Unfortunately, the sensitive body usually fares rather poorly in the city. On the double fronts of over and understimulation its senses are assailed and incapacitated. As Leder suggested, the disclosive power of the body itself recedes behind the clouding effects of sensorial duress and lassitude. Quite likely part of the eating disorders of the urbanized world stems from the sensorially beleaguered body's inability to feel too much or too little. Consequently, it either overeats or it starves. Of greater significance still, however, is the loss of sense and meaning that overtakes the innumerable acts of consumption in which the body does not play a productive, physical role. From this arises the mystification enshrouding most technological commodities, food included, of which both Orbach and Borgmann speak. The same process that makes industrialized food tasteless and unnatural also makes it nonsensical: namely, the ever-expanding attenuation of the physical relation that we humans have to the staff of our being. Only by a long, euphemistic stretch, for instance, do we call "fresh" the green groceries that appear in our supermarkets one, two, and sometimes three weeks after their harvest in another hemisphere.

The technological device separates production from consumption, machinery from commodity. The city instates this separation as a way of life, a determinate and rigid mode of being-in-the-world. Modern urban civilization orders the commodification of food and cannot survive without it. For these reasons, the city-as-world appears the paramount device, as it produces the most fundamental commodity. Repeating Berry's line, it is strange, but only apparently so, that the industrialized city, with next to no interest in or capacity for agriculture, could alone produce commodified food. But this technological productivity works on default. By drawing people off the land into an environment inhospitable to the twofold cultivation of food and bodily awareness, the metropolis at once creates the conditions and the hunger for commodified food. The mechanization of agriculture glutted the city with rural people dispossessed of their livelihood. Freed from their productive fields, the uprooted became subject to a new repossession of their bodily field, now the privatized terrain of commodified consumption. The twin fields of body and cultivated land could no longer rotate within the cycle of production, consumption, and return. Mass urbanization, isolating the first two moments of the cycle and eliminating the third, advances, so we read in the histories of many ancient cities, to its own final undoing.[20]

Somatic Truth

Historic urban civilizations have often fallen due to the linearity and momentum of their progress. This linearity is based on their unilinear structure: that one-way avenue of energies from the countryside without return lamented by Berry. After a critical point, a city's draw on the natural resources of its surrounding landscape becomes overly taxing. The momentum of the one-way movement will continue pulling in energies long after they have lost their regenerative capability. When it completely exhausts its landbase, the elaborate urban edifice collapses. City-dwellers have foreseen this danger from the dawn of urban settlement. Plato and Aristotle emphasized the political necessity for population control. Among the Greeks, infanticide was the less philosophical, expedient application of ancient political theory.

Of course, the technological city-as-world remains prey to these same environmental dangers. With respect to clean air, water, and soil, it draws on an increasingly alarming global deficit. These physical dangers, however, are of a piece with the less obvious, but for that reason potentially more disastrous, ontological perils. Put simply, the city-as-world occludes the earth, both literally, under concrete, and phenomenally. The phenomenal occlusion functions as a kind of optical illusion that makes the earth disappear from sense and significance. When a world onto itself, the city reflects man, once merely the *homo faber*, as the *prima causa*. The technological urbanite, confronted almost entirely by mass-manufactured objects, logically concludes that technological man is the determining measure of all things.[21] The city banishes from is vicinity anything that might contradict this conclusion. If perchance it does nominally recognize earth, it perceives the latter alternately as a handy font of natural resources, which includes "recreational wilderness," and a sink for its pollutants.

In his later works, particularly the essay "The Origin of a Work of Art," Heidegger uses "earth" as an ontological term to designate the essential counterpart of world.

> The world is the self-disclosing openness of the broad paths of the simple and essential decisions in the destiny of an historical people. The earth is the spontaneous forthcoming of that which is continually self-secluding and to that extent sheltering and concealing. . . . The world, in resting upon the earth, strives to surmount it. As self-opening it cannot endure anything closed. The earth, however, as sheltering and concealing, tends always to draw the world into itself and keep it there. The opposition of world and earth is a striving. . . . In the struggle each opponent carries the other beyond itself. (PLT 48–49)

Berry, as quoted earlier, complains that the city-as-world does not carry the earth beyond itself; it simply carries the earth away. To all appearances, the world, or human dimension, has indeed surmounted the earth and floats transcendent on its own powers. This Laputan adventure, however, is chimerical, no less for its physical than for its ontological groundlessness. Heidegger's rather vague and poetic ontological understanding of earth is well supplemented by Berry's profoundly physical understanding of it. In the earlier discussion on the body and food, I argued that the world of beings—that is, the world of meaning and significance—first arises from the primordial and ineluctable need of human being to eat. This need, at once the basis and the birthright of mortality, structures our ontological nature such that, so long as we exist, we must always remain open to the disclosure of beings without which we cannot live. Up to now in the study, our ontological nature has been formulated thus: food is need; need is the body; the body is mortality; mortality is essential openness to the meaningful world of beings. The formula must now be expanded to begin with the final element that bends this linear progression into its natural cycle: earth, or land as Berry favors, is food.

The expanded formula makes it clear that the world can never transcend the earth, for the very germination and growth of the world takes place in and out of the earth. A meaningful world is well rooted in the earth that physically and ontologically sustains it. The natural tendency for the earth to conceal itself has led to the crisis in agriculture warned of by Berry. It is at root the same ontological crisis that Heidegger called technological nihilism, the nearly absolute forgetfulness of Being. The crisis turns on the axis of distance. A physical separation of body from food-giving land creates a twofold absence, both of which threaten the meaning or sense of the world. Whether stuck in an office cubicle or the climate-controlled cab of a million-dollar grain-combine, the urbanized body, compelled to physical passivity and insensitivity, withdraws its world-defining somatic motility and senses. Itself severed from the onto-logically defining needs of the body, the world spins off into fantasy (the global entertainment industry) and abstraction (modern science and vir-tual reality).

As the body grows more alien to its world and to itself, the absence of the earth grows more decisive. Mystified by the immaterial and senseless objects that bombard it, the body loses its ability to respond sensuously and carefully to the earth, the physical source of all beings. A dulled, inert body can make sense only of a dead, inert earth, both of these troubled beings closing up within themselves their respective sensual and sense-nourishing upsurge that together give rise to beings. Both become, meta-physically conceived, mere substance, bereft of engaging properties, fit only to be trashed.

Divorce in the earth–body union destabilizes the world because the ontological roots that feed the world through sense (meaning and sensual-ity) fail to penetrate the opening of Being. Spengler puts it in these words:

> There, separated from the power of the land—cut off from it, even by the pavement underfoot—Being becomes more and more languid; sensation and reason more and more powerful. Man becomes intellect. . . . All art, all religion and science become slowly intellectualized, alien to the land, incomprehen-sible to the peasant of the soil. . . . The immemorially old roots of Being are dried up in the stone masses of the cities. And the free intellect—fateful word!—appears like a flame, mounts splendidly into the air, and pitiably dies.[22]

Spengler describes here the Icarus-like career of Western metaphysics from the earth–body union into the vertigous and empty heights of technological urbanization. Spengler's prophetic prose and pseudo-biological theories generally exclude him from the ranks of rigorous philosophers. Nonetheless, "despite disdaining Spengler's propositions and methods, early Heidegger began to conceive of his own work as an attempt to provide a philosophically sound account of the *symptoms* of decline popularized by Spengler."[23] And Spengler's account does have at least one major strength over Heidegger's in that it explicitly addresses the ontological significance of changes in our physical mode of being-in-the-world.

The ontological-agricultural crisis of modernity is one of absence where once was physical (*physis*) presence. As such, it hinges on distance and concealment. Heidegger and Berry both, while painfully aware of the mortal perils of the metaphysical condition, believe that it need not conclude pitiably. For Heidegger, thinking in a nonmetaphysical way, which eschews conceptual impositions on what is thought, might repair and finally replace the excesses of Western reason.[24] Such a willing, as opposed to a willful, way of thought would allow the history of Being to surface in its truth. Integral to nonmetaphysical thinking is mindful building and dwelling.[25] Although Heidegger unfortunately ignores the bodily implications of his triad, the latter clearly foreswears the possibility of disembodied intellection. No less than building and dwelling does thinking involve the cultivation and care of beings, through which the history of Being unfolds. In short, nonmetaphysical thinking becomes a practical affair, not in the sense of opposed to theory, but rather in the more basic sense of a practice, the careful and patient repetition that cultivates skill.

The Art of Farming

"If we are to challenge the rule of technology," Borgmann claims,"we can do so only through the practice of engagement."[26] Borgmann believes that the notion of a physically engaging practice supplies the missing ingredient to Heidegger's overly contemplative construal of nonmetaphysical thought. "The human ability to establish and commit oneself to a practice reflects our capacity to comprehend the world, to harbor it in its expanse as a context that is oriented by its focal points."[27] Borgmann offers a number of world-comprehending practices, most notably for us, the practice of preparing and celebrating a festive meal. Although his understanding of practices does "flesh out" Heidegger's to a good measure, the essential body of this thought remains even with Borgmann rather emaciated. Only with Berry does this body regain its native vigor. For him, the sole remedy for technological/metaphysical crisis is the age-old practice of agriculture.

Berry lays out the practical requirements for a truly ontological building-dwelling-thinking. They are, to the metaphysical mind, as reactionary and preposterous as they are elementary. The return of as many families as ecologically feasible to small agricultural landholdings will steer technological culture away from coming to grief on the shoal of absolute nihilism. Berry borrows his remedy from Thomas Jefferson's recipe for a democratic and independent state, constituted to cultivate equally the biological excellence of the land and the human excellence of those who live from it. This is not a question of reducing educated urban populations to nations of superstitious peasants. The vision, if marginally utopic, sees a resurrection of the dignity and worth of familial agricultural projects practiced in harmony with cultural pursuits. Berry's own person stands out as an exceptional model: his farm life animates his poetry, novels, lectures, and treatises. Although not equal to his genius, we can nonetheless recognize the sanity of his vision in light of "figures [which] describe a catastrophe that is now almost complete": "Between 1910 and 1920, [America] had 32 million farmers living on farms—about a third of our population. By 1991, the number was only 4.6 million, less than 2 percent of the national population. Also, by 1991, 32 percent of [American] farm managers and 86 percent of farmworkers did not live on the land they farmed."[28] Catastrophic is the nearly absolute disjuncture between the human body and its earth. Technological culture has taken this as a point of pride and progress because it fails to perceive the real ontological dangers deep within this chasm. Why does it amount to an ontological catastrophe?

If we look down from the peaks of civilization reached throughout history, we find that their base rests firmly in the earth. We still delight in the radiance of human achievement cast by ancient Greece. Yet Tierney reminds us how pastoral was the birthplace of philosophy, tragedy, democracy, epic poetry, and so on: "Despite the developments which were made in various trades and crafts, classical Greece was predominantly an agricultural civilization. It has been estimated that during the fifth century BC, nearly half of Athen's population lived in the countryside and worked the soil."[29]

The key point is that the culture wherein philosophy first bloomed was still fundamentally agricultural. We constantly hear snatches of the bucolic in the Socratic dialogues, where Socrates recruits time and again horses and craftsfolk in the defense of his arguments. Athens in its cultural glory was still a city enmeshed with its land, woven into it by the human bodies that physically worked its soil. At that time, the city instanced, at least in the West, the highest historical striving between earth and world, a striving that wed the two into a cycle of mutual cultivation. The world, through its cultural achievements, made sense of the earth, that is, it revealed it in a meaningful way. The earth, for its part, gave the world its sense, that is, put forth beings into the careful significance that nourished the meaningful world. For a time, it seems the two had struck a finely balanced cycle of return in which the harvested energies of the land were revitalized by "generosities of learning and art, conviviality and order" flowing out of the city.

Certainly the objectionable Athenian institutions of slavery, highly restricted citizenship, warfare, and the social and even physical confinement of women besmirch any romanticized portrait of ancient Greece. The so-called golden age contained a good measure of dross. All the same, it is difficult not to admire the fertility of its culture. A primary end of culture, on par in importance with the physical security it lends its human members, is to secure, preserve, and transmit the wealth of these members' existential experience. To qualify as viable and vital, in other words, a culture must participate in truth. For all its diversity of interpretations, truth invariably serves as the polestar to direct conscious human effort. Art, religion, and science all aim at what to each counts as truth. The quest for truth is known to be the task most proper to human being. Truth arises out of freedom as the oak from the acorn. Technology, with its emancipatory impetus, also promises the promotion of truth, and we must acknowledge its nobility of purpose. However, because it rockets truth and freedom into a metaphysical orbit beyond the reach of our existential, worldly experience, it unwittingly develops a culture based on mendacity, illusion, and dissemblance.

Truth and Presence

"From time immemorial," asserts Heidegger in *Being and Time*, "philosophy has associated truth with being" (BT 196). For the most part, the philosophical tradition has conceived of this association as an agreement or correspondence between a statement and its object. Such a conception presumes at least a kind of passive, removed, judging subject, a thinking substance whose only task is to assure that the expression of its intellection correctly describes its intentional object. Of course. a realist conception goes further, putting to rest any doubt concerning the identity between the intentional and the real material object. Heidegger's existential analytic of Dasein shows that every relation of correspondence between a judging subject and a perceived object (even if merely intentional) derives from the more basic relation of interconnection between Dasein and beings in general. The condition for the possibility of judgment, as well as of perception, for that matter, is the appearance or presence of phenomena. Beings have to be before any statement can be applied to them. When, furthermore, it is recollected that statements themselves are a sort of being, it becomes clear that truth fundamentally means the way that beings are.

Heidegger makes much of the Greek word for truth, *aletheia*, translating it variously as discovery [*Entdeckung*], disclosure [*Erschlossenheit*], unconcealment [*Unverborgenheit*] and truth [*Wahrheit*].[30] Each of these terms aims at suggesting how beings truly are. Beings are disclosed, discovered; they emerge into presence through a process of unconcealment. Truth, thus, is a revelatory relation between revealed beings and the being whose essence consists in revealing—namely, human being, or Dasein. Dasein discloses beings by understanding them within a relational context made meaningful ultimately by its concern with its own mortal being. Since the mortality of human being is no human feat, but rather the primordial bestowal of Being, the proper concern or care for it that leads to disclosive understanding performs an ontological and not merely utilitarian service.

> "The Dasein in man" is the essence which belongs to Being itself, in which essence, however, man belongs, indeed such that he has this Being to be. *Da-sein* concerns man. . . . Man becomes essentially himself when he enters properly into his essence. He stands in the un-hiddenness of being as the hidden place at which Being is present from its truth.[31]

Otherwise put, by inhabiting a world of significance, the human being evokes into this revelatory dimension other beings, all of which relate to its essential existential concern, that itself ultimately answers to the need of Being to manifest. Thus, the ontological relation of truth is at once world-constitutive and world-confirming. The significance of the world sets up an order wherein beings are meaningfully disclosed as what they are, while this disclosure perpetuates the significant world. Truth interrelates beings through meaning.

The obvious worry brought forward by the ontological interpretation of truth is, as Heidegger later recognized, its susceptibility to relativism and subjective arbitrariness. If truth relates to meaning, and meaning resides, existentially speaking, in Dasein, then it would seem that the latter has complete jurisdiction over truth and could therefore dispense with both objective beings and any sort of correspondence they may or may not have to our ideas of them. This misgiving, however, mistakes the nature of disclosure and is rectified with due consideration paid to this nature. Our earlier discussion of *physis* described how beings emerge into presence from concealment. *Physis* or nature is the partner of Dasein in the historical/phenomenal process of Being. We disclose beings meaningfully because these already put themselves forth into the contextual dimension opened up by our careful needy existence. Here it helps to harken to the English language. Truth occurs when and where Dasein discloses a being as it truly is. Disclosure involves interpretive, attuned understanding. As etymology implies, to understand something truly means to stand under or support it as it is. Consistent with the revelatory relation of truth, understanding functions receptively, upholding beings in a manner that protects their revealed presence. Understanding without the autonomous spontaneity of nature (*physis*) has neither material nor meaning. It is, borrowing from Kant, both empty and blind.

For Heidegger, truth and "untruth" are ontologically coeval, the presence of one entailing the fact of the other. Each disclosive event has the potential to cover up the being of the revealed phenomenon. This potential opens the sluice to a flood of paradox. How can a phenomenon appear and yet remain concealed? How can Dasein understand or, as I have phrased it, support a being in a manner that fundamentally misinterprets it? Heidegger motions to the answers of these questions without articulating them in the most compelling manner. He needed the persuasive pressure of the physical body.

The most basic relation of truth holds between Dasein and inner-worldly beings. "Being true as discovering is a manner of being of Dasein" (N 202). The disclosive relation is itself the essence of human being in that it arises out of the mortal need of humans to support their being by means of other beings.

> Discovering is a way of being of being-in-the-world. Taking care of things, whether in circumspection or in looking in a leisurely way, discovers inner-worldly beings. The latter become what is discovered. They are "true" in a secondary sense. Primarily true, that is, discovering, is Dasein. Truth in the secondary sense does not mean to be discovering (discovery), but to be discovered (discoveredness). (N 203)

Discoveredness relies on discovery, which is to say that truth relies on being-in-the-world. Our revision of Heidegger has shown that, essentially, Dasein is in the world as a needy body. The needs of the body, its mortality, makes beings ontologically possible, while the sense of the body make them ontically real, that is, apparent as phenomena. It is the body that first makes sense of beings, that understands them in a manner meaningful to its sensuous mortality. Beings become present in the presence of an embodied being-in-the-world. They are discovered to the extent that the needy body keeps open to discovery. Lived bodily absence—now the urban way of life—is a concealing way of being of being-in-the-world. It is therefore prone to ontological misunderstanding.

The absent body burdens the agricultural crisis with ontological gravity. That only 2 percent of a technological populace gathers food from the land signifies a colossal concealment. The overwhelming majority simply does not have the bodily presence to truly understand the beings that physically sustain them. Again, the absence is bi-faceted: technological humanity exists removed from the land and from its own sensitive corporeality. Consequently, the true being of food hides concealed beneath its technological disclosure. Food becomes a processed and packaged commodity: sterilized, eternalized, hypostatized, rationalized, and reduced to a simple alimentary calculus that balances grams of fat against grams of protein. The essential ontological relation between food and the mortal body is obliterated.

This same ontological gravity makes the agricultural crisis a cultural crisis. Just as soil is the basic matter of the earth, so is food the basic matter of the world. To culturally misunderstand and dissemble it is to conceal all the worldly properties that inhere in it. The city-as-world, unable to sense its constitutive food, must experience itself as meaningless. It tends, moreover, to complete concealment. Not only does it draw bodies off the land, it also covers the earth under concrete. Not only does it free its populace from food production, it also dissuades consumers from food preparation. The final, logical goal is to relieve humanity of consumption as well, by concealing an entire meal within a tiny, opaque capsule.

Obviously an abrupt and sweeping reversal of migration from country to city is neither feasible nor desirable. We need to preserve the rich cultural concentration of cities in a generous and beneficial relation of commensalism with the countryside that physically sustains them. For, apart from the the great urban contributions of education, arts, and humanism, there is simply not enough arable land worldwide to sustain over six billion subsistence farmers. We cannot abandon culture simply because it has reached a pitch of physical crisis. Nor can we all embrace agriculture as a "folk remedy" for this cultural crisis. Our timely response to the crisis and its accompanying metaphysical dangers does not have to be uniform or whole hog. The unconcealment of food can and has already begun to take place within certain urban communities. Community gardens, local organic markets, food cooperatives, community-supported agricultural initiatives, chapters of the international Slow Food movement, and shared kitchens all promote greater understanding of the truth of food among urbanites.

The city need not be a desert of lifeless consumption. It can provide fertile ground for the returns of production, appreciation, and health. We can begin granting citizenship to the presence of nature, which we have banished beyond our city walls. It can be as simple and grassroots as substituting vegetable plots for lawns, which per acre receive more chemicals in the name of cosmetics than conventional agricultural land in the name of commestible production. Many municipalities have already recommenced the tradition of returning to the county some of its organic generosity in the form of compost diverted from landfills. There exists a continuum of potential worldly engagement open to us, from off-grid homesteading to the mindful preparation of local crops for weekday suppers. If we do nothing more than decline our cars' constant invitation to convenience, we will already have taken a great leap forward. It behoves each individual to work toward the fullest engagement possible in her circumstances. This work keeps us true to our ontological nature and vocation.

Trash: A City Unto Itself

The technological city is both the sine qua non and the raison d'être of industrial agriculture. Insofar as rationalized food represents the paradigmatic commodity, the technological city must stand as the paradigm of devices. "In a device, the relatedness of the world is replaced by a machinery, but the machinery is concealed, and the commodities, which are made available by a device, are enjoyed without the encumbrance of, or the engagement with a context."[32] Borgmann's words perfectly describe the modern MacDonaldized city of everywhere and nowhere, in which disengagement meets its logical conclusion in mass unemployment. As the presence of multinational corporations, with their standardized operational codes, appearances, and products, exerts an homogenizing influence on all metropolitans around the globe, the cultural and even the geographical contours of local context flatten out. Place becomes, as Heidegger lamented, spatial, indistinguishable, hence interchangeable, with all other points on the grid.[33] Common experience teaches that a body in a scene without distinguishable landmarks quickly grows disoriented. Its surroundings cease to make sense to it and seem to withdraw into themselves, leaving the abandoned body feeling alein and isolated. Thus, the modern urban paradox: for all its loud conspicuous-ness, its traffic, its media, its pollutants, and its sensorially deactivated populace, the megapolis exists in a state of dark absence. These qualities, which compose the city's overtness, in fact cover over its covert tendency to conceal.

The heart of the device is its imperative to conceal by disengaging the human body from the world it needs. This renders the world untenable, which means not fit to be held or grasped or comprehended. The imperative to conceal extracts understanding from use and jettisons it. With the loss of understanding goes skill, which physical ease and competence so follow. A body thus dispossessed must encounter the device as a black box, a quasimagical object designed to operate within and to respond to a narrow and inscrutable set of parameters. These parameters are categorically ahistorical. They make no reference to the origin or the destination of the device they define. The device is therefore as timeless as it is placeless. The razing of the old and the headlong construction of the new that happen in most modern cities are another symptom of the city's temporal and geographical concealing of nature.

But cities need not absolutely conceal, nor have they always done so. As centers of art and learning, they have great revelatory potential. They have long been thought a distillation of the cosmos, or, in Lewis Mumford's words, "a simulacrum of heaven." Before the city appropriated the world, it disclosed it. Mumford explains: "The ability to transmit in symbolic form and human patterns a representative portion of a culture is the great mark of the city: this is the condition for encouraging the fullest expression of human capacities and potentialities, even in the rural and primitive areas beyond."[34] When vitalized by the cyclical principle of return, cities can bring forth and preserve the reclusive energies latent in the earth into the meaningful light of the world. The history of Being unfolds through such cultural productivity.

At the same time, however, it must be borne in mind that cultural productivity always involves some degree of physical destructiveness. The rational triumphs of the city come at the expense of the body's physicality. So long as the strife between world and earth remains mutually nourishing to both elements, then truth, that is, disclosive-embodied-being-in-the-world, prevails. When either side predominates, truth as an ontological mode of existence is upset and confounded. At this point, the fairly matched strife degenerates into slaughter and much is lost, including the possibility of truth as unconcealment. For reasons unknown, history has witnessed the world overpower the earth. A symbol of the world, the city inherits its historical destructiveness. "No matter how many valuable functions the city has furthered, it has also served, throughout most of history, as a container of organized violence and a transmitter of war."[35] The often palpable aggression seething in the city streets erupts, at least in part, from the frustration and subjugation that the concrete jungle afflicts on living human physicality.

Violence is a particular way of being-in-the-world, but, ontologically speaking, not a truthful way. Violence implies a negation of being that occurs at two levels. What typically goes for violence in everyday speech—ontic destruction or harm to a physical being—must be preceded by an ontological negation that denies the physicality of the physical being. Violence negates the physicality of the targeted being. This is most apparent in cases of human being. To do violence to a person means to deny that the person feels pain, suffers, cares for his existence, is mortal. The seeming paradox here is only seeming, for to fully identify the mortality of a human is to necessarily identify with it. In such a state of identity, violence against another has suicidal implications for the aggressor, who can perpetrate it only on the basis of a misunderstanding of himself and the victim. One can harm another when one does not discover oneself in the other. Violence, in other words, depends on not truly discovering the being of the other, not perceiving a person as a person.

That violence in general, and not solely against humans, negates the physicality of beings is more difficult to demonstrate. In the following chapter I try to clarify this point. I raise the specter of violence now as segue into that discussion. For if violence is a defective mode of disclosure that conceals rather than discovers the true being of a thing, then it gives further credibility to my claim that the container of violence—the city—has an ontologically destructive basis. By no means the originator of violence, the city very effectively concentrates it. Often the city raises the flag of human achievement up the pole of human depravity. Thomas Merton says the same, though much better in his colorful religious language:

> Everything in modern city life is calculated to keep man from entering into himself and thinking about spiritual things. Even with the best of intentions a spiritual man finds himself exhausted and deadened and debased by the constant noise of machines and loudspeakers, the dead air and glaring lights of offices and shops, the everlasting suggestions of advertising and propaganda. The whole mechanism of modern life is geared for a flight from God and from the spirit into the wilderness of neurosis.[36]

Even as it banishes the human spirit, the modern technological city rolls forward on the violent destruction of the physicality of beings. Urban being-in-the-world discloses beings not as they are but only as they are metaphysically rationalized. Destroying physicality, the metropolis conceals truth. I suggest that Merton's "flight from God" roughly translates Heidegger's forgetfulness of Being.

Metaphysics conceals the physical. The city conceals its waste. The nearly transcendent technological city cannot not abide any visual trace of its waste:

Scrupulously cleaning excrement off the body became a specifically urban and middle-class practice. In the 1750's, middle-class
people began to use disposable paper to wipe the anus after
excretion and chamber pots were by that date emptied daily.
The very fear of handling excrement was an urban fear, born of
the new medical beliefs about impurities clogging the skin.[37]

As I have shown, scrupulousness turned into practical necessity and
then paralyzing phobia with the discovery of the germ theory. The irony
of this discovery lies in its affinity for concealment. Themselves invisible
and unmanifest, germs seemed to have enjoined the disappearance of all
associated beings. "Out of sight, out of mind" is an effective code of
conduct for a rational, disembodied agent, for which *esse est percipi*. To
such an being, garbage is only an apparent problem; if it does not appear,
then it does not exist. When one puts together the traditional association
of being and truth with the original understanding of truth as unconcealment, then the technological method of dealing with waste—simply
conceal it and thereby deny its truth and being—amounts to a masterful
stroke of metaphysical genius.

Conclusion

Garbage indeed is an urban blight, and blights normally are conspicuous,
unsightly indicators of ill health and imbalance in nature. Technology has
cured this blight by making its matter trash. It has wiped out the signs of
disease. The modern city makes waste absolute by denying waste's phenomenal existence and thus negating its physical being. A being evacuated
of its physicality and truth is less than good for nothing. In fact, such a
being is as good as nothing. Since it does not physically touch our own
desensitized being, it cannot push us to question its ontologically unique
and likely dangerous essence. What is a being that is kept from being?
What is a substance experienced only as nothingness? Is it at all possible,
is it even conceivable, to discover the nature of trash?

CHAPTER FIVE

Trash

From the previous chapters a number of themes has surfaced: rationalization, disembodiment, convenience, the denial of mortality, dismissal of finitude, and, most recently, violence. Each one of these themes has arisen in some relation to waste and, when taken together, they combine to constitute the historically unique phenomenon of trash. With the elemental themes now gathered, their constitutive structure needs to be laid out in a way that will test the central hypothesis of this study. I have maintained that technological consumer trash signifies our failure at being human. Because I have construed this failure as ontological in nature, the hypothesis would seem to demand an ontological investigation of that which bears the failure's foremost stamp. But what in fact justifies an ontology of trash? Why not leave the mountainous refuse of the consumer society to the more expert and efficacious fields of public planning, politics, waste management, and engineering? Not to wipe our philosophical hands clean of trash is to take Heidegger's thinking seriously. For in the twilight of his life he declared solemnly that "the fundamental thought of my thinking is precisely that Being, or the manifestation of Being *needs* human beings and that, vice versa, human beings are only human beings if they are standing in the manifestation of Being."[1] This chapter will reveal how our everyday commerce and complicity in trash, by hurling us into the oblivion of Being, denigrates our humanity. Later, in chapter six, we will see how this also endangers our very existence.

An ontology of trash must support itself on what Heidegger rather forbiddingly calls in *Being and Time* "the formal existential totality of the ontological structural whole of Dasein" (BT 179). The single word, but by no means simple concept, used to name this arcane piece of prolixity is "care" [*Sorge*]. If care in fact defines our being, then ex hypothesi, our

121

failure to be truly human must involve a failure to care, to exist carefully. Yet how can we possibly fail in so essential a regard? Elaborating what has gone before, I will show that our metaphysical will to become superlatively human, that is, exclusively rational, actually forces us to neglect our being. In the name of convenience, we voluntarily, quite often voraciously, consume disposable commodities. We assume that the possibility for this is the positive actualization of the promise of technology. Technology promises to disburden us from the pressing concerns of the flesh so that we may maximally indulge our higher, rational, and creative faculties, those that distinguish us from purely animal beings. Technological progress has pursued this maximization through the unflagging development of increasingly "carefree" commodities. Thus, the technological value of a commodity resides in the extent to which it minimizes the care required of the consumer, a care grounded in physical engagement, as I have argued.

Our convenience items, those commodified objects that not only do not demand physical maintenance and our careful attention, but even practically frustrate all attempts at taking care of them, most easily and absolutely become trash. Their ability to minimize physical care in consumption necessitates that they maximize disposability. The polystyrene cup is effortlessly discarded and the consumer spared the trouble of washing it. This relative freedom from taking care of the object supposedly saves the consumer time. In the metaphysical ledger, all time not wasted on matters of bodily necessity gets recorded in the positive, rational column, the sum of which is presumed to equal our true humanity. "Carefreeness" is the real promise of technology, and its real fulfillment is trash.

From here one might hasten to conclusions. If care is our "formal existential totality"; furthermore, if technology directs its prowess at eradicating care, then we should confront technology as our archenemy. Clearly, this is not the case. We eagerly and enthusiastically promote its development and expansion. Technology benefits us with immense material wealth. It creates possibilities of existing hitherto unknown. The transformative mechanisms of industrialisation, for example, have ground down many of the gender and class inequities that have oppressed less scientifically sophisticated ages. It is, in this respect, patently false to oppose technology to human being. Our technological discoveries can better be said to express our concern for our being than to deny them. Care for our being makes use of the technological devices available in the service of our projects, goals, and needs. On closer inspection, it would seem that the mitigation of the exigency of physically taking care of things is technology's major contribution to our essential care. This simply reformulates technology's explicit promise of liberation and disburdenment.

Any confusion about this that could lead to a condemnation of technology would hinge on a prior confusion between care and taking care. In English, the terms are prone to ambiguity. Heidegger, however, has the linguistic means to keep the two conceptually distinct. He distinguishes the "formal existential totality"—care [*Sorge*] from "the expression 'taking care' [*Besorgen*] . . . used in this inquiry as an ontological term (an existential) to designate the being of a possible being-in-the-world" (BT 53). *Besorgen* presupposes *Sorge*; for "as a primordial structural totality, care lies 'before' every factical 'attitude' and 'position' of Dasein, that is, it is always already *in* them as an existential a priori" (BT 180). Care, which constitutes the very possibility of being-in-the-world, conditions every possible manner of being-in-the-world. Nothing in this permits the deduction that care logically necessitates taking care.

If care cannot be reduced to taking care of things, then technology, which aims only at the latter, would seem to leave the former intact. And, if that is the case, then the inevitable trash of technological consumption is, after all, no different from waste. It would imply only a failure to look after entities, but would not signify a failure to care, a failure to live up to our essential being. Yet, while mindful to keep the two distinct, Heidegger also claims that "even if only privatively, care is always taking care of things and concern" (BT 181). This suggests that deficiencies in taking care may in fact affect care itself.

I wish to argue that Being needs humans to take physical care of things, and that as humans we exist in our essential humanity only when we thoughtfully comply. Trash necessarily follows from the logic of care-free commodities, whose consumption necessarily excludes taking care of them. In other words, the commodified consumption that inexorably concludes with trash does not let beings be and this ontological refusal likewise prevents us from entering into our own being. To prove that the consumption of care-free commodities in fact conspires against our own essential being as care, we must first come to a clear understanding of what Heidegger means by care. Then we must explore the depth to which taking care of things penetrates it. Next, the demonstration will require an accurate measurement of the extent to which commodity consumption entails uncaring. At that point, it will become evident that uncaring as the mode of a possible being-in-the-world is an existential mode of violence that negates the being of beings. This ontological violence is the progenitor of trash.

Heidegger's Care

Due to the familiarity of the term in common discourse, Heidegger takes pains to convey that his "care" "is used in a purely ontological and existential way. Any ontically intended tendency of being, such as worry or carefreeness, is ruled out" (BT 180). Obviously, when he speaks of care as the existential totality of human being, Heidegger has more in mind than the pervasive anxious preoccupation that colors most, if not all, of our conscious lives. But neither does he mean what has become known as care-giving. Care for Heidegger is not primarily nursing, or healing, or fostering or tending. While each of these activities flows from the spring of possibilities fed by care, none of them can be equated with it. The author of *Being and Time* would not agree with Milton Mayeroff who writes that "in caring, the other is primary; the growth of the other is the centre of my attention."[2] On the contrary, the ontological direction of care always points back to oneself.

The reason for its inescapable self-reflexivity is that "care is being-toward-death" (BT 303). This unswerving orientation makes human being essentially ontological.

> Dasein is a being that does not simply occur among other beings. Rather it is ontically distinguished by the fact that in its being this being is concerned *about* its very being. Thus it is constitutive of the being of Dasein to have, in its very being, a relation of being to its being. And this in turn means that Dasein understands itself in its being some way and with some explicitness. It is proper to this being that it be disclosed to itself with and through its being. *Understanding of Being is itself a determination of Being of Dasein.* The ontic distinction of Dasein lies in the fact that it *is* ontological. (BT 10)

Mortality is the all too painful mark of this distinction. Our being concerns us because we understand, though most often dimly, its inherent fragility. The presentiment of its end and impermanence, even when rendered nearly insensible by the distracting defenses or our everyday habituations, obtrudes our finite being into the center of our present existence. Whatever forms it may subsequently take, care, for Heidegger, begins as the basic existential relation of one's being to its impending end.

This concern for her own being, erupting from the individual's understanding of her ultimate nullity, makes understanding in general possible. The individual encounters a world of objects more or less intelligible with respect to the relationship they bear to the projects of her existence. Care refers all beings back to the fundamental self-concern that grounds every human existence. *Being and Time* has a distinctive pragmatic tenor. It teaches that beings appear in the world only in relation to the understanding that refers them back to, as I have earlier translated it, the needs of human finitude. "Relevance is the being of innerworldly beings, for which they are always and already initially freed. . . . What the relevance is about is the what-for of serviceability, the wherefore of usability" (BT 78). Postponing comments on *Being and Time*'s pragmatism, I wish here to stress the essential disclosive capacity of care. Care discovers being only in reference to itself. "The primary 'what-for' is a for-the-sake-of-which. But the for-the-sake-of-which always concerns the being of Dasein which is essentially concerned *about* this being itself in its being" (BT 78). For Heidegger, this means that Dasein's being-in-the-world, the fundamental cause of concern ("What *Angst* is anxious for is being-in-the-world itself" [BT 175]) coordinates all beings. Establishing the contextual horizon of significance wherein every being appears as the being it is, care draws all phenomena into the opening of understanding. For "only as long as Dasein *is*, that is, as long as there is the ontic possibility of an understanding of being, 'is there' [*gibt es*] being" (BT 196).

As the ontological structure of Dasein, care brings things into being. I have argued the same earlier, though in less technical language. The vulnerable physical finitude in which we always helplessly find ourselves solicits a world of beings that emerge in response to our constitutive neediness. Unfortunately, Heidegger, despite the pragmatic leanings of his early thought, plays down to the point of disappearance the physical foundation of care and being-toward-death. He generally overlooks the fact that mortality is corporeality and that the most pronounced articulation of care is physical need. However, this is not so much an unbridgeable gap as a shadow in his work; despite his philosophical abstraction, he still arrives at the heart of the matter: that human limitation serves Being as a condition of its possibility.

Care Versus Taking Care

In his small treatise *On Caring*, Milton Mayeroff attempts his own analysis of the various phenomena of care in order to expose "a common pattern" underlying them all. While his basic thesis may seem to resonate well with Heidegger's later thought, it sounds initially dissonant with the utilitarian strains of *Being and Time*. "In the sense in which a man can ever be said to be at home in the world," Mayeroff proclaims, "he is at home not through dominating, or explaining, or appreciating, but through caring and being cared for."[3] Although Mayeroff here does in a way connect being-in-the-world and care, his link is, from a Heideggerean perspective, ontic rather than ontological. This becomes evident upon inspecting his "basic pattern of caring, understood as helping the other grow": "I experience the other as an extension of myself and also as independent and with the need to grow; I experience the other's development as bound up with my own sense of well-being; and I feel needed by it for that growing. I respond affirmatively and with devotion to the other's need, guided by the direction of its growth."[4]

The external orientation of Mayeroff's caring clearly shows that it belongs to solicitude [*Fürsorgen*] rather than to care itself [*Sorge*]. Yet Mayeroff maintains that just such caring for other persons and things is essential to human beings. He implies that authentic human existence, what he calls individual self-actualization, necessarily depends on solicitous caring for other beings beyond one's limited self. Granted the plausibility of this from a psychological point of view, it remains nonetheless ontologically problematic in that it completely disregards an ontological interpretation of the being both of that which is cared for and of that which does the caring.

The problem becomes all the more urgent when we consider how taking care of beings often stands at odds with care as the authentic existential mode of human being. Heidegger reminds us that "the everyday interpretation of the self has the tendency to understand itself in terms of the 'world' taken care of. When Dasein has itself in view ontically *it fails to see* itself in relation to the kind of being of the being that it itself is. And that is particularly true of the fundamental constitution of Dasein, being-in-the-world" (BT 296). More often than not our taking care takes the form of dispatching business. We lose ourselves in our attachment or aversion to other beings and become distracted and consumed by the world. Precisely this preoccupation with taking care of innerworldly things, which is always conditioned a priori by our ontological concern for our own being, blinds us to the truth of world, to wit, that it is a constituent of care. "The being of Dasein means being-ahead-of-oneself-already-in(the world) as being-together-with(innerworldly beings encountered)" (BT 180). In short, taking care of things typically obscures the unity of human being and makes it seem that being-in confronts a world of beings encountered. Everyday taking care reinforces the subject/object dualism native to metaphysical reasoning and calculation that reduces being to raw material for the subject's exploitation.

Heidegger calls this inveterate tendency of human being "falling prey" and characterizes it precisely by the dominating and scientific attitudes against which Mayeroff contrasts caring. "With regard to care,"

Michael Zimmerman explains, "falling leads me to neglect my possibilities (future) and fate (past) by letting me become too absorbed in everyday worldly affairs."⁵ Yet this absorption leading to neglect is itself a mode of care. Only out of a concern for our being do we seek to secure it by means of innerworldly beings. But the very quest for security through absorption in and exploitation of things deflects our understanding away from our ontological nature. We mistake ourselves as enduring, if not eternal substances, the qualities of which we long to fix as immutable. The notion of substance, however, goes forcefully against our existential being. The metaphysical tradition conceives substance as self-sufficient, independent, and more or less atemporal. Such a conception veils the finite and empty essence of human existence. It causes us to forget what I have stressed as our neediness. Thus, our very concern for our being-in-the-world for the most part takes us out of the world by allowing us to perceive ourselves as substantial subjects existing, as it were, merely accidentally amid external objects.

Insofar as everyday taking care of things in our fallen state seems to split apart the unity of care—being-ahead-of-oneself-already-in (the world) as-being-together-with (innerworldly beings encountered)—it is in fact more world-negating than world-affirming. It fails to understand how our neediness, over which we have no control, constitutes the world wherein we project our possibilities. What I prefer to designate "neediness," because the word carries connotations of physical limitation, corresponds to Heidegger's idea of facticity. Our neediness throws us into the world that always provides the context whereby we understand and live out our possibilities. Binding the past and the future in its response to our projective neediness, the world integrates the temporal structure of care. Once we ostensibly dissolve the temporal unity through forgetful taking care, the world loses its ontic integrity. The temporal totality of the world hence narrows to a spatial point, that of immediate preoccupied absorption "in everyday worldly affairs." Lacking any means of integration into a greater whole, these affairs are experienced as a series of busy and urgent "nows" whose incessant succession leaves no time to discover their meaning within the historical temporal unfolding. We lose time in taking care because "the primary phenomenon of primordial and authentic temporality is the future" (BT 303). Yet the future has its dwelling in the past, for "the authentic future . . . reveals itself as *finite*" (BT 303). Sending us toward death, the future always contains the facticity of our needy mortality. Any denial, therefore, of this essential neediness initiates the simultaneous contraction of time and dissipation of world.

The existential structure of human being, care, is not something we can either take or leave. So long as we are human we must be careful, that is, concerned about our very being. In throwing us into the world, however, care jeopardizes itself. Just as the lived body absents itself from perception, and Being as such conceals itself behind the manifestation of beings, so, too, does care cover over its vital truth in the process of taking care. Now, since the promise of technology proclaims to make us more human, it can do so only by making us more careful, that is, more sensitive and aware of our finite, temporal nature. Technology goes about fulfilling this humanitarian promise by assuming the care taken of things. According to the foregoing analysis, this technique should prove successful. By freeing us from the distracted care-taking that leads to the neglect of our careful essence, technology world seem capable of bestowing on us the time, that is, the temporal clearing, in which we could cultivate an authentic understanding of care. Mitigating the need for worldly absorption, does not technology place us back into our true existential and primordial world of care?

No doubt we all have anecdotal evidence that answers in the negative. With every acceleration of technological innovation we somehow feel that time passes us by more swiftly. The pace of life in consumer urban culture has reached a sprint. Rather than bringing greater unity to our lives, technological progress seems to have dissected them into autonomous members of leisure and work, family and state, intellect and psyche, duty and freedom, all moving in counter and incompatible directions. Much of this has to do with a geographical separation that transportation technologies promote. Many of us neither work nor recreate where we live. Thus, we spend much of our time as absentee citizens and absentee parents. All that civil society can expect from someone who is neither fully here nor there is regular taxes and the occasional vote. As consumers, many of us have experienced outcomes of carefree commodities contrary to those promised. On top of obesity, cancer, and cardiac arrest, their easy consumption seems often to breed flippancy, capriciousness, and indifference instead of a sensitive and grateful awareness. Of course, the reductive, exploitative, and domineering stance that Mayeroff opposes to care predominates throughout scientific technology and its vast utilization. All this indicates something ontologically amiss in the technological assumption of taking care.

By again probing the ambiguity of care, we come to appreciate the full complexity of the problem. Technology promises to liberate us from taking care of things—primarily our own physical bodies—so that we may freely pursue our more distinctively human concerns. From this point of view, technology appears to serve care. As his thought matured from *Being and Time*, Heidegger began to use the word "care" negatively. He began to trace back the ontological danger of technology to its allegiance to the utilitarian obsession that has seized hold of modern humanity. In his essay of 1946 entitled "What Are Poets For," Heidegger states that authentic human being must be "without care": "The caring here has the character of purposeful self-assertion by the ways and means of unconditional production. We are without such care only when we do not establish our nature exclusively within the precinct of production and procurement of things that can be utilized and defended."[6] The charge here amounts to this: that even as it presumes to disburden us from the weight of taking-care, technology embroils us in the absorption of "everyday worldly affairs." Whereas in *Being and Time* Heidegger privileges "the precinct of production and procurement" as Dasein's basic ontological orientation, he later specifies this as the dangerous and dehumanizing site of technological man. Does this then signal a radical turning in his thought? More important, by what differences, if any, can we distinguish technologically procured carefreeness from the poetic and truly human condition, as Rilke puts it, "outside all caring" (PLT 119)?

The question brings the discussion back once more to the relationship between taking care and care as ontological concern; it is this inevitable return that inclines me to regard Heidegger's famous turn as not as sharp as sometimes presumed. On either side of the turn what animates Heidegger's thought is the astounding insight that finitude conditions Being, even as Being determines finitude. This is witnessed by the constant emphasis that Heidegger attaches to the supreme ontological significance of death. In *Being and Time* he subordinates *Besorgen* to *Sorge* as a mode of the latter: "Since being-in-the-world is essentially care, being-together-with things at hand could be taken in our previous analyses as *taking care* of them. . . . Being-together-with is taking care of things, because as a mode of being-in it is determined by its fundamental structure, care" (BT 180). Since, moreover, "care is being-toward-death" (BT 303), taking care of things is, by extension, also a mode of being toward-death. Insofar as an authentic understanding of death grasps it "as the possibility of the impossibility of existence in general" (BT 242) taking care, when modified authentically, must also involve at some level a corresponding comprehension. That is, if "care itself is in its essence thoroughly permeated with nullity" (BT 263), then its authentic mode of taking care will reflect and preserve this very nullity qua nullity. Directed toward our mortality, taking care attends to death.

When in "What Are Poets For" Heidegger urges metaphysical man to move "outside all caring" he obviously does not mean that humans should transgress the limits of death. In fact, the danger of the modern era lurks in the darkness of death's absence: "The time remains destitute not only because God is dead, but because mortals are hardly aware and

capable even of their own mortality. Mortals have not yet come into ownership of their own nature. Death withdraws into the enigmatic" (PLT
96). Although death may withdraw into the enigmatic, the withdrawal
itself is not mysterious. It has demonstrable causes:

> The parting self-assertion of objectification wills everywhere the
> constancy of produced objects, and recognizes it alone as being
> and as positive. The self-assertion of technological objectifica-
> tion is the constant negation of death. By this negation death
> itself becomes something negative; it becomes the altogether
> inconstant and null. (PLT 25)

Evidently, the freedom from taking care promised by technology and
effected through the perpetual production of commodities consists
precisely of the care that Heidegger believes authentic mortals must
be without.

Technology's technique of taking care strikes at the very heart of true
care, that is, mortality, with multiple blows. First technological objectification wrenches "being-in" from its constituent world, thus enthroning
an unworldly transcendent subject over innerworldly objects. The counterpart of constant objectifying, the posited subject comes to interpret
itself by means of the metaphysical concept of permanent substance. This
interpretation forecloses the possibility of an authentic understanding of
care. "Care, the being of Dasein, thus means, as thrown project: being the
(null) ground of a nullity" (BT 263). The self-assertion of technological
objectification and its a priori subjectification negate death by sweeping
away the possibility of experiencing its mortal truth in a torrent of incessant production and consumption. Technological carefreeness means
immortality. Such a promise sounds the death knell for any and all beings
essentially finite.

Worldly Care

With this, we reach the interpretive limit of Heidegger's language.
Because Heidegger by and large avoids philosophical discussion about
physicality and corporeality, his interpretation of technology, although
complete, remains abstract. Recalling Tierney's observation that "the trajectory of modernity is to render everyone free not only from the limits
which are imposed by the body, but even from the body itself,"[7] we get a
more vivid sense of how technological taking care jeopardizes ontological
care. My argument has implied that, when authentic, Dasein's care is tan-

tamount to the state of being without care that Heidegger later contrasts to technological production. In *Being and Time*, authenticity blossoms in an individual's appropriate and appropriative relation to her death, namely, a relation that does not dissemble its total and essential nothingness. Authentic care senses the truth of death and discloses it accordingly. In previous chapters I sought to establish philosophically the otherwise obvious fact that mortality rests on the cornerstone of embodiment. The insatiable neediness, the immense finitude of our bodies hand us over, a priori and continuously, to death. Technology does not negate death by means of some sort of metaphysical black magic. Its technique is much more mundane. It negates death through an incremental process of dismantling the experienced limits of the lived human body. Since its physical limits define the body, their effacement means the negation also of the sense of human embodiment. Disembodiment stands for the physical negation of death.

On the macro level, the autonomy that Heidegger concedes to technology is credible. It is true that "no single man, no group of men, no commission of prominent statesmen, scientists, and technicians, no conference of leaders of commerce and industry, can brake or direct the progress of history in the atomic age. No merely human organization is capable of gaining dominion over it."[8] Likewise, no single shopper, nor the federacy of all consumers can choose that the world of consumption should appear other than a collection of commodified goods ranked according to market value. On the micro level, however, each of us knows why we avail ourselves of a certain technological device, especially one with a disposable commodity. We value such devices to the extent that they are convenient. Convenience, for its part, has a basic temporal criterion; it is measured according to the amount of time saved. The notion of saving time is, we must and occasionally do admit, patently absurd. Time is incessant passing-away. Knowing that we can never add even a second to the objective time of the twenty-four hour day, when we seek to save time, we are in fact pursuing something other than time per se. Saving time simply means not spending it on certain activities. Of what do these activities consist? Tierney answers: "The demands of the body are no longer thought of as requiring careful attention and proper planning. They are seen instead as inconveniences in that they limit or interfere with the use of time."[9] In other words, we feel that caring for the body, caring for our mortality, is a waste of time. But if "care is being-toward-death" then it seems that care itself, that is, human existence, has also become a waste of time.

An elaborated treatment of time will follow in the next chapter on human extinction. Before we can fully appreciate the odd phenomena of saving and wasting time, we must arrive at an adequate understanding of the transformations undergone by their physical locus and basis: the human body. Technology promises to take over the care of the body that we perceive as inconvenient to our being. Medical science fulfills this promise directly. Surgery, pharmaceutical products, and, most recently, bioengineering all take care of the troublesome human body in a way that leaves the embodied agent so taken care of more or less passive, in the dark, and out of play. In the realm of consumption, the method is less direct, though in the end it has the same outcome. Devices deliver care-free commodities, that is, they assume the care taken of the those things that answer the demands of the body. Commodities, like all innerworldly beings, ultimately refer to the final for-the-sake-of-which of embodied, that is, mortal human existence. It is, as I have argued, the neediness of the body that situates all phenomena within the meaningful context of the world. Consequently, taking care of things is always done in the service of the neediness and limitation of the human body. Existential care thus expresses itself in the manner and intention with which humans take care of the beings that always somehow impinge on our physicality.

Its essence metaphysical, technology always strives to surpass rather than to serve the limits of physicality. As a technique of taking care, it contains an inherent contradiction. Technology, in the form of devices at once takes care of objects that cater to the needs of the body while also promising to eliminate those said needs. The contradiction, in itself not impossible, has disturbing ontological ramifications. Devices take care of phenomena in a way that undermines their phenomenal being. Striving to eliminate the neediness of the body, technological devices end up unravelling the world-constitutive capacity and contextualizing power of mortal embodiment, by reference to which every commodity appears as it is. The world of beings orbits around the mortal neediness of the human body. Any being that denies or destroys that center of gravity sets the ground of its own being spinning into the void.

The problem, we can say, is one of authenticity, so long as we keep in mind this term's fundamental connection to truth. If taking care is a mode of care, the former ought to disclose the truth of the latter. Care is, in my reformulation of Heidegger's concept, physical neediness, which the mode of technological taking care denies and obscures. When we consume commodities in the unacknowledged interest of care, we almost invariably forget the true significance of our action. We look out over a huge totality of available objects, but are blind to the ontological miracle of an incomprehensible event whereby fragile, finite neediness cries out for succour and is blessed with a marvelous, responsive world. Ignorance of this wondrous truth of Being is, I would argue, fundamental to inauthenticity. It is the average everyday state of human existence. Technology, however, entrenches it so deeply that it all but negates its alternative. By lightening our physicality and our bodily engagement with things, technological devices make us insensitive to the truth of our mortal finitude. Consuming commodities takes care of our physicality instantaneously, safely and easily. These very selling points, howsoever attractive, also prevent us from truly experiencing, with all the force of somatic evidence, the essential limitedness of our being. Only real bodily work with the heavy, at times unyielding members of the world can uncover this truth to us. Without this practical engagement or essential neediness, our ontological being-in-the-world and all that this entails remain not only theoretical, but largely ignored, forgotten, denied. We begin, as a technological collective, to conceive of ourselves as other than we in truth are. We begin posturing as the unrivaled lord and master of all creation. In this sense, Zimmerman correctly remarks that "modern mankind is the inauthentic individual 'writ large'."[10]

Interest

None of this implies that we all must drop our books for hammers and march out intent on pounding boulders into gravel. We do not have to haul water eight miles over rocky ground in bare feet to get a true sense of our mortal fragility. It does suggest, however, that authentic care means taking interest in our physicality. Interest does not mean the obsessive preoccupation with "body-image" that the fashion and sports industries excite to a fever in the "health"-consumer. Nor do I wish to promote the idle curiosity bordering on boredom that Heidegger associates with the word:

> interesting is the sort of thing that can freely be regarded as indifferent the next moment, and be displaced by something else, which then concerns us just as little as what went before. Many people today take the view that they are doing great honor to something by finding it interesting. The truth is that such an opinion has already relegated the interesting thing to the ranks of what is indifferent and soon boring.[11]

I use interest in opposition to this indifference, which Simmel thought characteristic of the blasé attitude of modern urban existence. That attitude, we saw, results from an atrophy of sensorial and motile capacities suffered by the human body in an urban environment at once overwhelming and restrictive. The city houses the consumer society whose commodities likewise desensitize the senses and disengage the body. Interest in human physicality means, borrowing from Tierney, that "the demands of the body . . . are thought of as requiring careful attention and proper planning."[12] Interest implies that taking care of things, in such a way that brings this careful attention to the nature of those bodily demands, has deep ontological significance. This interest is physical attention to truth as revelation.

The Latin root of "interest" means literally to be among. Our physical neediness, our facticity, throws us into a world of beings. To be interested in these is to be among them in a way that resonates with this ontologically constitutive neediness. It is, therefore, to recognize the limits of one's own human being in the being of all phenomena. This type of interest deconstructs the metaphysical dualism of subject over against object. Ontologically speaking, being-in-the-world must include necessarily being-of-the-world for the double reason that human existence continues by grace of the world, while the world manifests itself out of the abyss of physical finitude, that is, mortal nullity. Interest, the careful practical concern with finite existence, clears away the illusion of subjectivity by revealing the basic and inviolable unity of being-in-the-world. Because it exists only among beings, interest is never speculative, but is only as practiced through taking care of beings that all refer back to finitude.

This definition of interest corresponds to one of the elemental teachings of Mahayana Buddhism. D. T. Suzuki translates it as the doctrine of interpenetration:

> It is, philosophically speaking, a thought similar to the Hegelian conception of concrete-universals. Each individual reality, besides being itself, reflects in it something of the universal, and at the same time it is itself because of other individuals. A system of perfect relationship exists among individual existences and also between individuals and universals, between particular objects and general ideas. This perfect network of mutual relations has received at the hand of the Mahayana philosopher the technical name of Interpenetration.[13]

Thus technically explicated, the doctrine has a metaphysical air rather unnatural to it. Thich Nhat Hahn plants the concept in more worldly terms:

> If you are a poet, you will see clearly that there is a cloud floating in this sheet of paper. Without a cloud, there will be no rain,

and without trees, we cannot make paper. The cloud is essential for the paper to exist. . . . If we look into this sheet of paper even more deeply we can see sunshine in it. . . . And if we continue to look, we can see the logger who cut the tree and brought it to the mill to be transformed into paper. And we see wheat. We know that the logger cannot exist without his daily bread, and therefore the wheat that became his bread is also in this sheet of paper. . . . The fact is that this sheet of paper is made up only of "non-paper" elements, and if we return these non-paper elements to their sources, there can be no paper at all. Without non-paper elements, like wind, logger, sunshine and so on, there will be no paper. As thin as this sheet of paper is, it contains everything in the universe in it.[14]

For Buddhists, realizing the truth of interpenetration, or "interbeing" as Nhat Hanh prefers, awakens one to the groundlessness of all phenomena. There is no such thing as a thing-in-itself because every being exists only as the confluence of similarly conditioned beings. The being of each entity refers beyond itself, and when regarded in the totality of this "perfect network of mutual relations" must be seen as intrinsically empty. This bears up my own interpretation. For the final reference of all beings is the mortal finitude of human being, that null ground of a nullity. Nothingness gives rise to Being.

We need not, however, journey to the East to reach an appropriate understanding of the cosmic breadth of every being. Heidegger conveys as much in his writings on the thing. The true being of a thing consists of its ability to gather a meaningful universe out of nonthing elements, what Heidegger christens the "fourfold." The interplay between these elements constitutes the world that situates each phenomenon within the abiding context that allows it to appear as the being it is. "The thing stays—gathers and unites—the fourfold. The thing things world. Each thing stays the fourfold into a happening of the simple onehood of the world" (PLT 181). This is accomplished by the demonstrative nature of things; they constantly refer beyond themselves to each member of the fourfold: earth, sky, mortals, and divinities. The association between these four can constitute a world because their combination exhausts all phenomenal possibilities. Earth harbors the dark potential for growth. Sky elicits this concealed force into the openness of light. Mortals bridge the expanse of sky and the closure of earth with the length of their neediness. The divinities infuse whatsoever appears with mystery, sanctity and grace.

The thing "brings the four into the light of their mutual belonging" (PLT 173). Heidegger illustrates this with an earthen jug rather than a sheet of paper. The jug holds and pours out liquid—wine, for example. But, looking more deeply, we see that

> in the water of the spring dwells the marriage of sky and earth. It stays in the wine given by the fruit of the vine, the fruit in which the earth's nourishment and the sky's sun are betrothed to one another. In the gift of water, in the gift of wine, sky and earth dwell. . . . The gift of the pouring out is drink for mortals. It quenches their thirst. . . . But the jug's gift is also given for consecration. . . . The outpouring is the libation poured out for the immortal gods. . . . In the gift of the outpouring, mortals and divinities each dwell in their different ways. Earth and sky dwell in the gift of the outpouring. In the gift of the outpouring earth and sky, divinities and mortals dwell *together all at once*. These four, at one because of what they themselves are, belong together. (PLT 172–173)

Although the jug itself is none of these elements alone, its being gathers and unites them all in its meaning qua jug. If it could not pour out the gift in the way Heidegger describes, it would not be the thing it is. Its thinghood and being are inseparable and codetermining.

I have quoted at length here to highlight the ontological significance of things. The being of a thing depends on its thinghood, that is, its ability to gather the world around it, which, in turn, gives it its meaning. It follows that the world also depends on the things that unite it. But the thinghood of things, for its part, depends on their appropriate disclosure. Things are disclosed as things only by our taking care of them in a manner that allows them to refer their being back to our essential embodied neediness. By promising to free us from the uniquely human practice of taking care, technology destroys the possibility of thinghood. This sets off a train of ontological annihilations ending in the negation of the world and the extermination of its intrinsic being-in, to wit, human being.

Disposability

In chapter three I introduced Borgmann's distinction—an elaboration on Heidegger's thought—between things and devices. Borgmann bases the distinction on the bodily engagement that things necessitate and devices alleviate. Such engagement calls for the growth of skill and, therefore, the physically engaging practices requisite for this. At the same time, this physical engagement also entails social interaction, for we learn the practices from others who have mastered the skill to a greater degree than ourselves. "The human ability to establish and commit oneself to a practice reflects our capacity to comprehend the world, to harbor it in its expanse as a context that is oriented by its focal points."[15] The points constellate in focal things. Keeping in mind that "focal things can prosper in human practices only,"[16] and that all practices have a physical fundament, then we find ourselves in good position to assess the ontological necessity of taking care.

Let us, in contrast to Heidegger's jug, look deeply into a disposable polystyrene (Styrofoam) cup. As an ingredient to the commodity of convenient liquid consumption, the cup is presumably not a thing in the sense here developed. What basis does this presumption possess? We can test it by discovering what type of world the disposable cup gathers or, in other words, revealing the nature of its reference to the overarching context wherefrom its phenomenal being receives its meaning. Immediately we run up against a kind of epistemological impenetrability intrinsic to the cup's very material. Most of us can say with some confidence that polystyrene is a form of air-blown plastic. We might add that plastic itself is a petroleum product, the beginnings of which reach back into prehistory with the accumulation of massive amounts of dead vegetive matter.

Our comprehension, already rather tenuous, breaks down at this point. The majority of people have never had a hand in manufacturing polystyrene cups, likely never entered a factory where they are made, and probably never even saw, touched, or smelled its raw material, which usually lies buried somewhere, if not in the bowels of the earth, then in the darkness of tanks and pipes. From a literal empirical perspective, our knowledge of the cup's substance is abstract nearly to the point of vacuity. We have no real experience of it and therefore it fails at a visceral level to make sense to us. In its appearance as a commodity, the cup shows up shrouded in a veil of obscurity. Our "general mystification as to how the available goods are produced" intensified by "an increasingly less physical relation to the wealth of the society"[17] prompts us to conceive of the cup as an abstraction. Without sensible experience to correct our ideations, these are prone to sink to ever deeper levels of mystification.

The concept of disposability marks the bottom of the depth of mystified rational abstraction. Because our cognitive grasp of the matter of the cup, lacking the correctives of concrete experience, is so tenuous, even vacuous, it seems quite natural that the cup should strike us as immaterial, a substance imperceptible to the body. At any rate, this is the manner in which consumers comport themselves to the cup. Upon consumption, the cup is supposed to disappear. It no longer occupies a meaningful place in the world of available commodities. The consumer, when disposing of the cup, consigns it to the same experiential realm of obscurity from which it originated. General interest and knowledge of the procedures of waste management and recycling; of the technology of landfilling and incineration; of the life span of petrochemical products is, to all intents and purposes, nil on the consumer level. We know as much about the "away" to which we throw things as the distant "whence" from which they came. In this atmosphere of general ignorance, ontological anomalies can readily multiply. Our everyday consumer circumspection discloses material beings as if they had no physical being, no basis for presence. Meanwhile the mammoth tonnage of this phenomenally "immaterial" substance, puts forward a weighty, if silent, disputation.

Even if we were to force a parallel on the disposable cup and Heidegger's jug, aligning the former's "whence" with the dark productive energies of the earth, and its "away" with the celestial pull that draws the terrestrial powers out, we would still be constrained to admit that neither the "whence" nor the "away" dwell in the cup in the demonstrative way that earth and sky are said to dwell in the thing. This admission is crucial. The cup appears to a great extent self-enclosed. While it certainly refers to other commodities—"Would you like some fries with that?"—a similar experiential gap overshadows these as well. Since commodities exist only to the extent that they disengage the body, their overall network rests on no solid physical base. In their circulatory referrals to one another, commodities prevent any reference to the constitutive conditions that ground them. Commodities conceal the bulk of their being in their glossy, "showcase" appearing.

To smuggle in here the notion of ground might seem illicit. After all, does not the phenomenal immateriality of disposable commodities accord perfectly with the essentially groundless emptiness of all beings that the Buddhists uphold as primal truth? Yet, for the Buddhist, beings reveal this truth only to a proper understanding of them. That is, beings must refer to emptiness, the ultimate nonbeing of interpenetration, in a meaningful manner. To do so they must refer properly to human being, for, as Heidegger puts it, "only Dasein can be meaningful or meaningless (BT 142). Understanding characterizes human being. Moreover, human beings are meaningful for the same reason that they are "the null (ground) of a nullity." Their mortal finitude, their physical neediness, pries open the empty gap of nothingness through which Being passes. Only in reference to this null ground can beings reveal their truth.

There is little need to argue for the essential nullity of our existence. Humans have always understood themselves in the negative, as what we are not. Even a metaphysician of Descartes' stature recognized that "insofar as I participate in nothingness or non-being, that is, insofar as I am not the supreme being and lack a great many things, it is not surprising that I make mistakes."[18] Neither beast nor god, we must seek our definition in the open chasm between the two. Each philosophical yearning for knowledge, every psychic desire for fulfillment, all religious longings for completion and eternity in the afterlife confirm the reality felt in the pangs of physical hunger. Lack and nothingness define our being. How do disposable commodities refer to this immovable facticity of mortal existence? They do so in a distracting, dissembling, and ultimately dishonest fashion. Their referral is at bottom mendacious because it covers over rather than reveals the abysmal well of finitude.

The polystyrene cup does not manifest our neediness. The commodity substitutes for the brute fact of thirst the more "humane" or subjectivistic potential for pleasure. Thirst reflects a dearth, whereas pleasure connotes fullness. The semblance of choice between, say, tea or coffee, Coca-Cola or Pepsi masks with an illusory sense of freedom the total constraint imposed by our physicality. The uncontrollable and therefore disturbing fact that we must drink is overlaid by the choice that the consumer presumes to command over what she will drink. Selection, of course, relies on availability. This determinant of commodities, which ensures their ubiquitous, instantaneous, and easy access, gainsays the intrinsic limitations of nature. Commodities falsely represent the abundance of nature by ignoring the limits that naturally condition it.

Advertising, an essential component of the being of a commodity, also testifies to this. Commodities are not pitched to needs, which are limited, but rather to desires, which know no bounds. The disposable cup, as commodity, presents itself as bottomless, even if, *qua* individual, each cup has a set volume. However, since nothing distinguishes one cup from the next, the commodity as such, that is, convenient imbibition, subsumes all individuals into its limitless scope. Again the epistemological remoteness of the commodity, this time instantiated in the contents of the cup, allows for the process of subsumption. While most of us might know a roasted coffee bean to see one, few would recognize the plant in its natural state. As for soft drinks, the process of their becoming and the makeup of their being elude common comprehension. Indeed, they are tightly locked in trademark secrecy. Because Coca-Cola presents itself as thoroughly unnatural, the fountain of its creation seems untarnished by the limits of nature. To all appearances, it ought to flow interminably.

The absolute absence of any reference to finiteness in the commodity is not simply an ingredient that might be added or left out. The point and purpose of a disposable commodity, the sum value of its convenient being, are contained in its ability to save time. Essentially a time-saver, the commodity can bear no overt relation to that which wastes time: the human body. This sink down which our time seems irretrievably to drain constitutes, as I have endeavored to put beyond doubt, all sense, meaning, and experience we have of finitude. The raw and forever dying physicality of our being is a priori contraband in the market of commodities that circulates around the central value of convenience. The famed *memento mori* of the Middle Ages, that skeletal guest at every banquet, can never appear on the shelves of consumer society. There is simply no room for it to come into significant manifestation. Tierney explains this as a fallout of the death of God:

> The desire for a life of convenience, in which the limits of the body do not consume much of an individual's time, runs counter to the Christian idea that the toil and trouble of earthly life were a punishment for Adam's sin.[19]
>
> However, when one looks more closely at the direction in which modern consumption practices have developed, it becomes apparent that those practices continually assault the limits imposed by human embodiment. It is in this sense that the modern consumption of technology can be seen as a new way of denying the body, mortality, and necessity—as a new form of asceticism.[20]

While traditional forms used pain and austerity to lay bare the truth of corporeal finitude, the new asceticism uses pleasure to cover up this truth. It seeks to possess the world by indulging the flesh to the point of distraction. Forgetting that the world exists inseparably from our being-in it, and that both arise from the neediness of human finitude, the consumer encounters the world as a vast store of external and possessable objects. Such comportment is no less otherworldly and self-immolating as the extreme physical afflictions prescribed by traditional asceticism. Both scourge themselves with harmful dualisms. Both deny the present symbiotic existence of our being-in-the-world. However, as I will show, modern asceticism is more dangerous and destructive than its precursors. In its complete forgetfulness of the bodily finiteness that ontologically constitutes the world, it undermines the latter's very possibility of being. So whereas the old asceticism vainly strove to transcend the world, consumerism succeeds in destroying it.

The disposable cup does not relate to our embodiment because it prohibits being taken care of physically. Qua disposable, its presence makes no demands on us; we never think to wash the cup or return it to a safe and fitting place. To do so would be to mistake the commodified nature of the phenomenon, to disclose it in a manner incongruent with its phenomenal meaning. The appropriate treatment of the cup involves depositing it into some sort of refuse receptacle. We display our understanding for the essence of the cup through a physical act that in fact simply rehearses the a priori divorce and distance of the object from our bodily being; we throw it away, we pitch it out. This "out" and this "away" have no meaningful location, lying, as they do, beyond the phenomenal world of everyday consumption. The disposable object belongs to this unmanifest realm by virtue of the ontological rupture it instantiates between its own being and the condition for manifestness or disclosure, that is, the human body.

Its mortality makes the body a concern for us, which means our physicality embodies care, our essence. "However," as Heidegger avows, "only as long as Dasein *is*, that is, as long as there is the ontic possibility of an understanding of being, 'is there' being" (BT 196). Therefore "being (not beings) is dependent upon the understanding of being, that is, reality (not the real) is dependent upon care" (BT 196). The logical extension of this, which Heidegger has left for us to draw, is that reality depends on our bodily neediness. But logic need not carry the full burden of proof. Practical being-in-the-world supports it. The reason why "care is always taking care of things and concern" (BT 181) is that it is rooted in our physical need for things. "Accordingly, the relation to innerworldly beings lies in it ontologically" (BT 181). Since commodification intervenes in this relation and dissolves it by injecting into things a resistance to being taken care of, it necessarily also begins dissolving the world, the context for all understanding and disclosure. If taking care is always the primary articulation of care as embodied being-in-the-world, then technological freedom from care must come at the expense of our exile from the human world of disclosure and meaning.

One can exhibit "virtual reality" as evidence. The phenomena of this so-called reality appear as substantial objects despite the lack of matter that a physical relation to embodiment gives to things. Technology can temporarily deceive the senses into perceiving the phenomena as physical beings; however, the deception itself becomes conspicuous when the needful body attempts to take care of them. The virtual apple dangles mute and infinitely remote from the body's hungry pleas. The virtual building offers no shelter from inclemency. Virtual reality presents a metaphysical world in which the veneer of phenomenality enshrouds an ontologically hollow center. Its phenomena, bearing no relation to the embodied care on which reality depends, is in a basic sense devoid of being. Thus, they often appear fantastical, but, more important, preeminently disposable. The entire virtual world can be made to vanish at the press of a button with no sense of loss, pain, or anxiety on the part of the "wired" agent in charge. Since it does not relate at all to the fragile flesh of mortality, the brute ineluctable facticity of human being, only the caprice of subjective willing keeps it from descent into utter nothingness. Thus, virtual reality quite vividly images the oblivion of Being before our enthralled, subjective gaze.

Insofar as disposability signifies a complete physical separation of phenomena from body, it can be called the essence of commodities, whose purpose consists of freeing the subject from the time-wasting limits of the objectified body. Not only the polystyrene cup and all similar single-use items, but equally the ostensibly durable goods of consumerism, from automobiles to computers to household appliances, are determined by disposability. "Planned obsolescence" has become a household expression for this ontological fact. Yearly model changes, unnecessary multiplicity in the types and makes of components, materials with calculated short life spans, and incessant product development saturate durable commodities with the same evanescence intrinsic to plastic ballpoint pens. Although we do not generally discard houses, the increasing mobility of the still burgeoning urban populations leads us to consider our domiciles, or ourselves, as disposable, that is, removable, dislocated. Without rootedness in the subsoil of our own embodiment, we cannot hope to feel a solid footing in geographic and architectural place. When one neighborhood or city or even country becomes inconvenient, we simply pack up our troubles and leave. At the farthest extreme, even our relations with other people have taken on characteristics of disposability. Currently, the divorce rate hovers at over 50 percent of North American marriages. We quite blatantly dump the elder population into inconspicuous institutions. The obvious need for solicitude and physical care that the aged manifest, and the corresponding inconvenience, justify, if only tacitly, their disposal. As before, the complete metaphysicality of cyberspace provides the final test case. There, where no physical basis whatsoever grounds being-with-others, relationships, many between false personas, have the reliability and durability of paper serviettes.[21]

In the throwaway society, disposability has become more than a prevalent feature of commercial goods. It has become more than a way of life. Disposability now predominates as the primary mode of being of innerworldly entities that presents all phenomena as a priori trash. In *Being and Time* each ontological mode of being of innerworldly entities corresponds to a specific mode of being-in-the-world of human being. Our different ways of disclosing entities, dictated by our various ways of handling them, translates into different possibilities of disclosure. *Being and Time* concerns itself with two such possibilities: instrumentality or handiness, and objective presence (*Zuhandenheit* and *Vorhandenheit*). Since care constitutes our being-in-the-world, our primordial being-with-innerworldly beings discloses them in terms of the use they might have in our projects. Objective presence results from a hemorrhage in our initial practical comportment with the world:

> Being-in-the-world, as taking care of things, is *taken in by* the world which it takes care of. In order for knowing to be possible as determining by observation what is objectively present, there must first be a *deficiency* of having to do with the world and taking care of it. In refraining from all production, manipulation, and so on, taking care of things places itself in the only mode of being-in which is left over, in the mode of simply lingering with. . . . (BT 57)

This particular disinterested mode gives birth to modern empirical science, which reduces objects to assemblages of minute and useless parts. However, what Heidegger subsequently suggested, and what I have argued, is that a still more deficient mode of taking care discloses phenomena in a third ontological mode, namely disposability. Of course Heidegger himself does not talk of "disposability." He coins the word *Bestand*, which has been translated as "standing-reserve." Nonetheless, "disposable," to my hearing, more accurately captures Heidegger's intention. The word implies mobility, the capacity to be placed, displaced, and replaced. Thus, it expresses the ceaseless ordering from which this doubly deficient mode of disclosure never desists:

> The revealing that rules throughout modern technology has the character of setting-upon, in the sense of a challenging-forth. That challenging happens in that the energy concealed in nature is unlocked, what is unlocked is transformed, what is transformed is stored up, what is stored up is, in turn, distributed, and what is distributed is switched about ever anew. Unlocking, transforming, storing, distributing, and switching about are ways of revealing.[22]

Incessantly mobile, the disposable, like the standing reserve, cannot come to rest in the abiding presence that would make it physically real. "Whatever stands by in the sense of standing-reserve no longer stands over against us as object" (QCT 17). Instead it reveals itself as trash. The ontological hollowness of disposable commodities evacuates their phenomenal being of physicality. Lacking even objective presence— already a deficient modification of handiness—disposable commodities appear as always already disposed of. Their revelation presupposes their disappearance in the commodified order of technology.

While synonymous with standing-reserve, disposability has an important advantage over it in its common currency. We all know very well how to identify a disposable commodity, whereas picturing a standing-reserve requires more than a little philosophical imagination. Furthermore, we often explicitly base our relation to technology on the presumed convenience that disposability affords. There are times (e.g., should we have the misfortune of working on an assembly-line) that we may feel challenged forth to reveal all beings as mere units in "an inclusive rubric" (QCT 17). For the most part, however, technology cajoles us into not taking care of things. We voluntarily and happily buy disposables; they are not usually forced on us. We embrace disposability as the effective fulfillment of technology's emancipatory promise. Its direct connection to the metaphysical drive of technology makes "disposability" a more intelligible and illuminating term that "standing-reserve" in the world of convenient consumption. It indicates our own personal involvement with and responsibility for what can otherwise be misrepresented as the idol of unconditionally autonomous technology.

If the way of being of objective presence modifies the primacy of handiness through deficiency, then the still more deficient mode of disposability must nearly negate that primary possibility of being. The consumption of disposable commodities offers to eliminate the need we have for useful things, insofar as using something involves taking care of it. To need something, moreover, involves understanding it on some level with respect to our own mortal finitude. As the practical mode of care, taking care is cotemporaneous and coextensive with human existence; only because we are in essence careful can we be lured by a promise of freedom from taking care. This is why disclosing beings as objectively present takes care of them only deficiently. Disclosing them as disposable, where every trace of use for mortal need is completely obliterated, is likewise taking care of them, but in this case negatively. We reveal disposables within the signifying luminosity of care by not taking care of them. If the comportment corresponding to objective presence is a kind of passive reflection on objects, it would seem fit to call the comportment corresponding to disposability as active uncaring.

Uncaring

By uncaring I wish to stress the ontological, but by no means ontic, contradiction of a mode of careful being-in-the-world that seeks to avoid taking care of innerworldly beings. Otherwise put, it is the contradiction of an essentially embodied being, disinterested, indeed indifferent to its physicality, hence hostile to the basis of its embodiment. The true metaphysical promise of technology aims at freeing us from care, from being-in-the-world-toward-death. On the physical plain, however, its technique of attainment is constrained to practical measures; it must mitigate our need to take care of the physicality embodied both in our own flesh and in the finite matter of other beings. To do so, it empties phenomena of the primordial usefulness of their being that necessarily refers to the neediness of mortal human existence. Thus, technology, notwithstanding its inherent tendency to reduce things to means and ends, reveals them as ultimately useless. A climate of frivolity and triviality is created by the manifest uselessness of the world of consumption, which appears to the continuously vacationing consumer as already wasted. To be is to shop, for shopping becomes an end in itself—the consummation of all our busy production and consumption. *What* one buys matters less than the actual act of acquisition because intrinsic to this act is the moment of disposal, which subsequently permits and even prompts further acquisition. Shopping turns into a sport that awards trash as its trophies.

Although *Being and Time* does not incorporate an ontology of trash into the analytic of human being, its so-called pragmatism lays the necessary foundations. Heidegger's insistence on the ontological priority of instrumentality makes it possible to see how deficiencies in the primary practical concern with the world would lead to the disappearance of physically commanding innerworldly things. The reality of the world grows more virtual, hence disposable, as our physical engagement with it—our physical need to take care of it—wanes. We engage with the world first and foremost out of necessity. Our inherent insufficiencies throw us into the world that we must make use of and not merely observe, as if gods, unmoved. But does not this emphasis on the pragmatic concern of everyday existence make possible the technological subordination of all things to the gratification of the metaphysical will? Is technological exploitation of Being not its logical conclusion? Hubert Dreyfus poses these same questions pointedly:

> It follows that opposing the Cartesian subject/object distinction in terms of an account of Dasein as a user of equipment becomes an ambiguous form of opposition; for it is no longer clear whether such an analysis offers a critique of technology in the form of a transcendental account of the pre-technological understanding of equipment, or whether, under the guise of a transcendental account of everyday activity, such an analysis

reflects a transition in the history of the way equipment *is* which prepares the way for technology. In other words, it is not clear whether *Being and Time* opposes technology or promotes it.[23]

Dreyfus mounts a strong argument for the latter alternative. Consequently, he finds a marked difference between the supposedly failed early critique of technology and its successful successors after Heidegger's turn. Again my reading is less divisive. Although certainly incomplete, *Being and Time's* latent critique of technology contains seeds that later come to fruition.

The invaluable contribution of *Being and Time* to this critique lies in its sustained demonstration that, as A. T. Nuyen puts it,

> to be human is to be in a world, which means to have concernful dealings with entities in the world, including nature. To have human dignity, then, is to have concernful dealings with nature; it is not to adopt a "hands off" approach, or the attitude of "leaving nature to nature," if that means living "side-by-side" with, or co-existing with nature. In this manner of living, we face nature "non-circumspectively," even though we may not be doing so disinterestedly. In this manner of living nature is excluded from the *a priori* structure of human existence, and is brought into our "world," such as it is, only afterwards. For Heidegger. this manner of living is inauthentic. It is indeed undignified.[24]

Its inauthenticity lies in the obstacle such a mode of being-in puts before a dependent being-with that other beings need to manifest their truth. The parallel indignity comes from the consequent incapacity we suffer preventing us from comporting ourselves in a way that befits mortal humanity:

> Only because we have concernful dealings with nature as dwellers on earth can we cherish, care for, protect and preserve nature. The Indians in the Amazon forests care for their forests, their world, only because they live *in* it, much more so than if they merely lived *off* it, and much more so than anyone of us who thinks that those forests have some intrinsic value which obliges us to leave them alone.[25]

Indeed stronger arguments than Dreyfus's have been made that reveal the preoccupation of the North American environmental movement for wilderness preservation (the hands-off approach) as itself a by-product of technological consumerism.[26] Only once we have thoroughly subdued and anthropomorphized the earth do we develop a taste and will to regard nature in the impassive stance of the comfortable aesthete. By prioritizing the ontological significance of pragmatic human existence, Heidegger reinstates the ultimate authority of mortal finitude.

Uncaring contradicts the revelatory nature of use. By negating our concernful dealings with beings, uncaring does violence to their essence. A quarter-century after the publication of *Being and Time*, Heidegger elaborated its basic insight:

> "Using" does not mean mere using up, exploiting. Utilization is only the degenerate and debauched form of use. When we handle a thing, for example, our hand must fit itself to the thing. Proper use does not debase what is used—on the contrary, use is determined and defined by leaving the used thing in its essential nature. But leaving it that way does not mean carelessness, much less neglect. On the contrary: only proper use brings the thing to its essential nature and keeps it there. (WCT 187)

The essential nature of a thing resides in its thinghood, that is, its ability to refer beyond itself to the unifying interdependence of world. But this requires care, and not simply as an abstract ontological referent. It requires practical, manual taking care of the physical being of the thing. "'To use' means, first to let a thing be what it is and how it is. To let it be this way requires that the used thing be cared for in its essential nature— we do so by responding to the demands which the used thing makes manifest in the given instance" (WCT 191).

The demands for care of things echo the physical demands of our own needful bodies. The relation to ourselves that the used thing establishes by referring to our mortal care is not one of subordination. Rather it is one of equal kinship. Physically taking care of a thing in a way that lets it be what it is acknowledges, even if only tacitly, that the thing shares the same essential fragility of our embodied existence. This is not to say that things are mortal. No, "only man dies" (PLT 178). What practical taking care acknowledges is the tendency of all physical beings to degrade, decay, to lapse into nothingness. By caring for things, that is, using them properly, we of course preserve our own bodily being, but at the same time we keep Being as such from the abyss of nothingness that surrounds it.

Another way to see this is to recall the disclosive nature of practical concern. A hammer is most truly a hammer when we use it as such in the careful activity of construction. Our disclosive understanding of its being is primordially practical. Outside this concerned activity performed in the service of our needs, the object remains a hammer at best only nominally. Left to rust and rot in the rain, the object becomes no hammer at all, but instead waste. Its being actually disappears when we negligently leave it alone, because its being depends on its physical integrity and potential usefulness. The needs in the service to which the hammer is put to use, while fundamentally physical, also include so-called "higher" human needs for art and veneration. The hammer is no less a hammer when used to fashion a stage or shrine than when to construct an unadorned shelter. But the reason humans need physical theaters and houses of worship is that such concrete places establish the structure in which we can continue to work out the mystery of embodied being-in-the-world with our mind and spirit.

Acknowledging the fragility of things, useful taking care a fortiori understands the needy finitude in the service of which such things are used. When we take time to maintain the physical integrity of those things that help sustain our own embodied being, we provide ourselves with an opportunity to remember our complete dependence on other beings. Without the opportunity for mindfully taking care of things, we tend all too quickly to forget that our own being is essentially in a world with others. We then take things for granted, which in itself is bad enough. But worse, we lose sight of the truth of our being and begin posing as self-sufficient, eternal subjects who can flex willful authority over the being of beings. We throw things out and presume to negate their being. All we have succeeded in doing thereby, however, is to bereft ourselves of the most valuable service any thing can offer, namely, the thing's ability to "stay the fourfold into a happening of the simple onehood of the world" (PLT 181). "The thing things world" (PLT 181) only by revealing the mutual dependencies, the interpenetration of all worldly beings, ourselves included. Because our embodied being-in-the-world is the field for all revelation, the very thinghood of the thing itself depends on a proper understanding of our own finite nature. Thus, the primary ontological function of a thing is to act as a mnemonic to call to mind our mortality. Proper use implies a truthful recollection of the finitude of Being.

As Levin has said, this recollection belongs to the body. For care to recognize itself, it must see itself in the mirror that attentive and manual taking care of physical things puts before it. Otherwise care remains blind to its constitutive finitude. It fails to grasp, sense, and comprehend the meaning of its essentially physical being when it no longer feels the need to handle the physical things that respond to it. The thing's reflection of cosmic finitude is perhaps the clearest interpretation of what Heidegger obscurely calls "the mirror-play of the worlding world" (PLT 180). It shows that Being occurs within the frame of Nothingness and at the same time that "Death is the shrine of Nothing" (PLT 178). It follows that, because everything has its place within the precincts of this shrine, each demands its proper sacrificial and reverent use. "Out of the ringing mirror-play the thinging of the thing takes place"([PLT 180). Any technological freedom from taking care of things must necessarily eliminate their thinghood. At the profoundest ontological level, disposability is the annihilation of things, which means the disintegration and ruin of the world. With that goes all possibility of being-in it.

Trash ultimately signifies the disposal of the truth of our humanness. Since this humanness alone harbors an ontological understanding, trash equally disposes of Being as such. While fallenness and forgetfulness are inevitable elements of the human condition, the promise of technology at once exacerbates, legitimizes, and institutionalizes them. Technology promises freedom from taking care that amounts to ignorance of the careful nature of our finitude. As Tierney suggested, this promise supplanted its predecessor; the death of God made void the old promise of religion. The earlier promise, although spiritual in intention, was physically demanding. To this day, religion focuses around practical, though consecrated, worldly engagement. Part of the surviving ritual, for instance, of the Catholic Mass is the careful preparation of the Paschal Feast followed by the attentive washing of the chalice and the return of the uneaten Eucharist to the tabernacle. Few priests, one suspects, entertain the idea of substituting the chalice for a disposable polystyrene cup, despite the possible gain in convenience afforded by the substitution. We can now appreciate the Buddhist's, not to mention the Shakers' and Saint Benedict's emphasis on not only the physical but also the spiritual necessity of humble, manual work. It cradles us in the truth of Being.

Compassion

Authentic taking care, properly using things, lets them be by allowing our ontological disclosive mortality to enter into its most appropriate relation to Being. When we recall that Heidegger's notion of *Gelassenheit*, letting be, originated from the Christian mysticism of Meister Eckhart, where the same notion means spiritual detachment from objects, we begin to sense the sacredness of Heidegger's pragmatism. Heidegger never opposes earth to sky, mortals to divinities, but insists that the being of each relies on the unity of all. As unifying foci, things, with the worldly engagement they demand, can serve as lenses through which we gain sharper insight into the true relation of finitude to its source. Heidegger's ontological reverence for things simply modifies the proper spiritual reverence for them that Thomas Merton considers crucial to an authentic Christian life:

All things are at once good and imperfect. The goodness bears witness to the goodness of God. But the imperfection of all things reminds us to leave them in order to live in hope. They are themselves insufficient. We must go beyond them to Him in Whom they have their true being.

We leave the good things of this world not because they are not good, but because they are only good for us insofar as they form part of a promise. They, in turn, depend on our hope and detachment for the fulfilment of their own destiny. If we misuse them, we ruin ourselves together with them. If we use them as children of God's promises, we bring them, together with ourselves, to God.

"For the expectation of the creature waiteth for the revelation of the sons of God. . . . Because the creature also itself shall be delivered from the servitude of corruption into the liberty of the children of God." (Romans 8:19–21)[27]

The imperfection of things is none other than their goodness; the two are not distinct. In their demand that care be taken of them, things remind us of the essential insufficiency of our common physicality. Our taking care of them is thus an act of remembrance of our own dependent imperfection that needs them to be. Reminded of our utter dependency and fragility, we may grow humble, thankful, and purified of the ontologically divisive egoism that posits existence as a confrontation between willful subject and inert object. Proper use of things allows us to become careful in the rich, selfless way that Mayeroff describes: "in caring as helping the other grow. I experience what I care for (a person, an ideal, an idea) as an extension of myself and at the same time as something separate from me that I respect in its own right."[28]

Indelible marks of the large intellectual debt that Heidegger owed to Christian thinkers such as Eckhart and Kierkegaard, and the spiritual debt he owed to his Catholic heritage appear throughout his philosophy. In case his interpretations of humans as the shepherds of Being; of things as imperfect principles of unity, of the inclusion of divinities in the fourfold of the world sound too culturally relative, we need only consider the profound affinities of his thought to various Asian religions, especially Buddhism. Zimmerman draws out the mutual sympathies well:

Regarding the technological disclosure of things, Buddhists would argue that even though all beings are merely temporary experiential gestalts, they are nevertheless sentient. It is wrong to inflict pain on sentient beings in the hopeless technological quest to make the ego immortal, all-powerful, and permanent. Because some beings are apparently more "sentient" than others, many Buddhists emphasize alleviating the suffering of humans and animals. Yet Buddhists also maintain that because all beings are interrelated, sentience cannot be restricted to a particular class of beings, especially if such restriction leads to a hierarchical scheme that justifies domination of some entities by others.

Clearly, issues concerning what sorts of suffering people may inflict on nonhumans in order to feed, clothe and house themselves are important and thorny, though they cannot be discussed here. Buddhism, Heidegger and Naess [the intellectual founder of deep ecology] argue that puncturing the illusion of permanent selfhood would alleviate the infliction of such suffering by freeing one from the illusory quest for total control. Being liberated from the illusion of egocentrism also frees one for spontaneous compassion toward other beings, human and nonhuman alike. One "lets things be" not for any external goal, but instead simply from a profound sense of identification with all things.[29]

What Buddhists call infinite compassion, compassion that encompasses all beings, springs from finiteness itself. For what weaves all beings into the vast web of interdependence, whose pattern reveals itself as the manifest world, is the revelatory finitude of our needy, careful, physical being. Disposability signifies the unravelling, not of the web of interdependence, which is immutable, but rather of its apparent pattern. In the chaotic mess of trash we fail to pick out our being in other beings.

Our failure to feel a sense of identification with all things severely cramps our innate capacity for compassion . Compassion literally means to suffer with and implies a common sensuality. At its root, our compassion has a physical basis and extends only as far as our potential sensibility. Commodities, we have seen, desensitize us in a number of ways. They often overwhelm the senses, as in the case of junk food, with excessive stimuli, causing the senses to withdraw in self-defense. Reducing the need for manual interaction and comprehension with things, commodities also decrease the skillful sense we make of beings through a practical familiarity with their physicality. We gradually become insensible to the mystifying commodities we seldom grasp or understand. The insensitivity of technological existence inures us to the mostly concealed cruelty and destruction that perpetuates the consumer society. The techniques, for example, of industrial meat production are nothing short of rationalized savagery. As an ontological mode, disposability can only presence to a being-in-the-world grown insensate to the "worldly," in Heidegger's sense, nature of things. A disembodied being cannot itself suffer, let alone experience compassion for what it cannot feel. The uncaring bred by our consumption of commodities steels us against the attentive compassion that all entities, by virtue of their being, deserve.

Applying the concepts of suffering and compassion to animals and even to inanimate beings may seem to stretch them to the point of tearing. Do these not become empty terms when extended beyond the human or, at very most, higher animal species? I see no method of arguing for or proving the universality of compassion. All one can do is to look to figures believed to instantiate this virtue in order to discover its acceptable range. In the Western tradition, Saint Francis stands out as a paragon of compassion and lover of humanity. Whether apocryphal or real, the stories we read and admire of him present us with a "mirror of perfection" and of infinite compassion. On an occasion when his clothes caught fire he forbade their extinguishment for fear that the fire would suffer hurt. "For whatever necessity urged him, he would never extinguish a fire or a lamp or a candle, with so much pity was he moved toward it."[30] And "when he washed his hands, he used to choose such a place that the water which fell should not be trodden by his feet."[31] Who can picture this generally accepted incarnation of human compassion thoughtlessly disposing a cup or newspaper?

Saints and their Buddhist peers, bodhisattvas, may well have attained the detachment requisite for proper use, but for the rest of fallen, unredeemed humanity infinite compassion looks a grand impossibility, not to mention an economic catastrophe. To care for water with as much solicitude that a mother brings to her child would be to paralyze oneself in the business of the workaday world. Our physical neediness, the very thing that weaves our being inextricably together with all other beings, also blunts our sensitivity to their affliction in order to expedite its own temporary satisfaction. So while a necessary condition for compassionate caring, our neediness is far from sufficient for the practice of compassion. An otherwise puzzling passage of Heidegger's becomes intelligible in this respect: "Proper use is neither a mere utilizing, nor a mere needing. When we merely need, we utilize from the necessity of a need. Utilizing and needing always fall short of proper use. Proper use is rarely manifest and in general is not the business of mortals. Mortals are at best illumined by the radiance of use" (WCT 187). The detachment of the saints divinizes them, yet they remain fully, indeed perfectly, human. Still mortal, they conduct themselves as if they had become immortal. Their human immortality does not result from an elimination of need but rather from a joyful acceptance of the latter. Saints exist as if already resurrected. Resurrection of the actual, physical body is, at least for Catholics, central to their doctrine and faith. Similarly, the bodhisattvas are thought to have escaped the cycle of birth and death by grace of their superlative virtue and to have entered the paradisiacal nirvana. Yet their profound sympathy for the afflictions of all phenomenal beings compels them to assume again a physical body to assuage the immensity of worldly suffering. The fact that humans cleave to such personages for solace and edification demonstrates that we uphold their lives as models for our own needful conduct. Their illumination is of no use if imitation does not try to rise up to meet it. Proper use may well not be the everyday business of mortals, but it certainly is their appropriate concern and aspiration.

Violence

While fallen everyday being-in-the-world prevents the practice of proper use, its specific mode of uncaring destroys the possibility of compassion. Violence permeates commodity consumption. This violence is foremost ontological, but, owing to the interdependence of being, it wreaks physical havoc as well. So as to again avoid the objection of distorting a notion through its wrongful application, let us first deal with the physical violence inherent in technological uncaring.

The science of ecology teaches that species coexist in such a finely balanced state of mutual dependency that any adverse effect on one member of an ecosystem ripples deleteriously throughout the whole. We all know, though care not to let it be known, that trash, together with the many polluting processes involved in its creation, harms the environment. At some level, we also intuit that any harm done to the world must eventually damage a being that cannot exist otherwise than essentially in it. If forcefully withholding food from a hungry man counts as a form of violence, then so must the assaultive techniques of industrial agriculture, which strip the soil of its fertility, poison the surrounding watertable, decimate biodiversity, and generally undermine all the many conditions necessary for the continued cultivation of healthful food. Agribusiness thus amounts to the starvation of future generations. If we do not hesitate to consider slavery a violent social institution, then can we come to any other conclusion about the rapid growth of dangerous and unjustly compensated sweatshop labor that hides behind the illusorily inexpensive availability of disposable commodities?

By failing to realize the universal breadth of care, technological uncaring has entangled us moderns in a unique and precarious ethical situation. Simply leading our everyday lives of ordinary consumption causes us to act immorally, that is, implicates us directly in the undue suffering of others. We read the various statistics in the newspaper, but, due to our technological insensitivity and security, the magnitude of their moral condemnation does not impress or disturb us. The industrialized world, containing only 20 percent of the planet's population, helps itself to 80 percent of its natural resources. By all reasonable standards, an inequity of this stature towers as a fearsome monument to violence, especially when set against the very credible argument "that economic growth in the West has historically rested on the economic and ecological exploitation of the Third World."[32]

These overt demonstrations of violence against humans are symptomatic of a deeper and covert ontological violence at the heart of technological uncaring. By trashing entities, we intend to annihilate their being. Baudrillard simply elaborates the economic imperative for disposability, legitimized by a capitalistic system under the constant threat of overproduction and market saturation, when he writes:

> The consumer society needs objects in order to be. More precisely, it needs to destroy them. The use of objects leads to their dwindling disappearance. The value created is much more intense in violent loss. This is why destruction remains the fundamental alternative to production: consumption is merely an intermediate term between the two. There is a profound tendency within consumption for it to surpass itself, to transfigure itself in destruction. It is in that that it acquires its meaning.[33]

The economic meaning of destruction implies relentless capitalistic expansion, whereas the ontological meaning signifies the contraction or withdrawal of Being. The violence of consumption concentrates on the disappearance of beings; when consumed, disposable items are supposed to vanish. Although their material remains, it is willfully denied presence within the contextualized disclosure of the meaningful world. We want no sight of our trash. Jettisoning all responsibility for the physicalness of the commodity, the consumer forcefully falsifies its being. We do not let the disposed disposable appear, do not let it be as it is in the open truth of worldly disclosure.

The refusal on our part to let beings be indicates that, once again and at its profoundest level, technological violence essentially assails humans. In other words, the violence of technology is fundamentally ontological because it wrenches us away from our ontological nature. This nature sends us out to take care of things, yet commodities physically hinder, if not altogether prohibit, the manual expression of our essential care. We falsify our own careful being in the destructive disclosure of beings as trash, as evacuated objects not worthy of appearance. When only nothing, not even ourselves, is left to be, then nihilism prevails. The oblivion of Being swallows up our own self-diminished being.

Conclusion

We have just now caught a glimpse of human extinction. It approached us out of the ontological shadows surrounding the modern phenomenon of trash. In this sense, the ontology of trash comes to appear as the study of the impossibility of ontology. Of course, there could not be any ontology without human inquiry to pursue it. More important, however, there can be no Being without an ontological nature to receive it. In all the many ways discussed, trash is antithetical to nature. It contradicts our careful disclosure. It conceals and dissembles the interdependence of all beings. By so doing, trash expels things from their essence, which consists in referring beyond themselves to the multiplicity of phenomena in such a way as to unify and integrate them into a sensible world. As the result of the abnegation of our own physicality, trash signifies the negation of physicality as such, on which all worldly existence, that is, Being relies. Technology promotes an uncaring way of being-in that, unsurprisingly, discovers objects as uncared for, as disposable. The grand ontological paradox of this is that, a priori trash, the phenomena of disposables counteract every stage of the process of disclosure that makes phenomenal existence possible. Trash thus piles high in free suspension over an abyss of nothing. But this abyss must not be confused with the ultimate emptiness of all beings within the web of its worldly interdependence. This abyss dissolves every relation by destroying the thread that relates all things. Out of this abyss appears the phenomenon of human extinction.

CHAPTER SIX

Human Extinction

But for the time being—we do not know for how long—man finds himself in a perilous situation. Why? Just because a third world war might break out and bring about the complete annihilation of humanity and the destruction of the earth? No. In this dawning atomic age a far greater danger threatens—precisely when the danger of a third world war has been removed. A strange assertion. Strange, indeed, but only as long as we don't meditate.

In what sense is the statement just made valid? This assertion is valid in the sense that the approaching tide of technological revolution in the atomic age could so captivate, bewitch, dazzle, and beguile man that calculative thinking may someday come to be accepted and practised *as the only* way of thinking.

What great danger might then move upon us? Then there might go hand in hand with the greatest ingenuity in calculative planning and inventing indifference toward meditative thinking, total thoughtlessness. And then? Then man would have denied and thrown away his own special nature—that he is a meditative being. Therefore, the issue is the saving of man's essential nature. Therefore the issue is keeping meditative thinking alive.

—Martin Heidegger, *Discourse on Thinking*

We are trying to learn thinking. Perhaps thinking, too, is just like building a cabinet. At any rate, it is a craft, a "handicraft." "Craft" literally means the strength and skill in our hands. The hand is a peculiar thing. . . . The hand is infinitely different from all grasping organs—paws, claws, or fangs. Only a being who can speak, that is, think, can have hands and can be handy in achieving works of handicraft.

—Martin Heidegger, *What Is Called Thinking*

Nomadic peoples do not put time into permanent dwellings. Their transience prevents their future from abiding in any one place, and nothing lasts that does not somehow participate in an abiding future. Modern

157

technological consumers do not put time into beings. The triumph of convenience means that we need not expend ourselves in the maintenance of things. But there is more to it than this. Enthralled by disposability, we encounter objects as essentially evanescent, instantaneous. The disposable commodity, already cast out of the foreseeable future, is deprived of all temporal duration. Because it does not figure in our world-disclosing projects, the disposable, like the firmly established domicile of the nomad, remains unfounded and unreal. Lacking access to the future, commodities are imprisoned in immediacy.

When, during the Peloponnesian War, a plague besieged Athens, the city gates gave way to an onslaught of licentiousness. Thucydides reports that the otherwise sober citizenry

> reflected that life and wealth alike were transitory, and resolved to live for pleasure and enjoy themselves quickly. No one was eager to persevere in the ideals of honour—it was so uncertain whether they would be spared to attain the object; present enjoyment, and all that contributed to it, was accepted as both honourable and useful. Fear of gods or law of man were no restraint. They thought that it made no difference whether they worshipped God or not, as they saw all alike perishing; no one expected to live to be brought to trial for his offenses, but each felt that a far severer sentence had already passed upon them all and hung over their heads, and before this felt it was only reasonable to enjoy life a little.[1]

The terrifying possibility of no future facing Athens compressed time into an instant. For the condemned city, only the present existed; it alone had meaning. But its meaning was corrupted by its own confinement. The present began to rot in its own hopelessness and self-enclosed futility. Pleasure became the principle of pointlessness.

The hedonism and materialism of consumer culture have also, one could say, become principled, in the sense that they are accompanied by a certain moral exigency. At all costs, the consumer must enjoy herself now. Does the consumer society exist under a similar temporal compression as that which plagued Athens? Might not its pleasure imperative derive from a future made abysmal by the possibility, simultaneously acknowledged and ignored, the real possibility of human extinction?

Although harboring nomadic ambitions on a galactic scale, modern terrestrial humanity has not yet become nomad. We still reside in cities. However, in our mobility, now foreshadowed by extinction, we surround ourselves with objects that share our transience and instantaneity. What use is it to build tools that will outlive *homo faber*? Why put time into durables when we ourselves are apparently disposable? The same lack, even but dimly perceived, of the future that sends us reveling to the shopping outlets also stocks them full of trash. Impermanence, that chief characteristic of disposables, seems a likely derivative of the temporal void created by the possibility of human extinction. In this respect, both consumers and their commodities appear as products of this titanic possibility.

Such an interpretation is as partial as it is plausible. It touches but half the matter. Disposable commodities, whose convenience purportedly saves time, would seem the reasonable response to the sharp abridgement of time implied by our extinction. Time's imperilled state would seem to justify our obsession for trying to save it. When faced with imminent destruction, prudence dictates living in the moment, which consistently includes consuming momentary objects. That the threat of extinction motivates the production of disposables is itself an intriguing thesis, one that satisfies certain psychological questions. Nevertheless the interpretation is ontologically insufficient.

Dissatisfaction with this interpretation arises when explanation shifts from the being of commodities to the being of extinction. Stating that extinction brings forth the phenomenon of trash simply buries the basic ontological problem one level deeper. How does the phenomenon of extinction come into being? What, in other words, produces human extinction and can account for its dismal present influence?

The troubling answer to these unsettling questions is ourselves. For the most part we assume a kind of anticipatory responsibility for human extinction. We know that our nuclear weapons, indeed even our nonmilitary nuclear generators, could snuff out all life on the planet many times over. International political protocols, such as the Kyoto Accord, acknowledge that disaster awaits our current rate and scale of consumption. Hollywood capitalizes on the underlying apprehension of a scientific people towards the audacity of their specialists' research and ingenuity. Such dubious accomplishments as the discovery of biological weapons make it painfully clear that, whether accidentally or intentionally, our curiosity could well prove fatal.

The human imagination has a penchant for the cataclysmic. Even in his infancy, civilized man suspected his end was nigh. Long before Greece gave birth to metaphysics, doom overshadowed the working days of Hesiod, who entertained small hope for the future of his species:

I wish I were not counted among the fifth race of men,
This is the race of iron. Neither day nor night
Will give them rest as they waste away with toil

And pain. Growing cares will be given them by the gods,
And their lot will be a blend of good and bad.
Zeus will destroy this race of mortals
When children are born gray at the temples.[2]

Plagues, famines, meteorological catastrophes, atmospheric upheavals, and sundry other natural disasters have long put the continuance of human habitation on planet earth into question. The intrinsic vulnerability of the individual person plays out on the aggregate level of humanity as a perpetual state of species-precariousness. Human extinction has always been a possibility. But only in the twentieth century did human extinction become a phenomenon.

When does possibility become phenomenon? What differentiates our perilous situation from the no more desirable circumstances of Hesiod's ferric fellows? Both groups face potential destruction, and, in fact, the ancient situation, on its own interpretation, fares much worse than the modern. Whereas our perpetuity at times looks doubtful, the surety of a god guarantees the annihilation of Hesiod's. There is something of importance in this. We admit to the imminence of apocalyptic danger, yet we believe that fate lies in our own hands. If the planet and the human species do in fact need saving, we are the ones to save it. We presume that it is up to us to divert disaster and postpone indefinitely the actualization of the potentiality of our destruction. Such notions of grandeur have sent us chasing ludicrous fantasies like the colonization of Mars. Scientists zealously and with no small expense continue their philanthropic construction of the defensive missile system designed to deflect wayward comets. We have already begun hatching plans of escape from our solar system before its tired old sun betrays us and sputters out. All this busyness bespeaks our tacit assumption that any species that winds up extinct deserves its fate for not adapting quickly, boldly, and cunningly enough. Should we ever come to meet our end, we little doubt but that it will be by our own hand. Whether through nuclear warfare, environmental despoilage, or some gross scientific miscalculation, we feel that our demise will bear our signature. We claim sole authorship over it, assuming, not without arrogance, that nothing less than ourselves has the strength to defeat us. If allowed to happen, human extinction will be the final product to roll off the assembly line of our global industrial–military complex.

Those who contemplated human extinction before the age of technology feared the wrath of God. They thought that the fate of humanity was left to the discretion of supernatural intelligence. This gave the execution of humanity tragic overtones. Such is not the case today. The tragic element has bled out of the modern phenomenon of extinction.

Because "we multiply our opportunities for waste as we improve our control and prediction of events,"[3] by presuming exclusive control over our collective existence, we can perceive its loss only as a waste. Howsoever regrettable, we cannot even call our extinction unfortunate, since we have deprived fortune of any role in it. As waste, the phenomenon of human extinction implies neglect and failure, and an absolute failure at that. For if extinction means the negation of existence, then the failure it represents is existential and ontological. Literally, it is the failure to be and, specifically, the failure to be human. When we exterminate ourselves, we neglect and fail our being.

I have argued that the absolute waste of trash is also our ontological failure at being human. In this final chapter I hope to complete the argument by revealing the underlying identity between the twin phenomena of trash and human extinction. Intimations of their relatedness have emerged throughout. The technological effacement of the body prefigures the total elimination of embodiment accomplished in extinction. Likewise, the denial of needy mortality articulated through carefree commodity-consumption is affirmed retroactively by the annihilation of mortals. Trash attacks the contextualizing integrity of the world by substituting self-enclosed disposables for the referential, expansive essence of things that safeguard worldly integrity. Human extinction, for all intents and purposes, marks the end of the meaningful world.

These many relations between the two phenomena suggest that their kinship is closer than cause is to effect. They are, I argue, identical phenomena, trash being merely the present phenomenal manifestation of the possibility of extinction. Both result from our negative being-in-the-world in the mode of violence. Thus, the more commonsense interpretation—that trash leads us to extinction—and the earlier psychological interpretation—that extinction elicits trash—unite in the ontological interpretation that understands our technological existence as violently destructive of beings and, therefore, of our humanity, which is the shelter of Being as such. The last interpretation does not undermine the former pair, but rather furnishes them with a foundation of sufficient depth. However, before pronouncing any further identity statements, we must become clear on the present phenomenal nature of extinction.

The Phenomenon of Negation

Our study of trash excavated several layers of ontological contradiction resting on the void of technological nihilism. Disposable objects contradict the world-gathering power of things by preventing the human practice of care through which that power works. Since the contextual totality of the world conditions the possibility of all significant phenomenal appearing, the phenomenon of disposables also contradicts the conditions of the possibility of its own disclosure. Trash, in other words, consumes its own being. The phenomenon of extinction contains an identical contradiction. Jonathan Schell construes it this way: "The perplexity underlying the whole question of extinction, then, is that although extinction might appear to be the largest misfortune that mankind could ever suffer, it doesn't seem to happen to anybody, and one is left wondering where its impact is to be registered and by whom."[4] Extinction, in other words, happens to nobody. Its concept logically obliterates the possibility of human intelligence that supports all concepts. Inasmuch as no human understanding can survive to interpret and disclose the extermination of humanity, the latter can never come forth into meaningful presence. The very thought of extinction effaces itself, in that it necessarily entails the impossibility of thinking. "It is, above all, the death of mankind as this immortal source of all human subjects, not the death of mankind as an object, that makes extinction radically unique and 'unthinkable'."[5] Extinction means the obliteration of the very world that embeds all phenomenal appearances into the disclosive ground of meaning. Without this embeddedness, extinction itself could not ominously loom as an obtrusive feature of modern life haunting our media and collective consciousness.

On this account, extinction seems best regarded as an antiphenomenon. Its sheer potentiality might influence us, but its actuality cannot. The moment that extinction really presences as a worldly phenomenon coincides exactly with the moment that the possibility of any innerworldly presence has vanished. If "*phainomenon* means what shows itself, the self-showing, the manifest" (BT 25), then clearly extinction cannot be a modern phenomenon at all because its manifestation necessarily includes the absence of beholders. As Berkeley might say, *non esse sine percipi*. By what right, then, do we call human extinction a phenomenon unique to our day and radically different from the apocalyptic fears of previous eras?

We do so by the same right that we distinguish trash from waste. Waste, we saw, is obvious and offensive. Trash, on the other hand, has an intrinsic tendency to conceal itself and deceive. Trash dissembles the truth of its being by presenting itself as immaterial, innocuous substance divorced from the relations to physicality that weave all beings into the interdependent context of the manifest world.

Although no one who has ever eaten at a fast-food restaurant could, in good faith, deny the existence of disposables, the consumer encounters their useless objective presence as ontologically deficient. Trash appears as a negative phenomenon out of all meaningful joint with the convenient context of consumption. When, as consumers, we treat disposable objects as if they were nothing, we do not act inconsistently. "From time immemorial, philosophy has associated truth with being" (BT 196). An essentially deceptive phenomenon must show itself as empty and meaningless. However, since every mode of disclosure corresponds to a specific mode of disclosing, or being-in-the-world, the vacuum in the phenomenon of trash results from the subtraction of physical care from technological existence. Regarded ontologically, trash reflects our consumptive uncaring.

In a word, the truth of trash indicates our inauthenticity, our everyday deficient, technologically enhanced being-in-convenience. The same goes for extinction, which is a phenomenon of modernity that mirrors the deficiencies of trash. Like trash, the phenomenon of human extinction dissembles the truth of our basic disclosive mortality. Its deception makes it ontologically vacuous, able only to appear negatively, disassociated, ironically, from our embodied existential concerns. Thus, also like trash, even though extinction permeates modern existence, it never comes to its full, disturbing presence. We casually entertain various speculations concerning the perpetrator and the target of nuclear war or biosphere collapse, calculate the probability of their occurrence, dream up desperate science-fiction scenarios, and blithely continue to carry on our courtship of them. Because, again like trash, it covers over the truth of death, human extinction appears relatively harmless, out of touch with our consumer "reality" and, to that extent, cannot appear precisely as the destruction of thoughtful beings in a meaningful manner at all.

The question now becomes how does extinction, which implies universal human demise, dissemble death? What sense, if any, can Schell's statement have that "death is only death; extinction is the death of death"?[6] Our discussion anticipated the answer in the previous chapter when it cited this passage from Heidegger: "the self-assertion of technological objectification is the constant negation of death. By this negation death itself becomes something negative; it becomes the altogether inconstant and null" (PLT 125).

Objectification is the unfeeling, hence compassionless, attempt to technologically transmute our vulnerability and neediness into security and self-sufficiency, goals that have irresistible appeal. But willfully denying the truth of mortal embodiment, objectification generates the trash of disposables which prevents all careful activity that might recollect mortality. Death becomes a displaced object utterly forgotten, inconstant, and null. As its presence evaporates, it ceases to impress our present existence.

The absence of death poses a grave danger to Heidegger's ontology, so reliant is it on the "possibility of grasping Dasein as a whole" (BT 221). An individual becomes whole only through a resolute authentic relation to death wherein she understands and embraces her coming end as vital to her present being. Thus, an ontological understanding of death regards it as fully positive. Inauthenticity, on the contrary, as the prefix indicates, means a lack, an existential deficiency. For Heidegger, "a proper analysis of death remains purely "this-worldly" in that it interprets the phenomenon solely with respect to the question of how it *enters into* actual Dasein as its possibility-of-being" (BT 230). But the uncaring consumption of disposables bars death from entering into significant possibility. The hypertechnology of consumerism leaves human being lacking the authentic wholeness that comes only by relating to "death (as) a way to be that Dasein takes over as soon as it is" (BT 228).

Technological uncaring contradicts Heidegger's ontological assertion that, "in the broadest sense, death is a phenomenon of life" (BT 229). By evading the embodied needs of care, technology negates the world-constitutive power of mortal embodiment in relation to which all phenomena enter into appearance. Technological humanity does not disclose death as a phenomenon; it barely apprehends death as a possibility. For all the violence, both covert and celebrated, of the consumer world, death as the existential reality of every individual figures not at all in the rational calculations of convenient being. However, just as the technological negation of the positive, manifest phenomenon of waste engendered the negative, deceptive phenomenon of trash, so the negation of the positive phenomenon of death also has its negative pole: human extinction.

Because, existentially, mortals cannot escape "being toward the end of being" (BT 228), when death no longer signifies that end, some other phenomenon must takes its place. Due to its ontological deficiencies, the antiphenomenon of human extinction fills the gap most conveniently. Human extinction simply pushes the lacking, inauthentic, everyday understanding of death to its technological extreme.

> Entangled, everyday being-toward-death is a constant *flight from death*. Being *toward* the end has the mode of *evading that end*—reinterpreting it, understanding it inauthentically, and veiling it. Factically one's own Dasein is always already dying, that is, is a being-toward-its-end. And it conceals this fact from itself by reinterpreting death as a case of death occurring every day with others, a case which always assures us still more clearly that "one oneself" is still "alive." (BT 235)

In being-toward-extinction, I substitute for my own private death the public death of all. If I evade the distinctness of my own death by smudging it with the death of others, then my technique of evasion becomes exponentially more effective when I include the death of all others. The universal demise of humanity equals only the death of *das Man*, someone, luckily enough, I have never met. The antiphenomenon of extinction does not trouble us not simply because it never actually appears, never enters into our company. Over and above this, it tranquilizes us, lulls us into a blissful forgetting of our inescapable personal mortality.

We talk of the possibility of human extinction, perhaps soberly and earnestly, yet the incomprehensibility of its actualization removes it to an infinite, and therefore infinitely safe, distance. Human extinction may happen, but certainly not to me, not to my generation. Insofar as I have cast my lot with technological humanity, I have received inoculation against the bug of species annihilation. Technological man assures himself that it remains strictly in his power to pose and to answer the question of extinction. I know myself, and know that I am not suicidal. As technological man, therefore, I can rest comfortably in the confidence of continued survival. Giving up my little death to the unthinkable grandeur of human extinction, I attain a sort of immortality.

Extinction is the death of death, we now can see, because it eliminates mortality. It accomplishes this by dilating the limits of the mortal body so far beyond their native field that they lose all form and definition. The individual loses sight of the unique face of her own death in the threatened masses of a globalized humankind. Universalized mortality is infinite and thereby sheds its finitude. Finite human being quits mortality in the metamorphosis to the technological consumer. The evolutionary direction of this mutation, whether forward or back, is disputable. Tierney thinks it regressive:

> And if I may speculate on what the future holds for humanity's struggle against death, I think that death will eventually be overcome as a limit, and the body will indeed be eliminated as the source of limits or necessity. However, these so-called "achievements" will only be won at the cost of a greater dependency on the technological order, socialist or capitalist, which provides them.[7]

Others, however, view the same prospect more buoyantly. We have already heard Dewdney's sanguine prophecy: "It is possible that the next few generations will be among the last to die, and, if this is the case, future humans will regard the tragedy of death as an inconceivable horror and a cosmic waste."[8] But to repeat: whatsoever being does manage to survive "the next few generations . . . among the last to die," it will not be human. Having finally shuffled off the mortal coil, the essence of our being, our technologically consummated successors may bear passing resemblance but no existential relation to our present needy and human selves.

Time Gap

The metaphysical view from nowhere that looks with uncomprehending sadness on the cosmic waste of death is little dismayed by the universal trashing of meaningful being brought on by extinction. On the contrary, it takes consolation in the spectacle. As earlier discussed, trash does not concern the consumer because it is categorically denied access to the consumer's existential, embodied concerns. Unfit to be taken care of, the disposed commodity falls outside the disclosive relations of care. The unseen mountains of trash silently measure the spectacular heights of the technological good life. They testify to a mode of existence unencumbered by the demands of physicality and thus aver the fulfillment of technology's promise. The phenomenon of human extinction makes the same avowal, only more vociferously. The total elimination of embodied mortality is the logical terminus of metaphysical technology. This explains our otherwise irrational behavior that, even while cognizant of the their destructive nature, we eagerly continue to consume commodities and multiply trash. Both in consumption and in consequence (e.g., environmental degradation, ill health, sterility, etc.), disposable commodities pander to our metaphysical taste for transcendence.

Death conditions time. This fact lies open to various interpretations. Metaphysics construes the conditioning negatively, as an imposition of unwanted natural limits. Death, and its necessary accomplice, the always dying body, "are seen . . . as inconveniences in that they limit or interfere with the use of time."[9] In the previous chapter I already motioned toward the problem of treating time as an innerworldly being. The implication of the metaphysical position is that time is either something ready to hand, as when we efficiently "use it," or something objectively present, that conspicuously gets in our way. Every innerworldly being primordially disclosed in the mode of equipment has a purpose, a "what-for." When we ask the obvious question—what purpose could time possibly have?—we catch sight of the diminutive status given time by metaphysics. Time is forced into a station of subordination as the degraded mode of eternity. Metaphysics fixes on the eternal as the real and the true, the final what-for of time. Reason must use time as an instrument somehow to overcome temporality itself. But the changeable nature of time, its liability to limitation and its recalcitrance to rational control make it an unwieldy tool, ill-suited for its presumed task. Metaphysics, therefore, would better dispense with time than struggle to skillfully master it.

If finite time can serve the infinite eternal only in its self-destruction, then metaphysics must adopt the same violent attitude toward time as it does toward the body. Metaphysics no more wants to "save time" than it wants to take compassionate and patient care of mortal neediness. For time and embodiment are wedded together indissolubly by the bond of finitude. Just as technology strives to overcome the mortal body, it aims ultimately to transcend time. However, whatever success it achieves in this dual project is challenged by the contrary undercurrents experienced within the consumer culture. It seems that the more that consumers effectively efface the essential neediness of embodiment through commodified consumption, the more central a position the fetishized object of the body assumes in their lives. Right in the middle of the rationally illuminated world of technology there flourishes a veritable cult of the body. So, too, does time become an object of increasingly anxious, obsessive concern, the nearer that technology approaches time's elimination. These inconsistencies stem naturally from the core contradiction of a metaphysical attempt to base physical transcendence on the grounds of a scientific, reductive materialism.

Metaphysics, it was seen, regards the body as the source of waste. Metaphysics overcomes the natural, physical associations of waste through a process of rationalization and sublimation that transforms waste into trash. Because disposables appear as the willed fulfillment of the technological promise, and, by consequence, because technology presumes to design and control the existence of trash, the latter does not, metaphysically speaking, reflect finitude or failure. The antiphenomenon of trash wipes out the physical blemish of waste/body. A parallel effacement, occurring on the temporal plain, is effected by the antiphenomenon of human extinction. Of course, as already mentioned, extinction also implies the complete disappearance, or call it transcendence, of wasteful, mortal corporeality. But extinction attacks the threat of finitude especially and uniquely on the front of time. In terms of metaphysical destructiveness, human extinction is to time as trash is to the body. Both these antiphenomena, the first on the temporal level, the second on the physical, enter into a hostile and contrary relation to the finitude essential to human being.

We saw how technology takes care of the solicitous concern intrinsic to embodiment. It does so by a process of elimination that shrinks the possibility for that concern's expression through the physical taking care of things. Consuming commodities, the consumer surrenders her need to the rationalized care of technology. The greater her surrender of her mortal neediness, the less able she is to express her existential care through physical service to her finiteness. On the temporal plain, human extinction likewise corrodes the conditions of the possibility of care. By eliminating the future, just as trash eliminates embodied neediness, extinction undermines the foundations of human finitude.

"Of all the crimes against the future," writes Schell, "extinction is the greatest. It is the murder of the future."[10] Exactly how extinction manages to commit so capital a crime will be dealt with shortly. Prior to that explanation we need to understand why the death of death murders the future and how this prohibits care. That is, we require an interpretation of the phenomenon of extinction that displays it truthfully, not as the superlative evolutionary failure, but as our own absolute failure at being human.

Heidegger's characterization of care as being-toward-death is meant to make explicit the ecstatic forward momentum of our being. Lacking a demonstrable and determinative quiddity, our existence leans more to the side of possibility than actuality. To be sure, our existential concern orbits around our present being, but this being is always understood in light of what it might become. Even our most immediate engagements and preoccupations project purpose, intentions, assumptions, or conjectures onto the future.

But not only does becoming permeate our being, nonbeing determines it yet more profoundly. Death, the impossibility of our being, circumscribes every possibility of our existence. While the anticipatory nature of this circumscription associates it primarily with the temporal moment of the future, its circumference is nevertheless measured by the radius of the past. What we are and have been conditions what we may become. Our past conditions the future in the restrictive sense of limiting it, but equally our past establishes the existential platform necessary for all possible projections.

Existing as our conditioned possibilities, our being is, as Heidegger says, always ahead of itself. "The primary phenomenon of primordial and authentic temporality is the future" (BT 303). The past has no room for disclosure; its fullenss cannot let beings be. Only the empty but circumscribed openness of the future provides the clearing where phenomena may enter into the relation with our mortal projects that coordinates each phenomenon into the meaningful whole of worldly manifestation. Without the horizon of the future to receive the innumerable, though limited, projections of possibility, our being would remain inert, dumb, and meaningless. Thus, it is only nominally contradictory to call the future the site of present appearing. Because all beings presence in relation to the essentially anticipatory concern for mortality, they all arise, as it were, out of the unknowable darkness of the future. In other words, the world gathered and preserved in things is constitutively mortal and, as such, is essentially futural.

There could be no world without the future because without the future there would be nowhere for mortality to exist. Death, as the present "phenomenon of life," constantly throws our careful being beyond its present settled state into the void of conditioned possibility. Ontologically, as well as psychologically, death unsettles us, forever preventing us from resting full and complete, which is as much to say self-sufficient. Always being toward death but never reaching it as an actual innerworldly experience, our existence receives its lack, its incompleteness from the mortal essence of the future. "The ecstatic quality of the primordial future lies precisely in the fact that it closes the potentiality-of-being, that is, the future is itself closed and as such makes possible the resolute existentiell understanding of nullity" (BT 303). This coupled with the fact that "temporality temporalizes itself primordially out of the future" (BT 304) yields the conclusion that, "primordial time is finite" (BT 304).

Metaphysics hears this as a declaration of war. Primordial time, streaming out of mortal temporality, stands in the way of eternity. Such time is immanent, worldly, natural, and physical, it therefore is at odds with metaphysics' transcendent ambitions. Eternity can coexist with finite time no more than a mortal man can live forever. Limited time, just like the limitations of death, must, metaphysically speaking, be eliminated. Both sets of phenomena vanish with the disappearance of the future. Since the enclosed horizon of conditioned time cages in metaphysics' upward flight, full transcendence depends on the destruction of that mortal horizon. Thus, the death of death, death's overcoming, is accomplished in the metaphysical murder of the future.

How could the future possibly be murdered? A sort of sterile eternity would result from the annihilation of beings in which the primordial mortal future exists. With the extinction of all projecting beings metaphysics realizes itself. In other words, the actualization of metaphysics coincides with the categorical impossibility of all possibilities, that is, universal death. Given that temporality, with its inherent bias toward the mortal future, is the chief target of metaphysical hostility, the phenomenon of human extinction is more accurately called extermination. The death of death is also and necessarily the demise of time. Overcoming time overthrows human being.

According to Heidegger, our being-in-the-world necessarily and essentially includes being-with other such beings. While death individuates each person, it does not isolate the individual because, as a worldly, existential phenomenon, death is continually taking place with and through all other mortals who constitute the world. Schell, via Hannah Arendt, picks up the intrinsic community of mortality to investigate the dual crimes against death and time perpetrated by the present phenomenon of extinction. Although his language is not outwardly ontological, his conclusions are. Thus, he interprets the futural orientation of mortality in terms of a common world that encompasses all temporal and historical phenomena. "Death lies at the core of each person's private existence, but part of death's meaning is to be found in the fact that it occurs in a biological and social world that survives."[11]

Without this shared context of meaning, the phenomenon of death looks utterly nonsensical. It ceases to have significant presence within life, since "man, who has been described as the sole creature that knows that it must die, can know this only because he lives in a common world, which permits him to imagine a future beyond his own life."[12] An insignificant and unimaginable death—a death surrendered to the phenomenon of extinction—becomes vacuous and can no longer bear relation to our disclosive mortal concerns. In the absence of a personal relationship with death, our ecstatic being heads toward nothing, making our present existence absurd and literally unintelligible. Extinction contradicts the common world. But the "common world is not something that can be separated from the life we now live; it is intrinsic to our existence—something as close to us as the words we speak and the thoughts we think using those words."[13]

The phenomenon of extinction is the technological ersatz for death. But our being-toward-extinction can never be authentic because it occludes the mortal being-in-the-world-with-others, whose resolute acceptance authenticity requires. Unlike death, extinction cannot summon authentic individuals to their possibilities. Rather it addresses isolationists and solipsists, for "the lack of others is the defining feature of extinction."[14] So long as we exist toward this lack, we cannot exist as whole, as healthy. "Being human, we have, through the establishment of a common world, taken up residence in the enlarged space of past, present and future, and if we threaten to destroy the future generations we harm ourselves, for the threat we pose to them is carried back to us through the channels of the common world that we all inhabit together."[15] We fail to be human as long as we project a hostile indifference onto the possibility of perpetuity. Here again, the ontologically inconsistent phenomenon of extinction undermines its own being, for it dismantles the temporal platform from which all projections are cast. "We need the assurance that there will be a future if we are to take on the burden of mastering the past—a past that really does become the proverbial "dead past," an unbearable weight of millennia of corpses and dust, if there is no promise of a future."[16]

Schell's use of Arendt's notion of a social and biological common world convincingly demonstrates how the phenomenon of human extinction stymies our careful being-in-the-world-with-others. It does not, however, manage to exhaust the structural totality of care: "the being of Dasein means being-ahead-of-oneself-already-in (the world) as being-together-with (innerworldly beings encountered)" (BT 180). Our being-with extends beyond other humans to encompass all innerworldly beings. Thus, the lack of others definitive of extinction must include a lack of beings in general. The being of trash is ontologically deficient to the point of phenomenal disappearance. The more the common world fills up with disposable commodities, the more it becomes ontologically empty, hence worthless and dispensable. Consequently, a thorough interpretation of human extinction requires an ontology of trash. Schell moves toward this necessity without meeting it when he writes:

> Like death, extinction is felt not when it has arrived, but beforehand, as a deep shadow cast back across the whole of life. . . . Extinction saturates our existence and never stops happening. If we want to find the meaning of extinction, accordingly, we should start by looking with new eyes at ourselves and the world we live in, and at the lives we live. The question to be asked then is no longer what the features and characteristics of extinction are but what it says about us and what it does to us that we are preparing our own extermination.[17]

In the technological era, the lives we live are lives of consumption, and the world we live in teeters on a mountain of trash high above an infernal abyss. The ontology of trash comes to its end in the discovery of the full meaning of extinction. The twin phenomena appear as one in the destruction of time, the extermination, that is, the detemporalization of human being.

Saved Time Lost

We consume commodities, so we tell ourselves, in order to save time. Although commodities also furnish us with a degree of security and pleasure, they do so generally at an overall net loss. We consider it a rather uncultured palate that actually prefers the taste of fast food to a meal skillfully prepared from fresh, whole ingredients and presented on well-crafted dinnerware. When we consume fast food we willingly compromise taste and nutrition for celerity. Addictive additives aside, it is the "fast" that sells highly processed foods. This "fast," of course, also includes the supposedly inexpensive price, for in any culture where time is money, fast means profit. Thus, we drive cars on occasions when it lies well within our capacity to walk; we employ dishwashers rather than clean up after ourselves, so as to hasten to our rendezvous with the television; we finger remote-controls in order to obtain most quickly the maximum of distraction. Finally, we buy single-use cameras, pens, utensils, containers, and countless other disposables for the speed and ease, but rarely for the quality they offer. By metaphysical measurements, time as well as money are saved when they are not spent taking care of the demands of embodiment. Since our physical natures waste time, time is safe only in an atmosphere purified of physicality. The phenomena of disposables has minimal physical purchase. Disposable commodities relieve the demands of the body and make no further physical demands themselves. Their negative relation to physicality makes them immaterial beings, unapparent phenomena. Disposablity is the metaphysical essence of convenience because it aims at the creation of a virtual world emptied of limitation and resistance.

Heidegger distinguishes primordial time, which issues from our mortality, from derivative time. To the extent that commodities mitigate our mortal neediness, they must also eliminate the primordial time that passes through this. But since humans exist as primordial time rather than in it, we cannot objectively reckon its loss. The time we want to save is derivative, the "clock" time within which we conduct our daily lives. We would not feel the loss of primordial time if it were compensated by an addition of its derivative. However, the consumption of commodities, contrary to all promises, also squanders the latter. Derivative time, the time with which we reckon, is measured by our worldly engagements, our taking care of things. Heidegger explains:

> Initially and for the most part, care is circumspect taking care of things. Expending itself for the sake of itself, Dasein "uses itself up." Using itself up, Dasein uses itself, that is, its time. Using its time, it reckons with it. Taking care of things which is circumspect and reckoning, initially discovers time and develops a measurement of time. Measurement of time is constitutive of being-in-the-world. Measuring its time, the discovering of circumspection which takes care of things lets what it discovers at hand and objectively be encountered in time. (BT 305)

Carefree commodities thus elude encounter within time. The technological mode of being-in of uncaring, which retards the development of a measurement of time, diminishes time itself. Rather than saving time, commodities destroy time by conflicting with the conditions of its possibility. Thus, every new messianic gadget betrays itself a false prophet as it further spurs the mindless gallop of our consumer lives.

Given our temporal nature, we can only lose time when we err from our essential being. We feel that taking care of things, primarily our physical needs, wastes time because, tending to become absorbed in our worldly business, we mistake ourselves as wilful subjective agents in contest with a recalcitrant, objective world. Misdirected preoccupation with our material subjectivity leads us into the illusion where we find ourselves fixed, substantial egos. We forget that we exist as empty temporality, that is, mortal beings. Losing sight of our mortality, we also fail to see the possibilities that our authentic being-toward-death opens up for us. Blind to possibility, we feel ensnared by the truncated instantaneity of the present. We feel no temporal extension, as if we had no time. When, on the other hand, our taking care of physicality recalls our mortality in such a way that our own possibilities become illuminated, we reconcile time with our finite temporality. When creatively absorbed in physical work, hobby, or sport, we easily drop our temporal covetousness. Time becomes for us engaging experience rather than possession, unfolding existence rather than morbid obsession. Precisely at these moments of careful indwelling of the present, when all our futile fretting about the "upcoming" grows still, we feel the full expansion of time. Time is saved in the recollection of primordial time flowing from our careful embodied being. Only by taking care of our mortal needs can we encounter our essential finitude; and only by embracing this finitude can we understand time not as a possession to be hoarded, but as way of existing, an openness and service to the passage of Being.

Time derives from mortal temporality. It must therefore be embodied. What Wendell Berry writes concerning human energy equally applies to time:

> as a people, we must learn again to think of human energy, *our* energy, not as something to be saved, but as something to be used and to be enjoyed in use. We must understand that our strength is, first of all, strength of body, and that this strength cannot thrive except in useful, decent, satisfying, comely work. There is no such thing as *potential* bodily energy. By saving it— as our ideals of labor-saving and luxury bid us to do—we simply waste it, and much else along with it.[18]

Similarly, by saving the time needed to take care of our mortal finitude, we waste our temporality, our being. The waste is ontological in essence, signifying our failure to exist as human, reflecting our extermination.

Between debilitating drudgery and luxurious convenience there must lie a golden mean along which time runs its course at its natural pace. We certainly do not want to be pinched by necessity. If all our hours we burn in the fire of bare survival, we cannot live fully human lives. But neither should we want to be out of touch with necessity, straining to avoid it all costs. The supposed freedom granted by technology means little outside the context of physical necessity. It becomes spurious and superficial; the freedom to choose between Coca-Cola Classic or Diet Coke, between Pepsi, or Pepsi Clear; the freedom to discard perfectly serviceable items because repair, which requires human labor, is more expensive than robotic production. Beyond the reach of necessity, we fail not only to live fully, but also to live humanly. Taking care of things in a mindful manner that recollects us to our mortal temporality is our special, dignified, and proper work. When we forget ourselves, in the crush of overwhelming physical neediness as in the heady inebriation of physical carefreeness, we wrong our essential being.

Our harried obsession to save time springs directly from our ignorance and inability surrounding a proper expenditure of time. The mortal rhythms and ages of our bodies set primordial time into motion. The finer our attunement to the miraculous being of embodiment, the wider our finite temporality enlarges. Hatha yoga, a physical discipline originating in ancient India, has accumulated thousands of years of careful empirical observation of this miracle. "The yogi's life is not measured by the number of his days but by the number of his breaths."[19] However, as we stray from the vast ground of our body, we stumble into ever tighter temporal strictures. Omitting to use our embodiment in careful, gainful work, we cast aside the standard that measures and elongates time. The omission fires the starting-shot for the race of urban consumer modernity:

> In time-famine cultures, the balance between accomplishment in work and leisure has been destroyed as worker productivity has accelerated, "increasing the yield" on an hour of work. . . . In terms of our psychological perception of time there is an unambiguous effect produced by increased productivity—time becomes perceived as "scarce" as its economic value increases. . . . As the "yield" on time at work increased, people tried also to increase the "yield" on time devoted to leisure in similar fashion, trying to get more out of it in order to balance the increasing productivity at work. In time-famine cultures, people's leisure is transformed into

a frantic race to get as much as possible out of every minute spent in leisure activities. *To do this, goods are combined with activities in a variety of ways to increase the "yield" on time, much as technology increased the yield on time at work.*[20]

These goods, or commodities of convenience, are, unfortunately, counter-productive. Because they estrange and objectify the body by disengaging its natural capacities, commodities shrink the standard of time-measurement. At work, technology, in the name of productivity, puts the body, as it were, on the dole. Machines produce more quickly and accurately than the capricious body. If not completely unemployed, the body becomes a mere appendage or at most an apprentice to the machine. At leisure, technology pushes the body to unnatural extremes. In both cases the objectified body loses its mortal ability to tell time. Since the body idles during work, leisure, work's counterpart, can no longer be restive, contemplative, and restorative—the very qualities that inspired Descartes and his fellow scientific revolutionaries to apply technology to the procurement of leisure. Chased by ever more alienating production, leisure becomes harried and exhausting. Given "free time," the consumer either "shops 'til she drops," goes for a "workout" or quite blithely volunteers for grave injury by diving into the folly of any number of new extreme sports. Evidently, the consumer body has become so unfeeling that any outdoor activity not undertaken at speeds upward of one hundred miles per hour does not register with it.

At least since Aristotle, the West has deemed leisure prerequisite for philosophical achievement. Only in the repose of metaphysical contemplation, so the tradition holds, can people fully indulge their humanity. The irony here is that the metaphysical disdain for physical work that has spurred technological commodification runs roughshod over leisure itself. Today work mocks our bodily nature while leisure excites it to distraction, leaving no time at all for the cultivation of our human being. Thus, metaphysics fails by its own criterion. Hurrying toward transcendence, it has left us humans behind.

In the technological absence of the body, in the forgetful oblivion of our mortal temporality, time itself curls and shrivels up to a dry, brittle point. Lacking depth in our temporal dimension, we fail to relate meaningfully to the past, and especially to the future. We further the unconditionally absurd amassment of nuclear weapons, the unconscionable plunder of our natural inheritance, the highly dubious manipulation of our genetic constitution with little to no consideration of what consequences our successors may suffer. Indeed, we even knowingly wager the future in our technological crap game, comfortable in the untried belief that subsequent generations will deal appropriately with our nuclear and toxic wastes and repay the titanic debt to nature that our prodigality has accrued. While such selfish and puerile behavior certainly bodes ill for coming generations, it more loudly scandalizes our present one. The phenomenon of extinction is, as Schell claims, our current way of life, our uncaring being in the world cut off from others. What Richard Sennett says of the multicultural city applies all the more fittingly to the multigenerational community of the common world:

> For people in a multi-cultural city to care about one another, I believe we have to change the understanding we have of our bodies. We will never experience the difference of others until we acknowledge the bodily insufficiencies in ourselves. Civic compassion issues from the physical awareness of lack in ourselves, not from sheer goodwill or political rectitude.[21]

Care for others begins with authentic care for ourselves, that is, skillful taking care of things in a gentle manner reminiscent of our fragile mortality. So long as we elevate convenience above all other values, so long as we refuse to eschew trash, we will live under the selfish, solipsistic cloud of human extinction. Since the phenomenon of trash appears as a deficit in our ontological structure of care, it amounts to a negation of our being. Trash, with its heap of ontological paradox and destructiveness, is the manifestation of extinction.

Fallacious Man

Whether called original sin, or the veil of Maya, inveterate ignorance or existential guilt of being a nullity, fallibility stands as the human quintessence. Where does this leave our study's central thesis? How can we fail to be human, when the very act of failure only confirms our humanity. In this respect, are not trash and human extinction the phenomena most affirmative of our nature? Possibly, but only in the same sense that jealousy, anger, cowardice, and hatred are distinctively human qualities. The negative connotations of these qualities suggest that, while they may stubbornly adhere to our nature, our indulgence of them somehow diminishes our proper being. The violence inherent in trash represents a similar ethical failure. But the more profound ontological failure involves a logical inconsistency. Trash is the product of metaphysics, the attempt to surpass the inalienable fallibility of mortal, carnal man. Its failure consists, then, in its tendency to hide the truth of our basic faultiness. Trash contains a host of existential fallacies: that mortals can live as disembodied; that mortals can care for their being without taking care of that which preserves their being; that a temporal being can exist without time; that a communal being can exist without others.

The metaphysical mind finds none of these fallacies fatal to its position. Its logic is purely rational, not existential, and thus it can factor out the variables born of embodied being. Precisely these, however, create the uniquely human factor. So while it certainly is natural for us to pursue physical ease, comfort and immortality, the actual technological pursuit of metaphysical existence tends to degrade our humanity. We need not celebrate suffering and perishing to properly and graciously own our essential physicality. It is mindfulness, not morbidity, that keeps the feeling of mortality ever-present to our sensitivity. Doing so acknowledges the truth of our humanness. Consuming commodities in such a way that negates beings rather than lets them be categorically denies our closest truth. We allow technology to take care of things in the mode of uncaring. In all of this there rages the self-immolation and impossible contradiction implicit in the phenomenon of extinction.

We would do well, I should think, to treat technology as inhuman. Such an attitude, making us wary, could introduce a degree of awareness into our otherwise unconscious mode of consumptive being. But aware of technology as an inhuman force, we should by no means treat it as inimical. Heidegger spoke sanely half a century ago: "It would be foolish to attack technology blindly. It would be short sighted to condemn it as the work of the devil. We depend on technical devices; they even challenge us to greater advances. But suddenly and unawares we find ourselves so firmly shackled to these technical devices that we fall into bondage to them" (DT 53). Trash, as I have endeavored ontologically to describe it, forms the chains of these technological bonds. These chains manacle our minds by enfranchising our bodies. The danger of this bondage is "that the approaching tide of technological revolution in the atomic age could so captivate, bewitch, dazzle, and beguile man that calculative thinking may someday come to be accepted and practiced *as the only* way of thinking" (DT 52). Reason, by no fault of its own, is heartless. We need it and rightly celebrate it, but raising it to absolute authority dethrones the powers of compassion. The day that technology does revolutionize the globe through perfect rationalization is the day the world becomes radically inhumane, a veritable moonscape devoid of solicitude and truth.

It would be as foolish to condemn technology as the work of the devil as to praise it as heaven-sent. Yet in between these dual follies lies the more likely danger feared by Heidegger: that we continue mindlessly to embrace technology without an adequate understanding of its essence.

Technology, for the most part, cannot help but to tend to disembody us, and to this extent it inevitably harms the physical field that grounds and nourishes not only care and compassion, but equally mindfulness or Heidegger's "meditative thinking." For Heidegger, this latter is literally handicraft, which suggests that it is inseparable from a receptive manual engagement with beings in the world. "Only a being who can speak, that is think, can have hands and can be handy in achieving works of handicraft" (WCT 16). Even more so than eyes, our hands serve as portals to the world. All human emotions dwell in them. They can perform the most heinous of crimes and saintly acts of benevolence. Technology stifles the human expression of the hands. We know how the fluid and gentle rhythm of manual writing gives way to the staccato beat enforced by the keyboard, which in turn gives way to the jerky prodding of an electronic mouse. The more we reconfigure our bodies and their native capacities to better suit the machines we deploy, the more mechanical, both physically and spiritually, we become.

The technology productive of trash almost entirely effaces our embodiment and thus institutionalizes the disinterest or uncaring characteristic of all machines. Modern devices and the commodities they deliver are not in the least more devilish than any other implement of an earlier day. They do, however, dehumanize, that is, mechanize our careful, meditative physical being more effectively. If the history of technology is read as the progress of increased disembodiment and disengagement from the world, then the present era of thoughtless consuming and trash comes as the actualization and culmination of a possibility long since suspected by Chuang-tze in ancient China. Thousands of years before Heidegger, he told the following parable:

> A farmer dug a well and was using the water for irrigating his farm. He used an ordinary bucket to draw water from the well, as most primitive people do. A passer-by, seeing this, asked the farmer why he did not use a shadoof for the purpose; it is a labor-saving device and can do more work than the primitive method. The farmer said, "I know it is labor-saving, and it is for this very reason that I do not use the device. What I am afraid of is that the use of such a contrivance makes one machine-minded. Machine-mindedness leads one to the habit of indolence and laziness."[22]

We can read "machine-mindedness" as the perfect synonym for "metaphysical." First of all, the very structure of the term combines technology and intellect into a single structure. Curiously, the structure contains an ontological paradox. According to Western dualism, body is nothing more than a living machine, and its work has nothing essential to do with the immaterial mind. "Machine-mindedness" would seem to imply a fusion of body and mind rather heterodox to conventional dualism. On closer inspection, however, the term displays a neat encapsulation of the essence of metaphysics. "Minded" functions as a verbal adjective and as such it connotes a kind of intellectualization of the machine, that is, the body. To be machine-minded is precisely to experience the body as a de-animated device exploitable by the disembodied intellect. Because the mind has supposedly shed all physicality after it has intellectualized the needy mortal body, it nullifies these natural physical characteristics. This process transforms the lived body into an insensitive machine, raising it up to the metaphysical level of mind.

Chuang-tze's farmer fears that machine-mindedness will uproot him from the ground of his human being physically extended as the field of his mortal finite body. Indolence and laziness are not just morally repugnant to the farmer. More pointedly, they signify a neglect or refusal to care for one's embodied needs, one's essential being. D. T. Suzuki explains:

> Mechanical devices are far more efficient and accomplish more. But the machine is impersonal and non-creative and has no meaning. Mechanization means intellection, and as the intellect is primarily utilitarian there is no spiritual aestheticism or ethical spirituality in the machine. The reason that induced Chuang-tze's farmer not to be machine-minded lies here. The machine hurries one to finish the work and reach the objective for which it is made. The work or labor in itself has no value except as the means. That is to say, life here loses its creativity and turns into an instrument, man is now a goods-producing mechanism.[23]

Suzuki describes the greatest of all ontological perversions, where the care for one's being gets subordinated to the inhuman end of convenience and efficiency. In this way, authentic and active care for one's well-being devolves into passive dread about one's bare survival.

Salvaging Trash

Chuang-tze's farmer was not innocent of all mechanical sophistication. He used a bucket rather than transporting the water in the cup of his hands. Moreover, he practiced the art of irrigated agriculture instead of living off whatever windfalls nature would chance him. While as a parabolic figure he comes across as reactionary and extremist, he nevertheless offers clues as to how we might forge a human and healthy relation with technology. In a way he exemplifies Heidegger's conception of this relation:

> We can use technical devices, and yet with proper use also keep ourselves so free of them, that we may let go of them any time. We can use technical devices as they ought to be used, and also let them alone as something which does not affect our inner and real core. We can affirm the unavoidable use of technical devices, and also deny them the right to dominate us, and so to warp, confuse and lay waste our nature. (DT 53)

The farmer weighs devices in the balance of our essential physicality. What he suspects may cover over the mortal truth of his being, what uproots him from the corporeal ground of his human care, compassion, and thought, he forgoes. He does not live beneath the cloud of extinction because his manner of existing gives prominence to the reality of neediness that makes us take care of physicality. He neither wants to contradict his mortal being, nor annul its marriage with the physical world. His affirmation of the unavoidable use of technical devices above all affirms also his essential humanity.

We, too, can take up his work of affirmation through observing our technological patterns of consumption and production with awareness and intelligence. Do these patterns include the shapes of happiness, companionship, health, and love? First, in the name of common justice, we must wean ourselves off the unhelpful superfluities that glut our consumer lives. It is only too true, to our profound discredit, that a large portion of humankind has trouble simply living because we have such trouble living simply. How do we distinguish a superfluity from a necessity? I propose the following criterion: if featured on a television commercial, internet site, in a glossy magazine ad, colorful newspaper flyer, or insistent junk mail, the trumpeted commodity is more than likely something we do not need. Nor must we imprison ourselves in bare necessity. For example, most North Americans own a gross excess of clothing. Were we to curb this excess, we might still appreciate the convenience of a washing machine. However, I suggest that most circumstances would leave us hard pressed to assent with intelligent awareness to the use of clothes dryers. When for a few minutes effort we can cooperate with the liberal air to dry our garments without expense or expenditure of energy, the highly wasteful use of electric dryers seems senseless and indefensible. So, too, the unquestioned consumer right to command cars to conduct our idle bodies across distances easily covered on foot or bicycle. These are but examples. The principle behind them states that with every consumption of a device we must remain sensitive to the effects it has on our physicality, which inevitably includes the physicality of other beings. Does it foster thoughtful gratitude, generosity, and gregariousness or frustrated isolation, competition, and greed? Answers to such questions ought to guide our use of technology.

Such a recollected use that mindfully implants our mortal being in the world would recoil from trash. Like its twin, the phenomenon of extinction, trash nullifies our essential nature. Obviously, we must consume and dispose of things, but these unavoidable activities can also be done in a spirit of humility and thankfulness more becoming of our finite interdependent being than the uncaring violence at reign over the consumer culture. The majority of commodities, when distractedly consumed in the name of convenience for which they were made, rot our natural capacities for gratitude, compassion, mindfulness, and skillful practice. The phenomenal immateriality of trash makes it weightless in the balance of our physicality. Thus, a proper use of technology does not generate trash.

Machine-mindedness or calculative thinking forms part of our faculty of reason, and thus is a vital constituent of our human condition. Like its crutch, technology, we cannot help using it to support our existence. But we must understand that machine-mindedness, which calculates strictly in terms of efficiency and convenience, is essentially compassionless. When allowed to dominate, if not eradicate other modes of thinking, it inevitably sinks into cruelty—not, to reiterate, because it is evil and inimical, but because it is insensate. It does not feel. Nor do we modern consumers feel to the extent that our labor-saving devices vitiate our sensitive physicality. Our indifference to trash and all the violence it contains proves this.

Unintentionally, we have grown savage in our efficiency. The industrial procedures involved in commodified beef production alone suffice to damn us as inhuman. Here all beings concerned, both bovine and human, are effectively brutalized. "Violence today," attests Thomas Merton, "is white-collar violence, the systematically organized bureaucratic and technological destruction of man."[24] Now even those who work in blue collars wear white ones when they go shopping. Technology has implicated all consumers, rich and poor, into its uncaring insensitivity. That means human destruction is as universal as empty aluminium cans, dirty plastic bags, and spent Bic lighters.

Trash is the collapse of the ontological/physical structure of human being. A history of technological alienation, beginning with our removal from food-bearing lands and food-rearing bodies, has brought us before the real prospect of our extermination. Machine-minded and uncaring consumers, we lack the simple wherewithal to let beings be. All we can do is trash them and purchase another. The ontology of trash ends here where we despondently revel in and fully expend our inhumanity. To truly understand the contradictory ontological nature of disposable beings is to confront the cold failure of a dispossessed being-in that handles the world roughly and without comprehension. Trash, in other words, manifests our complete lack of grace, a despairing forfeiture of our receptive service to Being.

But if trash were only this, perhaps our indifference and disinterest in regards to it would have some measure of justification. It would simply be too dismal to contemplate. Yet trash can be more. It can be the mirror in which we suddenly perceive our own sickly aspect. It can help us resolve ourselves to better living. Therefore, although the ontology of trash itself naturally terminates in human extinction, its true, philosophical significance first emerges after.

Before the End

I well remember that those very plumes,
Those weeds, and the high spear-grass on that wall,
By mist and silent raindrops silvered o'er,
As once I passed, into my heart conveyed
So still an image of tranquillity,
So calm and still, and looked so beautiful
Amid the uneasy thoughts which filled my mind,
That what we feel of sorrow and despair
From ruin and from change, and all the grief
That passing shows of Being leave behind,
Appeared an idle dream, that could maintain,
Nowhere, dominion o'er the enlightened spirit
Whose meditative sympathies repose
Upon the breast of Faith. I turned away
And walked along my road in happiness.
　　　—William Wordsworth, *The Recluse, Book I*

With these words, Wordsworth depicts a radical human transformation—
one, moreover, not in the least metaphysical. The passage comes at the
end of the doleful story of a ruined cottage. Once the domestic sanctuary
of order, care, and humble industry, Margaret's "poor cottage/ Sank into
decay; for he was gone, whose hand,/ At the first nipping of October
frost,/ Closed up each chink and with fresh bands of straw/ Chequered
the green-grown thatch" (lines 901–904). The narrator sadly retells a history of negligence, indifference and carelessness that sinks the once proud
and comely home into dereliction. He mourns the wasteful loss, recalling
the former beauty, hospitality, and peace of the spot. But precisely there,
surrounded by ruin and decadence, with the rubble of memory giving
cold comfort to a tired body now bereft of its late shelter and rest, the

narrator's understanding suddenly penetrates the phenomenon of destruction and waste. Compassion seizes him out of the lethargic isolation of despondency and plants him in a world lush with wondrous manifestation. The signs of decay become revelations of beauty to "the enlightened spirit/ Whose meditative sympathies repose/ Upon the breast of Faith." Faith sanctifies the desolate present. No longer a spectacle of failure and loss, the meditatively apprehended ruin appears a signpost pointing in the direction of happiness.

Our world is now a ruined cottage. Like Margaret's abode, it suffers the loss of careful hands to tend and to keep it. Everywhere we look, our dwelling shows signs of grave decay. The forests are felled or falling; cities, rotten at their cores, collapse into social disorder; poisons and ill-begotten weapons settle to the floor of the seas; meanwhile, amid all this declension there rises up a mountain, confounding as the Tower of Babel, a mountain of trash. The magnitude of this obstacle to our careful human dwelling in the world makes it seem insurmountable. We know that we cannot continue unabated to consume and dispose of the world as we now do. Yet this mountain of used convenience, with its summit of spent promises, imposes itself between our present path and the road to happiness that lies beyond trash. We fear that we have neither the strength nor the will to go straight forward. We tell ourselves that we have not the desire to go back. So we wait helplessly at the base of our own indifference and uncaring, adding a little more mass to its bulk, and another cubit to its height every consumptive day.

The nature and content of this book are somewhat foreign to the philosophical tradition. Its conclusions, under the objective scrutiny of disembodied reason, may leave the reader at a certain loss. But the success of an ontology of trash is to be gauged not so much in what it proves as in what it exhibits and elicits. At its best, such an ontology ought to be transformative in a manner not unlike Wordsworth's history of Margaret's decline. When infused with compassionate understanding, Wordsworth's narrator is party to a double transformation. First, the whole sorry spectacle that so dismayed him transforms into a scene of beauty and promise and hope. At once the cramped decay of the world bursts open with possibility and vivacity. Suddenly, the ruined world appears hospitable again. This apparent external alteration coincides with an existential transformation within the narrator himself. To see hope and beauty in waste, he must rely on faith and careful thought. Only then can he turn away from the old aspect of ruin, not in disgust, fear, or callousness, but instead in happiness. He turns away and foots the road just newly cleared by the strength of a receptive, meditative sympathy.

I consider this ontology a success if it has, howsoever immeasurably, managed to portray trash—a phenomenon of inhuman destruction—as beautiful to the view of a compassionate eye, able to see with Keats that "Beauty is Truth, Truth Beauty." I count this success absolute because such a perception implies a definite attunement at work in the perceiver. It means the study, to whatever small degree, has roused compassion in the reader. It means that it has contributed, albeit minutely, to the humanization of modern humanity, to our rehabilitation in a world technologically depopulated, and comes as a salve, even if weak and temporary, for the burning wounds of human extinction.

If psychoanalysis accomplishes any good in a person's life, it does so by operating on the conviction that this person cannot change in herself what she does not understand. The relation between understanding and change extends beyond the human psyche. Without a proper understanding of disposability, all our scientific bustling to develop new technologies to combat trash and potential extinction serves only to aggravate the perceived problems. The single goal of this study was to prepare our field of understanding wherein the seeds of change might naturally grow.

To understand trash, and thus also the plight of a disposable world, we must become thoughtfully compassionate. First, we must feel the violence suffered by all beings under the autocratic rule of technology. Yet the attendant shame and sadness must eventually give way to hope and humility. When we can look into the mirror of trash and see not simply our own selfishness and failure, but also an opportunity for edification and transformation, only then can we turn away from the phenomenon and step toward a world of beings more commensurate with and true to our mortal existence. We then can give up the ill-fitting mantle of a lord and god; we can resume our natural place of service. By this return we do not at all demean ourselves. We simply quit the cosmic masquerade in which we have made of our human selves a ridiculous sight.

The irony is seldom relished that those who most adamantly denounce the slightest form of technological determinism are also those who most stridently cry "we can't go back." The idea of reducing the current and rising level of technological sophistication and dependency seems to them so impossibly absurd that they do not deign even to entertain it. Science and technology must advance, they contend, and so imply that linear progress is the inflexible nature of science. Technology is our tool, yet we can do little besides watch it break out of the human scale and balloon beyond all proportion suited to its proper use. The tacit logic of their argument is as simple as it is flawed: we can't go back because technology pushes us forward.

When you mistakenly turn down a blind alley and come to a dead end, you enter a situation of limited practical options. Either you can sit down, passive, frustrated, and trapped, to wait for the possibility that one day the way might clear of its own accord or you can retrace your steps, exit the cul-du-sac, and set off in a different direction. Prudence counsels for the latter alternative. Waiting for the phenomenon of human extinction to dissipate while we linger in the dead end of technological consumption is futile. It only speeds our destruction. Sanity itself screams "turn around." Thoreau's imperative, once simply morally intelligent, has become categorical: Simplify, simplify, simplify.

The balkers who find technological determinism so offensive a concept are also those who elevate the status quo to a sacrament. Any exhortation of change in a direction not perfectly parallel to the trajectory of technology is rebuffed with the generic-brand objection: "too much, too soon." Our society, much less our economy, they cry, could not possibly withstand such precipitous alterations. If we must voluntarily simplify, so be it, but slowly, and better tomorrow. After all, nothing happens overnight. Thus, they adapt St. Augustine's infamous prayer: "Lord, make me chaste, only not yet." Here again, mechanical thinking blinds us to the distortions of our own perspective. Throughout the entire twentieth century, vast, unimaginable changes repeatedly occurred all but overnight. Consider only the automobile's cometary rise to unconditional world autonomy. In less than two generations a single device has utterly transformed the face of the earth, the structure of societal life, and every level of economic production. The car is a veritable thunderclap in history. Yet very few have cautioned "too fast." On the contrary, the yearly extension of speedometers speaks only: "not fast enough." However, the astounding malleability of the human race to configure itself almost instantly to the rolling shape of the automobile gives us hope. If such transformations can take place so easily with little to no philosophical thought or awareness on our part, then we have some reason to anticipate great and redemptive change with the epiphany of understanding.

Such changes we cannot now in any detail foresee. Fortunately, prophecy is not among the philosopher's proper tasks. What we are called to do is to remain open through our questioning to the changes that present themselves. We must always bear in mind and cherish the humility that reminds us of our essential roles as receivers, stewards, and beneficiaries of Being. Yet reception does not equal passive acceptance; it involves continual active practice. To remain open, we must empty ourselves of the superfluities that clog our understanding. We need to practice simplicity—what prudent Christians have long called poverty, and Buddhists detachment.

Let me repeat that the imperative to simplify does not command us to go grubbing in the earth with sticks for edible roots and rodents. All of us do not have to flee the city, much less the world, to squat instead on a rocky patch of land and wring a subsistence out of it. We must, however, become careful, mindful, and meditatively compassionate. Trash presents us with an opportunity to comprehend the peril of our own existential and ontological failure. When we understand how contrary to our mortal essence is our technological treatment of worldly beings, convenient commodities will lose much of their luster. They will cease to comfort and sedate us in their old, advertised manner. Their a priori disposal will begin to alarm us, for therein we have caught a glimpse of our own insensitive rejection of ourselves.

Simplification happens incrementally and spans a continuum. It begins first with the practice of temperance with respect to trash. We stop consuming the most ludicrous and superfluous of disposables: polystyrene cups, plates, and bowls, ballpoint pens, cameras, anything excessively packaged, and so on. We gradually replace these replaceables with lasting goods of quality that we can take proper, useful care of. Slowly, the idle talk of newspapers, television, and magazines may start sounding harsh and cacophonous to our ears. We might become more selective and careful about what we give our mind's audience to. At the same time we refine our other senses, especially our palate, such that industrially commodified foods come to taste as unsavory and indigestible as the requisite plastic that encapsulates them. We return to our lived and living body with a solicitude vibrant with wonder and gratitude. We emancipate our limbs from the stocks and shackles of cars, giving them liberty to explore and enjoy their innate power of locomotion. We begin to ask ourselves whether for the sake of relaxation it is necessary to be airlifted to a holiday resort, whether for the sake of experience we must jet set to every corner of the globe that remains the least bit less tawdry than our shopping strips at home. In good time, the monarchy of convenience and luxury gets overturned by a more equitable democracy of values, where no single value holds absolute sway but is checked and balanced against others according to the varying needs of the present situation.

As Heidegger attests, we cannot simply throw out technology. We need it and need to continue to better it. At the same time, however, we need to follow Wordsworth's narrator who "turned away/ And walked along [his] road in happiness." Going back does indeed mean fewer landfills, fewer shopping malls, fewer televisions, fewer automobiles, fewer computers, fewer airplanes, fewer McDonald's, fewer Club Meds, and so on. But all this sounds like welcome news to "the enlightened spirit/ Whose meditative sympathies repose/ Upon the breast of Faith."

Notes

Introduction

1. Susan Strasser, *Waste and Want: A Social History of Trash* (New York: Metropolitan Books, 1999), p. 12.
2. Ibid., p. 266.
3. Immanuel Kant, *The Critique of Pure Reason* (New York: St. Martin's Press, 1929), p. 21.
4. Plato, *Complete Works* (Indianapolis: Hackett, 1997), pp. 57–58.
5. Strasser, *Waste and Want*, p. 192.
6. Jean Baudrillard, *The Consumer Society* (London: Sage Publications, 1998) p. 76.

Chapter One: Waste

1. Robert Elliot, *Faking Nature* (London: Routledge, 1998) p. 117.
2. Alexander Judd, *In Defense of Garbage* (Westport: Praeger, 1993) p. 213.
3. Ibid., p. 21.
4. Kevin Lynch, *Wasting Away* (San Fransisco: Sierra Club Books, 1990) p. 146.
5. Ibid., p. 146.
6. Mary Douglas, *Purity and Danger: An Analysis of the Concepts of Pollution and Taboo* (London Routledge, 1996), pp. 35–36.
7. Ernest Becker, *The Denial of Death* (New York: Free Press, 1973), p. 33.
8. René Descartes, *The Discourse on Method and Meditations on First Philosophy* (Indianapolis: Hackett, 1993), p. 82.

9. Baudrillard, *The Consumer* Society, p. 43.
10. Ibid., p. 47.
11. Douglas, *Purity and Danger*, p. 62.
12. Thorstein Veblen, *The Theory of the Leisure Class* (New York: Modern Library, 1931), p. 7.
13. Ibid., p. 29.
14. Ibid., p. 88.
15. Ibid., p. 110.
16. Marshall Sahlins, "The Original Affluent Society," in *Culture and Practice: Selected Essays* (New York: Zone Books, 2000), p. 98.
17. Ibid., p. 132.
18. Michael Zimmerman, "Heidegger and Heraclitus on Spiritual Practice," in *Philosophy Today* (Summer 1983), p. 88.
19. Comparing Heidegger to Buddhist thought, Zimmerman tells us that "it is precisely because the relatively ahistorical Mahayana tradition lacks the conceptual resources necessary to confront the emergence of planetary civilization that Nishitani and other members of the Kyoto school have looked to Heidegger's thought for insight regarding how to relate *sunyata* (emptiness) to history." Michael Zimmerman, "Heidegger, Buddhism and Deep Ecology," in *The Cambridge Companion to Heidegger* (Cambridge: Cambridge University Press, 1993), p. 260.
20. To cite one example, Hubert Dreyfus argues that the primacy of equipmentality in Heidegger's early thought philosophically establishes the supremacy of utility as the ultimate metaphysical value in the age of technology, thus "*Being and Time* appears in the history of the being of equipment not just as a transition, but as *the* decisive step towards technology."

> The account of worldhood in *Being and Time*, however, removes every vestige of resistance—that of *physis* and earth, as well as that of will and subjectivity—to the technological tendency to treat all beings (even man) as resources. Nothing stands in the way of the final possibility that for Dasein the only issue left becomes ordering for the sake of order itself. This is the understanding of Being definitive of technological nihilism, an understanding prepared but not consummated by the account of equipment in *Being and Time*.

Hubert Dreyfuss, "Heidegger and the History of Equipment," in *Heidegger: A Critical Reader* Dreyfus, Hubert, and Hall, eds. (Oxford: Blackwell, 1992), pp. 182–184.

21. Michael Zimmerman, *Heidegger's Confrontation with Modernity: Technology, Politics, Art* (Bloomington: Indiana University Press, 1990), p. 224.

In his article, "Heidegger and Dasein's 'Bodily Nature': What Is the Hidden Problematic?," David Cerbone defends Heidegger's reluctance to discuss embodiment.

> There are, I think, deeper reasons for Heidegger's refusal to incorporate an account of the body into his explication of Dasein. These reasons have to do with the kinds of conclusions he wishes to draw concerning Dasein's way of being. That is, Heidegger's aim is to conduct a kind of *transcendental* investigation, the purpose of which is to reveal various non-contingent features of Dasein's way of being. . . . Attending to Dasein's "bodily nature" may be seen to be at odds with this conception of what a phenomenology of everydayness is meant to achieve: our embodiment, especially our being embodied in this particular way, may be considered too contingent to be part of the existential analytic.

David Cerbone, "Heidegger and Dasein's 'Bodily Nature': What Is the Hidden Problematic?," in *International Journal of Philosophical Studies* (vol.8, no.2, June 2000), p. 214.

My argument, of course, contests the so-called contingency of embodiment with respect to the existential structures of human being. Given that no human being has ever existed disembodied, one wonders how contingent embodiment in fact is.

22. Martin Heidegger, *Vier Seminare* from the *Gesamtausgabe: Band 15: Seminare* (Frankfurt am Main: Vittorio Klostermann), p. 370.

23. Martin Heidegger and Eugen Fink, *Heraclitus Seminar* (Tuscaloosa: University of Alabama Press, 1970), p. 146.

Chapter Two: The Body

1. Zimmerman, "Heidegger and Heraclitus on Spiritual Practice," p. 88.

2. Heidegger, *Vier Seminare*, p. 370.

3. Emmanuel Levinas, *Basic Philosophical Writings* (Bloomington: Indiana University Press, 1996), p. 18.

4. Martin Heidegger, *Kant and the Problem of Metaphysics* (Bloomington: Indiana University Press, 1962), p. 237.

5. See Radhakrishnan, trans., *Bhagavadgita* (New Dehli: Harper Collins, 1993), pp. 300ff.
6. Heidegger and Fink, *Heraclitus Seminar*, p. 146.
7. Ibid., p. 146.
8. Vincent Vycinas, *Earth and Gods* (The Hague: M. Nijihoff, 1961), p. 136.
9. Thomas Tierney, *The Value of Convenience: A Genealogy of Technical Culture* (Albany: State University of New York Press, 1993), p. 42.
10. Martin Heidegger, *Poetry, Language, Thought* (New York: Harper and Row, 1971), p. 49.
11. Ibid., p. 42. Hereafter page references from this work will appear in the body of the text under PLT.
12. Michael Zimmerman, *The Eclipse of the Self: The Development of Heidegger's Concept of Authenticity* (Athens: Ohio University Press, 1981), p. 27.
13. Drew Leder, *The Absent Body* (Chicago: University of Chicago Press, 1990), p. 22.
14. Ibid., p. 14.
15. Ibid., p. 54.
16. Martin Heidegger, *The Question Concerning Technology and Other Essays* (New York: Garland, 1977), p. 26.
17. Ibid., p. 26.
18. cf. Martin Heidegger, "Nihilism and the History of Being," *Nietszche Volume 4: Nihilism.* (San Francisco: Harper and Row, 1977), pp. 244 ff.

Being is compelling in a twofold, harmonious sense: it is unrelenting and needful in relating to an abode that essentially occurs as the essence to which man belongs, man being the one who is needed. What is doubly compelling is, and is called, the need. In the advent of the default of its unconcealment, Being itself is need.

But need veils itself by staying away. At the same time the default is hidden by omission of the truth of Being in the history of metaphysics. Within the unconcealment of the being as such, which the history of metaphysics determines as the fundamental occurrence, the need of Being does not come to the fore. The being *is*, and gives rise to the illusion that Being is without need.

But the needlessness that establishes itself as the dominion of metaphysics brings Being itself to the utmost limit of its need. Need is not merely what compels in the sense of the unyielding claim that occupies an abode by using it as the unconcealment of the advent; that is, by letting it unfold essentially as the truth of Being. The relentlessness of its usage extends so far in the default of its unconcealment that the abode of Being—that is, the essence of man—is omitted; man is threatened with the annihilation of his essence, and Being itself is endangered in its usage of its abode.

Again, it is physicality that Heidegger's otherwise incisive interpretation lacks. The annihilation of man's essence is the destruction of his mortal nature or the mechanization of his lived, fragile body.

19. Leder, *The Absent Body*, p. 86.
20. Ibid., p. 108.
21. Ibid., p. 133.
22. David Levin, *The Body's Recollection of Being* (London: Routledge and Kegan Paul, 1985), p. 56.
23. Becker, *The Denial of Death*, p. 35.
24. Martin Heidegger, *Being and Time* (Albany: State University of New York Press, 1996), p. 261. Hereafter citations from this work will be referred to as BT in the body of the text.
25. Leder, *The Absent Body*, p. 3.
26. Eric Havelock, "The Orality of Socrates and the Literacy of Plato: With Some Reflections on the Historical Origins of Moral Philosophy in Europe," *New Essays on Socrates*, E. Kelly, ed. (Lanham: University Press of America, 1984), p. 90.
27. Martin Heidegger, *Basic Writings* (New York: Harper and Row, 1977), p. 375.
28. David Abram, *The Spell of the Sensuous* (New York: Pantheon, 1996), p. 108.
29. Plato's *Phaedrus* in *Dialogues of Plato*, B. Jowett, trans. (New York: Random House, 1937), p. 77.
30. Abram, *The Spell of the Sensuous*, p. 124.
31. Havelock, "The Orality of Socrates and the Literacy of Plato," p. 72.
32. Ibid., p. 79.
33. See, for example, Heidegger, "The Word of Nietzsche," in *Question Concerning Technology*, p. 100.

All that is, is now either what is real [*das Wirkliche*] as the object or what works the real [*das Wirkende*], as the objectifying within which the objectivity of the object takes shape. Objectifying, in representing, in setting before, delivers up the object to the *ego cogito*. In that delivering up, the *ego* proves to be that which underlies its own activity (the delivering up that sets before), i.e., proves to be the *subiectum*. ... Man, within the subjectness belonging to whatever is, rises up into the subjectivity of his essence. Man enters into insurrection. The world changes into object. In this revolutionary objectifying of everything that is, the earth, that which first of all must be put at the disposal of representing and setting forth, moves into the midst of human positing and analyzing. The earth itself can show itself as the object of assualt,an assualt that, in human willing, establishes itself as unconditional objectification. Nature appears everywhere—because willed from out of the essence of Being—as the object of technology.

34. Abram, *The Spell of the Sensuous*, p. 71.
35. Leder, *The Absent Body*, p. 122.
36. Ibid., p. 123.
37. Heidegger, *Basic Writings*, p. 239.
38. While some people find the impermanence of word-processing liberating because it mimics the flow of oral dialogue, freeing the hands from the work of writing has affected both the style and content of modern literature. The ease of word-processing makes pulp readily available. Heidegger thought that the movement of the hand is essential to the art of composition. "Every motion of the hand in every one of its works carries itself through the element of thinking, every bearing of the hand bears itself in that element. All the work of the hand is rooted in thinking. Therefore, thinking itself is man's simplest, and for that reason hardest, handiwork, if it would be accomplished at its proper time." Martin Heidegger, *What Is Called Thinking* (New York: Harper and Row, 1968), p. 16.
39. Maurice Merleau-Ponty, *The Phenomenology of Perception* (London: Routledge and Kegan Paul, 1962), p. 143.
40. Ibid., p. 144.
41. Jerry Mander, *Four Arguments for the Elimination of Telelvision* (New York: Morrow, 1978), p. 26.
42. Levin, *The Body's Recollection of Being*, p. 43.
43. Mander, *Four Arguments for the Elimination of Television*, p. 79.
44. Albert Borgmann, *Technology and the Character of Contemporary Life* (Chicago: University of Chicago Press, 1984), p. 41.
45. Ibid., p. 35.
46. Tierney, *The Value of Convenience*, p. 156.

47. Ibid., p. 157.
48. Becker, *The Denial of Death*, p. 51.
49. B. K. S. Iyengar, considered one of the great living practitioners and teachers of hatha yoga, writes:

> The yogi realises that his life and all its activities are part of the divine action in nature, manifesting and operating in the form of man. In the beating of his pulse and the rhythm of his respiration, he recognizes the flow of the seasons and the throbbing of universal life. His body is a temple which houses the Divine Spark. He feels that to neglect or to deny the needs of the body and to think of it as something not divine, is to neglect and deny the universal life of which it is a part. The needs of the body are the needs of the divine spirit which lives through the body. The yogi does not look heaven-ward to find God, for he knows that He is within, being known as the Antaratma (the Inner Self). He feels the kingdom of God within and without and that heaven lies in himself.
>
> Where does the body end and the mind begin? Where does the mind end and the spirit begin? They cannot be divided as they are interrelated and but different aspects of the same all-pervading divine consciousness.

    B. K. S. Iyengar, *Light on Yoga* (London: Thorsons, 2001), p. 41.
50. Thomas Merton, *No Man Is an Island* (New York: Harcourt, Brace, 1955), p. 128.
51. For the full quotation, see note 18, chapter two.
52. Tierney, *The Value of Convenience*, p. 42.
53. Christopher Dewdney, *Last Flesh: Life in the Transhuman Era* (Toronto: HarperCollins, 1998), p. 168.
54. John Gregory Burke, *Les Rites Scatologiques* (Paris: Presses Universitaires de France, 1981), p. 33.
55. Zimmerman, *The Eclipse of the Self*, p. 198.
56. To appreciate the complexity involved, consult Alan Durning and John Ryan, *Stuff: The Secret Lives of Everyday Things* (Seattle: Northwest Environment Watch, January 1999) in which the authors attempt to track the hidden history and future of common commodities. They admit to having to make wide generalizations in their method due to the magnitude of interrelations, variables, and sums.
57. Leder, *The Absent Body*, p. 31.

Chapter Three: Food

1. Radhakrishnan, trans., *The Principal Upanisads* (New Delhi: Harper-Collins, 1994), p. 543.
2. Ibid., p. 457.
3. George Armelagos and Peter Farb, *Consuming Passions: The Anthropology of Eating* (Boston: Houghton Mifflin, 1980), p. 9.
4. A. F. Raum, *Chaga Childhood* (Oxford: Oxford University Press, 1940), p. 318.
5. Ibid., p. 109.
6. See William Rathje and Cullen Murphy, *Rubbish: The Archaeology of Garbage* (New York: HarperCollins, 1992), p. 46.
7. See Judd, *In Defense of Garbage*, p. 67.
8. William Rahtje, *Rubbish: The Archaeology of Garbage* (New York: HarperCollins, 1992), p. 62.
9. Borgmann, *Technology and the Character of Contemporary Life*, p. 41.
10. Ibid., p. 42.
11. Ibid.
12. See Lewis Mumford, *The Myth of the Machine* (London: Secker and Warburg, 1966).
13. Tierney, *The Value of Convenience*, p. 88.
14. Borgmann, *Technology and the Character of Contemporary Life*, p. 44.
15. Marc David, *Nourishing Wisdom* (New York: Bell Tower, 1991), p. 2.
16. Tierney, *The Value of Convenience*, p. 82.
17. Eric Schlosser, *Fast Food Nation: The Dark Side of the All-American Meal* (New York: Houghton Mifflin, 2002), p. 9.
18. George Ritzer, *The McDonaldization of Society* (Thousand Oaks, Cal.: Pine Forge Press, 2000), p. 186.
19. Ibid., p. 95.
20. See Schlosser, *Fast Food Nation*, p. 33.
21. Strasser, *Waste and Want*, pp. 176–177.
22. Schlosser, *Fast Food Nation*, p. 8.
23. Judd, *In Defense of Garbage*, p. 68.
24. Harvey Levenstein, *Paradox of Plenty: A Social History of Eating in Modern America* (New York: Oxford University Press, 1993), p. 130.
25. bid., p. 127.
26. Alan Durning, "Junk Food, Food Junk" in *World Watch Magazine*, Sept. 1991, p. 7.
27. Levenstein, *Paradox of Plenty*, p. 249.
28. As already noted, the convenience of food commodities has helped allow women to move out of the home into the workforce, which in turn has promoted gender equality, though this still remains far from

perfect. Freedom from the home, however, has been accompanied by a certain enslavement to the industrial franchisers that supply our commodified food. For those consumers who simply do not know how to prepare a meal, there will never be time enough or an opportunity to cook. Simple eating need not be laborious or tasteless. Finally, when we learn from *Statistics Canada* that the average Canadian watches twenty-one hours of television in every week— approximately equivalent to half a full-time work week—it seems hard to defend our modern technological foodways. Our taste for convenience seems to have developed more out of ignorance, indifference, or indolence than from social, political, or humanitarian passions.

29. Tierney, *The Value of Convenience*, p. 193.
30. Schlosser, *Fast Food Nation*, p. 54.
31. Jeffrey Sobal, "Sociological Analysis of the Stigmatisation of Obesity," in *A Sociology of Food and Nutrition*, Germov et al., eds. (Oxford: Oxford University Press, 1999), p. 189.
32. Durning, "Junk Food, Food Junk," p. 7.
33. Ritzer, *The McDonaldization of Society*, p. 39.
34. Ibid., p. 104.
35. Ibid., p. 41.
36. Schlosser, *Fast Food Nation*, p. 94.
37. "The roughly 3.5 milllion fast food workers are by far the largest group of minimum wage earners in the United States." Schlosser, *Fast Food Nation*, p. 6.
38. Ibid., p. 154.
39. Ibid.
40. Ritzer, *The McDonaldization of Society*, p. 65.
41. David, *Nourishing Wisdom*, p. 2.
42. Abram, *The Spell of the Sensuous*, p. 47.
43. Schlosser, *Fast Food Nation*, p. 121.
44. Descartes, *Discourse on Method and Meditations on First Philosophy*, p. 67.
45. See Heidegger, "The Origin of the Work of Art," *Poetry, Language, Thought*, p. 34.

> The equipmental quality of the equipment consists indeed in its usefulness. But this usefulness itself rests in the abundance of an essential being of the equipment. We call it reliability. By virtue of this reliability the peasant woman is made privy to the silent call of the earth; by virtue of the reliability of her equipment she is sure of her world. World and earth exist for

her, and for those who are with her in her mode of being, only thus—in the equipment. We say "only" and therewith fall into error; for the reliability of the equipment first gives to the simple world its security and assures to the earth the freedom of its steady thrust.

46. Strasser, *Waste and Want*, p. 22.
47. Ibid., p. 66.

Chapter Four: The City

The epigraph to this chapter is from Martin Melosi, *Garbage in the Cities: Refuse, Reform and the Environment 1880–1980* (College Station: Texas A and M University Press, 1981), p. 3.

1. Strasser, *Waste and Want*, p. 133.
2. Karl Marx, *Essential Writings*, Bender, ed., (New York: Harper and Row, 1972), p. 71.
3. Marx phrases the sense of personal helplessness of the wage-laborer in economic terms:

> But just as nature affords the *means of existence* of labor in the sense that labor cannot *live* without objects upon which it can be exercised, so also it provides the *means of existence* in a narrower sense; namely the means of physical existence for the worker himself. Thus, the more the worker *appropriates* the external world of sensuous nature by his labor the more he denies himself of *means of existence*, in two respects: first, that the sensuous external world becomes progressively less an object belonging to his labor, and secondly, that it becomes progressivly less a means of existence in the direct sense, a means for the physical subsistence of the worker.
>
> In both respects, therefore, the worker becomes a slave of the object; first in that he receives an *object of work*, i.e., receives *work*, and secondly, that he receives *means of subsistence*. Thus the object enables him to exist, first as a *worker* and secondly as a *physical subject*. The culmination of this enslavement is that he can only maintain himself as a *physical subject* so far as he is a *worker*, and that it is only as a *physical subject* that he is a worker.

Marx, *Essential Writings*, p. 72.

4. See Locke's *Second Treatise of Government*, sections 27 and following:

> 27. Though the Earth, and all inferior Creatures be common to all Men, yet every Man has a *Property* in his own *Person*. This no Body has any Right to but himself. The *Labour* of his Body, and the *Work* of his Hands, we many say, are properly his. Whatsoever then he removes out of the State that Nature hath provided, and left it in, he hath mixed his *Labour* with, and joined to it something that is his own, and thereby makes it his *Property*. It being by him removed from the common state Nature placed it in, it hath by this *labour* something annexed to it, that excludes the common right of other Men. For this *Labour* being the unquestionable Property of the Labourer, no Man but he can have a right to what that is once joined to, at least where there is enough, and as good left in common for others.

> 31. It will perhaps be objected to this, That if gathering the Acorns, or other Fruits of the Earth, etc. makes a right to them, then any one may *ingross* as much as he will. To which I answer, Not so. . . . As much as any one can make use of to any advantage of life before it spoils; so much he may by his labour fix a Property in. Whatever is beyond this, is more than his share, and belongs to others. Nothing was made by God for Man to spoil or destroy.

John Locke, *Two Treatises of Government*, Peter Laslett, ed. (Cambridge: Cambridge University Press, 1964).

5. Susie Orbach, *Hunger Strike*, p. 34.
6. See Ritzer, *The McDonaldization of Society*.
7. Georg Simmel, *Classic Essays in the Culture of Cities*, Sennet, ed., (New York: Appleton-Century-Crofts, 1969), p. 49.
8. Ibid., p. 48.
9. Mander, *Four Arguments for the Elimination of Television*, p. 62.
10. Ibid., p. 64.
11. Abram, *The Spell of the Sensuous*, p. 62.
12. Simmel in *Classic Essays in the Culture of Cities*, Sennet, ed., p. 51.
13. Ibid., p. 51.
14. Oswald Spengler in ibid., p. 70.
15. Douglas Dowd, *The Waste of Nations: Dysfunction in the World Economy* (Boulder: Westview Press, 1989), pp. 9–10.
16. See Melosi, *Garbage and the Cities*.

17. Orbach, *Hunger Strike*, p. 34.
18. Wendell Berry, *The Unsettling of America: Culture and Agriculture* (New York: Avon, 1978), p. 85.
19. Ibid., p. 137.
21. Archeologist Ronald Wright writes:

> The fall of the Classic Maya Civilization in the ninth century has long intrigued archeologists. Now answers are emerging that should worry us all. Tikal, the greatest city, seemed a Manhattan of art deco pyramids (Maya architecture influenced the modern style) presiding over a conurbation of 120 square kilometres. It took 1,500 years to reach that size, yet all of Tikal's skyscrapers were built in its final century, an extravagent flowering on the eve of collapse.
>
> Copan is less grandiose, with exquisite sculpture, the statues of its kings radiating order and refinement. Yet excavation has shown that this city, over centuries, smothered the rich soil from which it grew. The best land was paved, the hills were stripped for farms and timber. The ruling class (revealed by their bones) grew tall and fat; the peasants became stunted. The end was an agony of ecological and social chaos, a scramble for resources in a top-heavy, shrinking world. Diggings at Dos Pilas have exposed a final moment, the people huddling in the centre, tearing stones from the temples to throw up barracades.
>
> Earth is full of dead cities. Civilizations, like individuals, are born, flourish and die. Except ours. Ours, we feel, is different, the beneficiary of all the rest. The sunny afternoon in which we thrive will stretch forever. In this belief, we carry on our own lives against the evidence of time.

"Civilization Is a Pyramid Scheme," in *The Globe and Mail* (August 5, 2000), p. A15.
21. "In this way the impression comes to prevail that everything man encounters exists only insofar as it is his construct. This illusion gives rise in turn to one final delusion: it seems as though man everywhere and always encounters only himself. . . . In truth, however, precisely nowhere does man today any longer encounter himself, i.e., his essence." Heidegger, *The Question Concerning Technology and Other Essays*, p. 27.
22. Spengler in *Classic Essays in the Culture of Cities*, Sennet, ed., p. 67.
23. Zimmerman, *Heidegger's Confrontation with Modernity*, p. 27.

24. See, for example, Heidegger, "The End of Philosophy and the Task of Thinking" in *Basic Writings*, p. 391:

> Perhaps there is a thinking which is more sober-minded than the incessant frenzy of rationalization and the intoxicating quality of cybernetics. One might aver that it is precisely this intoxication that is extremely irrational. Perhaps there is a thinking outside of the distinction of rational and irrational, more sober-minded than scientific technology, more sober-minded and hence more removed, without effect, yet having its own necessity.

25. Heidegger, "Building Dwelling Thinking" in *Poetry, Language, Thought*, p. 177.

> Building and thinking are, each in its own way, inescapable for dwelling. The two, however, are also insufficient for dwelling so long as each busies itself with its own affairs in separation instead of listening to one another. They are able to listen if both—building and thinking—belong to dwelling, if they remain within their limits and realize that the one as much as the other comes from the workshop of long experience and incessant practice.

26. Borgmann, *Technology and the Character of Contemporary Life*, p. 207.
27. Ibid.
28. Wendell Berry, *Another Turn of the Crank* (Washington, D.C.: Counterpoint, 1995), p. 8.
29. Tierney, *The Value of Convenience*, p. 31.
30. See Heidegger, *Being and Time*, pp. 29, 202ff; "On the Essence of Truth" and "The End of Philosophy and the Task of Thinking" in *Basic Writings*, pp. 132ff and 388ff.
31. Martin Heidegger, *Neitzsche, Volume II* (San Fransisco: Harper and Row, 1961), p. 358. Hereafter cited as N in text.
32. Borgmann, *Technology and the Character of Contemporary Life*, p. 47.
33. Heidegger, "The Thing," in *Poetry, Language, Thought*, p. 177: "Today everything present is equally near and equally far. The distanceless prevails. But no abridging or abolishing of distance brings nearness. What is nearness? . . . Nearness brings near—draws nigh to one another—the far and, indeed, *as* the far. Nearness preserves farness."
34. Lewis Mumford, *The City in History: Its Origins, Its Transformations, and Its Prospects* (New York: Harcourt Brace Jovanovich, 1961), p. 93.

35. Ibid., p. 46.
36. Merton, *No Man is an Island*, p. 108.
37. Richard Sennet, *Flesh and Stone: The Body and the City in Western Civilization* (New York: Norton, 1994), p. 262.

Chapter Five: Trash

1. "Martin Heidegger in Conversation with Richard Wisser," in *Martin Heidegger and National Socialism*, Harris, trans. (New York: Paragon House, 1990), p. 82.
2. Milton Mayeroff, *On Caring* (New York: Perennial Library, 1972), p. 29.
3. Ibid., p. 2.
4. Ibid., p. 9.
5. Zimmerman, *The Eclipse of the Self*, p. 67.
6. Heidegger, *Poetry, Language, Thought*, p. 120. Hereafter PLT in text.
7. Tierney, *The Value of Convenience*, p. 42.
8. Martin Heidegger, *Discourse on Thinking* (New York: Harper and Row, 1959), p. 52. Hereafter DT in text.
9. Tierney, *The Value of Convenience*, p. 36.
10. Zimmerman, *The Eclipse of the Self*, p. 225.
11. Martin Heidegger, *What Is Called Thinking* (New York: Harper and Row, 1968), p. 5. Hereafter WCT in text.
12. Tierney, *The Value of Convenience*, p. 36.
13. D. T. Suzuki, *Essays in Zen Buddhism*, third series (York Beach, Me.: Samuel Weiser, 1971), p. 87.
14. Thich Nhat Hanh, *Peace Is Every Step* (New York: Bantam, 1991), p. 95.
15. Borgmann, *Technology and the Character of Contemporary Life*, p. 207.
16. Ibid., p. 200.
17. Orbach, *Hunger Strike*, p. 34.
18. Descartes, *Discourse on Method and Meditations on First Philosophy*, p. 82.
19. Tierney, *The Value of Convenience*, p. 179.
20. Ibid., p. 186.
21. Albert Borgmann discusses this well in his *Holding on to Reality* (Chicago: University of Chicago Press, 1999), p. 190.

> The human body with all its heaviness and frailty marks the origin of the coordinate space we inhabit. Just as in taking the measure of the universe this original point of our existence is

unsurpassable, so in venturing beyond reality the standpoint of our body remains the inescapable pivot.

Sooner or later, the gravity of their bodily existence pulls MUD [Multi User Domain] players through the veil of virtual ambiguity into the entanglements of ordinary life. Sometimes a player is cast out of his virtual seclusion when his wife discovers his amorous multiplicity. More often, players get impatient with the vacancy of virtuality and allow themselves to be drawn into reality. They set out to meet the enchanting MUD persona face to face, most often with disappointing consequences. Or they try to satisfy their hunger for reality by devouring the traces of actuality that come with a new MUD friendship. As soon as the thrill of novelty is gone and the specter of virtual vacuity rises, they move on, endlessly reenacting their quest for real engagement.

22. Heidegger, *The Question Concerning Technology*, p. 16. Hereafter QCT in text.
23. Dreyfus, "Heidegger's History of the Being of Equipment."
24. A. T. Nuyen, "A Heideggerian Existential Ethics for the Human Environment," in *Journal of Value Inquiry* (vol. 25, October 1991), p. 362.
25. Ibid., p. 365.
26. See, for example, Ramachandra Guha's article, "Radical American Environmentalism and Wilderness Preservation: A Third World Critique," in *Environmental Ethics* (vol. 11, no. 1, Spring 1989):

> Here [in USA] the enjoyment of nature is an integral part of the consumer society. The private automobile (and the lifestyle it has spawned) is in many respects the ultimate ecological villain, and an untouched wilderness area the prototype of ecological harmony; yet for most Americans it is perfectly consistent to drive a thousand miles to spend a holiday in a national park. They possess a vast, beautiful, and sparsely populated continent and are also able to draw upon the natural resources of large portions of the globe by virtue of their economic and political dominance. In consequence, America can simultaneously enjoy the material benefits of an expanding economy and the aesthetic benefits of unspoilt nature.

27. Merton, *No Man Is an Island*, p. 19.

28. Mayeroff, *On Caring*, p. 5.
29. Zimmerman, "Heidegger, Buddhism and Deep Ecology," *Cambridge Companion to Heidegger* (Cambridge: Cambridge University Press, 1993), p. 263
30. *The Little Flowers of St. Francis; The Mirror of Perfection; and St. Bonaventure's Life of St. Francis* (London: Everymans Library, 1963), p. 292.
31. Ibid., p. 293.
32. Guha, "Radical American Environmentalism: A Third World Critique," p. 79.
33. Baudrillard, *The Consumer Society*, p. 47.

Chapter Six: Human Extinction

1. Thucydides, *History of the Peloponnesian War*, Livingstone, trans. (London: Oxford University Press, 1943), p. 121.
2. Hesiod, "Works and Days," *Classical Mythology: Images and Insights*, Harris and Platzner, eds. (Mountain View: Mayfield Publishing, 1995), p. 92.
3. Lynch, *Wasting Away*, p. 146.
4. Jonathan Schell, *The Fate of the Earth* (New York: A Knopf, 1983), p. 138.
5. Ibid., p. 128.
6. Ibid., p. 119.
7. Tierney, *The Value of Convenience*, p. 204.
8. Dewdney, *Last Flesh*, p. 168.
9. Tierney, *The Value of Convenience*, p. 36.
10. Schell, *The Fate of the Earth*, p. 168.
11. Ibid., p. 166.
12. Ibid., p. 119.
13. Ibid., p. 120.
14. Ibid., p. 144.
15. Ibid., p. 154.
16. Ibid., p. 165.
17. Ibid., p. 147.
18. Berry, *The Unsettling of America*, p. 219.
19. Iyengar, *Light on Yoga*, p. 23.
20. Geoffrey Godbey et al., "No Time to Waste: An Exploration of Time Use, Attitudes Toward Time, and the Generation of Municipal Solid Waste," in *Social Research* (vol. 65, no. 1, Spring 1998), p. 108.
21. Sennett, *Flesh and Stone*, p. 365.

22. Fromm, Demartino, and Suzuki, *Zen Buddhism and Psychoanalysis* (New York: Grove Press, 1963), p. 6.
23. Ibid., p. 8.
24. Thomas Merton, *Faith and Violence* (South Bend: University of Notre Dame Press, 1968), p. 6.

Bibliography

Abram, David. *The Spell of the Sensuous: Perception and Language in a More-than-Human-World*. New York: Pantheon, 1996.

Ames, Kaaulis, and Dissanayake, eds. *Self as Body in Asian Thoery and Practice*. Albany, State University of New York Press, 1993.

Baudrillard, Jean. *The Consumer Society: Myths and Structures*. London: Sage, 1998.

Baumrin, Bernard. "Waste," *Journal of Social Philosophy*. Vol. 24, No. 3, Winter 1993.

Becker, Ernest. *The Denial of Death*. New York: Free Press, 1973.

Berry, Wendell. *Another Turn of the Crank*. Washington, D.C.: Counterpoint, 1995.

———. *The Unsettling of America: Culture and Agriculture*. New York: Avon Books, 1978.

Blocker, Gene. *The Meaning of Meaninglessness*. The Hague: Martinus Nijhoff, 1974.

Borgmann, Albert. *Technology and the Character of Contemporary Life*. Chicago: University of Chicago Press, 1984.

———. *Holding on to Reality: The Nature of Information at the Turn of the Millennium*. Chicago: University of Chicago Press, 1999.

Bourke, John Gregory. *Les Rites Scatologiques*. Paris; Presses Universitaires de France, 1981.

Bull, Micheal. *Sounding Out the City: Personal Stereos and the Management of Everyday Life*. Oxford: Berg, 2000.

Caputo, John. *The Mystical Element in Heidegger's Thought*. Athens: Ohio University Press, 1978.

Cerbone, David. "Heidegger and Dasein's 'Bodily Nature': What Is the Hidden Problematic?," *International Journal of Philosophical Studies*. Vol. 8, No. 2, 2000.

Cussler, Margaret, and de Give, Mary. *'Twixt the Cup and the Lip.* Washington, D.C..: Consortium Press, 1970.

David, Marc. *Nourishing Wisdom.* New York: Bell Tower Books, 1991.

Descartes, René. *The Discourse on Method and the Meditations on First Philosophy.* Indianapolis: Hackett, 1993.

de Silguy, Catherine. *La Saga des Ordures du Moyen Age a nos Jours.* Paris: Editions de l'Instant, 1989.

Dewdney, Christopher. *Last Flesh: Life in the Transhuman Era.* Toronto: HarperCollins, 1998.

Douglas, Mary. *Purity and Danger: An Analysis of the Concepts of Pollution and Taboo.* London: Routledge, 1966.

Dowd, Douglas. *The Waste of Nations: Dysfunction in the World Economy.* Boulder: Westview Press, 1989.

Dreyfus, Hubert. "Heidegger's History of the Being of Equipment," *Heidegger: A Critical Reader,* Dreyfus and Hall, eds. Oxford: Blackwell, 1992.

Durning, Alan B. "Junk Food, Food Junk," *World Watch.* Vol. 4, No. 5, September/Oct.ober 1991.

Durning, Alan, and Ryan, John. *Stuff: The Secret Lives of Everyday Things.* Seattle: Northwest Environment Watch. January 1997.

Featherstone, Mike. "The Body in Consumer Culture," *The Body: Social Process and Cultural Theory.* London: Sage, 1991.

Fromm, DeMartino, Suzuki. *Zen Buddhism and Psychoanalysis.* New York: Grove Press, 1963.

Godbey, Geoffrey et al. "No Time to Waste: An Exploration of Time Use, Attitudes Toward Time, and the Generation of Municipal Solid Waste," *Social Research.* Vol. 65, No. 1, Spring 1998.

Griffiths, Sian, and Wallace, Jennifer, eds. *Consuming Passions: Food in the Age of Anxiety.* Manchester: Mandolin, 1998.

Grimm, Veronika. *From Feasting to Fasting, the Evolution of a Sin: Attitudes to Food in Late Antiquity.* London: Routledge, 1996.

Grosz, Elizabeth. "Bodies–Cities," *Places through the Body,* Nast and Pile, eds. London: Routledge, 1998.

Guha, Ramachandra. "Radical American Environmentalism and Wilderness Preservation: A Third World Critique," *Environmental Ethics.* Vol. 11, No. 1, Spring 1989.

Hardin, Russell. "Garbage Out, Garbage In," *Social Research.* Vol. 65, No. 1, Spring, 1998.

Harris, Lisa, ed. *Martin Heidegger and National Socialism.* New York: Paragon House, 1990.

Harris and Plaztner, eds. *Classical Mythology: Images and Insights.* Mountain View: Mayfield Publishing, 1995.

Havelock, Eric A. "The Orality of Socrates and the Literacy of Plato: With Some Reflections on the Historical Origins of Moral Philosophy in Europe," *New Essays on Socrates*, E. Kelly, ed. Lanham: University Press of America, 1984.

Heidegger, Martin. *Gesamtausgabe*. Frankfurt am Main: Vittorio Klostermann.

———. *What Is Called Thinking*. New York: Harper and Row, 1968.

———. *Discourse on Thinking*. New York. Harper and Row, 1959.

———. *Being and Time*. Albany: State University of New York Press, 1996.

———. *Basic Writings*. New York: Harper and Row, 1977.

———. *Kant and the Problem of Metaphysics*. Bloomington: Indiana Univeristy Press, 1962.

———. *Nietzsche*. San Francisco: Harper and Row, 1961.

———. *Poetry, Language, Thought*. New York: Harper and Row, 1971.

———. *The Question Concerning Technology and Other Essays*. New York: Garland, 1977.

Heidegger, Martin, and Fink, Eugen. *Heraclitus Seminar*, trans. Charles Seibert. Tuscaloosa: University of Alabama Press, 1970.

Howes, David. *Cross-Cultural Consumption: Global Markets, Local Realities*. London: Routledge, 1996.

Iyengar, B. K. S. *Light on Yoga*. London: Thorsons, 2001.

James, David N. "Risking Extinction: An Axiological Analysis," *Research in Philosophy and Technology*. Vol. 11, 1991.

Judd, Alexander. *In Defense of Garbage*. Westport: Praeger, 1993.

Kant, Immanuel. *The Critique of Pure Reason*. New York: St. Martin's Press, 1929.

Laporte, Dominique. *History of Shit*. Cambridge: MIT Press, 2000.

Leder, Drew. *The Absent Body*. Chicago: University of Chicago Press, 1990.

Leslie, John. *The End of the World: The Science and Ethics of Human Extinction*. London: Routledge, 1996.

Levenstein, Harvey. *Paradox of Plenty: A Social History of Eating in Modern America*. New York: Oxford University Press, 1993.

Levin, David. *The Body's Recollection of Being*. London: Routledge, 1985.

Levinas, Emmanuel. *Basic Philosophical Writings*. Bloomington: Indiana University Press, 1996.

Lhulier, Dominique, and Cochin, Yann. *Des Dechets et des Hommes*. Paris: Desclee de Brouwer, 1999.

The Little Flowers of St. Francis; The Mirror of Perfection; St Bonaventure's Life of St Francis. London: Everymans Library, 1963.

Locke, John. *Two Treatises of Government*, Peter Laslett, ed. Cambridge: Cambridge University Press, 1964.

Lynch, Kevin. *Wasting Away*. San Fransisco: Sierra Club Books, 1990.

Mander, Jerry. *Four Arguments for the Elimination of Television*. New York: Morrow, 1978.

Mayeroff, Milton. *On Caring*. New York: Perennial Library, 1972.

Marx, Karl. *Essential Writings*, Frederic Bender, ed. New York: Harper and Row, 1972.

Marx, Werner. *Towards a Phenomenological Ethics*. Albany: State University of New York Press, 1992.

Mauss, Marcel. *The Gift: Forms and Functions of Exchange in Archaic Societies*. New York: Norton, 1967.

McCracken, Grant. *Culture and Consumption: New Approaches to the Symbolic Character of Consumer Goods and Activities*. Bloomington: Indiania University Press, 1990.

Melosi, Martin. *Garbage in the Cities: Refuse, Reform, and the Environment 1880–1980*. College Station: Texas A and M University Press, 1981.

Mennell, Stephen. "On the Civilizing of Appetite and the Body," *The Body: Social Process and Cultural Theory*, Featherstone and Turner, eds. London: Sage, 1991.

Merleau-Ponty, Maurice. *The Phenomenology of Perception*. London: Routledge, 1962.

Merton, Thomas. *Faith and Violence: Christian Teaching and Christian Practice*. Suth Bend: University of Notre Dame Press, 1968.

———. *No Man Is an Island*. New York: Harcourt Brace, 1955.

Mumford, Lewis. *The City in History: Its Origins, Its Transformations, and Its Prospects*. New York: Harcourt Brace Jovanovich, 1961.

———. *The Myth of the Machine*. London: Secker and Warburg, 1966.

Nhat Hanh, Thich. *Peace Is Every Step*. New York: Bantam, 1991.

Nuyen, A. T. "A Heideggerian Existential Ethics for the Human Environment," *Journal of Value Inquiry*. Vol. 25, October 1991.

O'Meara Sheehan, Molly. "Where the Sidewalks End," *World Watch Magazine*. November/December 2002.

Orbach, Susie. *Hunger Strike: The Anorectic's Struggle as a Metaphor for our Age*. London: Faber and Faber, 1986.

Packard, Vance. *The Waste Makers*. New York: Rocket Books, 1960.

Pasi Falk. *The Consuming Body*. London: Sage, 1994.

Pieper, Josef. *Leisure: The Basis of Culture*. New York: Pantheon Books, 1952.

Plato. *Complete Works*. Indianapolis: Hackett, 1997.

———. "Phaedrus," *Dialogues of Plato*, B. Jowett, trans. New York: Random House, 1937.

Radhakrishnan, S., trans. *Bhagavadgita*. New Dehli: HarperCollins, 1993.

———. *The Principal Upanisads*. New Delhi: HarperCollins, 1994.

Rathje, William, and Murphy, Cullen. *Rubbish: The Archeaology of Garbage*. New York: HarperCollins, 1992.

Raum, A. F. *Chaga Childhood*. Oxford: Oxford University Press, 1940.

Richardson, Miles. "Culture and the Urban Stage," *Human Behavior and Environment Volume Four: Environment and Culture*, Altmann et al., eds. New York: Plenum Press, 1980.

Ritzer, George. *The McDonaldization of Society*. Thousand Oaks, Cal.: Pine Forge Press, 2000.

Sahlins, Marshall. "The Original Affluent Society," *Culture and Practice: Selected Essays*. New York: Zone Books, 2000.

Schell, Jonathan. *The Fate of the Earth*. New York: Knopf, 1983.

Schlosser, Eric. *Fast Food Nation: The Dark Sid of the All-American Meal*. New York: Houghton Mifflin, 2002.

Sennett, Richard. *Flesh and Stone: The Body and the City in Western Civilization*. New York: Norton, 1994.

Sennett, Richard, ed. *Classic Essays in the Culture of Cities*. New York: Appleton-Century-Crofts, 1969.

Sheets-Johnstone, Maxine. "The Materialization of the Body: A History of Western Medicine, A History in Process," *Giving the Body Its Due*, Sheets-Johnstone, ed. Albany: State University of New York Press, 1992.

Sobal, Jeffery. "Sociological Analysis of the Stigmatisation of Obesity," *A Sociology of Food and Nutrition*, Germov, John, et al., eds. Oxford: Oxford University Press, 1999.

Stambaugh, Joan. *The Finitude of Being*. Albany: State University of New York Press, 1992.

Steffney, John. "Man and Being in Heidegger and Zen Buddhism," *Philosophy Today*. Vol. 25, Spring 1981.

Strasser, Susan. *Waste and Want: A Social History of Trash*. New York: Metropolitan Books, 1999.

Suzuki, D. T. *Essays in Zen Buddhism, third series*. York Beach, Me.: Samuel Weiser, 1971.

Takeichi, Akhiro. "On the Origin of Nihilism—In View of the Problem of Technology and Karma," *Heidegger and Asain Thought*, Graham Parkes, ed. Honolulu: University of Hawaii Press, 1987.

Tierney, Thomas. *The Value of Convenience: A Genealogy of Technical Culture*. Albany: State University of New York Press, 1993.

"Trash," *Colours Magazine*. Milan: October/November 2000.

Veblen, Thorstein. *The Theory of the Leisure Class*. New York: Modern Library, 1931.

Villeneuve, Johanne, et al. eds. *La Memoire des Dechets: Essais sur la Culture at la Valuer du Passe*. Quebec City, 1999.

Vycinas, Vincent. *Earth and Gods: An Introduction to the Philosophy of Martin Heidegger.* The Hague: Martinus Nijhoff, 1961.

Westra, Laura. "Let It Be: Heidegger and Future Generations," *Environmental Ethics.* Vol. 7, No. 4, Winter 1985.

Whitaker, Jennifer S. *Salvaging the Land of Plenty: Garbage and the American Dream.* New York: Morrow, 1994.

White, Peter. "The Fascinating World of Trash," *National Geographic Magazine.* April 1983.

Wordsworth, William. *The Excursion: Preceded by Book I of The Recluse.* London: Macmillan, 1935.

Wright, Ronald. "Civilization Is a Pyramid Scheme," *The Globe and Mail,* August 5, 2000, p. A15.

Young, John E. "Discarding the Throwaway Society," *Worldwatch Paper 101,* January 1991.

Zimmerman, Micheal. "Heidegger, Buddhism and Deep Ecology," *Cambridge Companion to Hiedegger.* Cambridge: Cambridge University Press, 1993.

———. "Heidegger and Heraclitus on Spiritual Practice," *Philosophy Today,* Summer 1983.

———. *Heidegger's Confrontation with Modernity: Technology, Politics, Art.* Bloomington:Indiania University Press, 1990.

———. *The Eclipse of the Self: The Development of Heidegger's Concept of Authenticity.* Athens: Ohio University Press, 1981.

Index